Messenger of Death

Messenger of Death

Captain Nolan and the
Charge of the Light Brigade

David Buttery

Pen & Sword
MILITARY

First published in Great Britain in 2008 by
PEN & SWORD MILITARY
an imprint of
Pen & Sword Books Ltd
47 Church Street
Barnsley
South Yorkshire
S70 2AS

ISBN 978 1 84415 756 3

Printed and bound in Great Britain
by CPI UK

Pen & Sword Books Ltd incorporates the imprints of
Pen & Sword Aviation, Pen & Sword Maritime, Pen & Sword Military,
Wharncliffe Local History, Pen & Sword Select, Pen & Sword Military Classics,
Leo Cooper, Remember When, Seaforth Publishing and Frontline Publishing.

For a complete list of Pen & Sword titles please contact
PEN & SWORD BOOKS LIMITED
47 Church Street, Barnsley, South Yorkshire, S70 2AS, England
E-mail: enquiries@pen-and-sword.co.uk
Website: www.pen-and-sword.co.uk

Contents

Brethren, how shall it fare with me
When the war is laid aside,
If it be proven that I am he
For whom a world has died?

Rudyard Kipling, 'The Question', 1916

List of maps and illustrations

1. Captain Louis Edward Nolan of the 15th Hussars
2. The Military Pioneer School at Tulln, Austria
3. A parody on the British Army's purchase system
4. Holy Trinity Church, Maidstone
5. The former officers' mess for Maidstone Barracks
6. Nolan's recommended military seat or riding posture
7. Recruiting for the cavalry in London
8. Demonstrating the act of reining back
9. Demonstrating the pirouette
10. The slope before the two redoubts at the Alma
11. Allied guns bombarding Sevastopol
12. The small harbour of Balaklava
13. A view of the Causeway Heights across the South Valley
14. Looking into the South Valley and towards Balaklava
15. A view from the Sapouné escarpment near Raglan's position
16. View from the site of Redoubt No. 4 where Nolan is supposedly buried
17. Midway down the North Valley
18. A view of the North Valley from the eastern end of the Causeway
19. The first line of the Light Brigade charging into the Russian battery
20. Lord Raglan, commander-in-chief of the Allied forces in the Crimea
21. Lord Lucan, commander of the cavalry division
22. General Bosquet
23. General Prince Alexander Menshikov, commander-in-chief of the Russian Army
24. The North Valley beyond the guns
25. The charge of the French Chasseurs d'Afrique against Russian infantry and artillery
26. A Russian statue of Admiral Kornilov
27. Poor-quality track roads in use after the yielding of the Woronzov Road
28. The British memorial to those who fell at the Battle of Balaklava
29. Relics displayed at the Balaclava Festival, Alexandra Palace, London, 1875
30. A wounded soldier at the Military Hospital in Haslar
31. A cutting satire on the inquiry held into the Crimean War

Map Symbols

Maps: key to military symbols

INFANTRY
British
French/Turkish
Russian

CAVALRY
British
French/Turkish
Russian

ARTILLERY

REDOUBTS ⑤

REDANS

Preface

There can be few men whose last minutes have been as fiercely debated as those of Captain Louis Nolan (1818–54) of the 15th Hussars. The echoes of the gunfire that raked Balaklava's North Valley (Tennyson's infamous Valley of Death) had barely died away before recriminations were being exchanged over who was responsible for the Charge of the Light Brigade, one of the most famous incidents in military history. Some believe that Nolan died in a desperate attempt to avert a terrible mistake he saw unfolding before him, whilst others suspect him of urging on the brigade in an action he had purposely brought about. Doubtless some of his contemporaries would have preferred that he and the events that followed his death could have been quietly forgotten; but, though over 150 years have passed since the calamity, theories and speculation about Nolan's last moments are still contested.

The fame of this charge reveals an unusual trait in the British psyche. Almost any other country in the world would have emphasized the other famous incidents during the Battle of Balaklava in preference. Considering that the Heavy Cavalry Brigade mounted a highly successful charge almost immediately before the incident, this is strange. The charge had little strategic or tactical influence on the outcome of the campaign and historians' concentration on this event reveals a national passion for glorious and spectacular failure. In the light of almost unparalleled military success over the past 300 years it could be argued that it implies a certain conceit: the British feel they can afford to dwell on such incidents because, although many battles have been lost, Great Britain has rarely lost a war – the American Revolution was one of the rare exceptions.

It is Nolan's fate to be forever associated with the terrible blunder that brought about the charge, and the events of his last half an hour of life have eclipsed everything else he achieved during his thirty-six years. However, Nolan's earlier career was interesting and varied and won popular acclaim. He had been in two national armies and achieved considerable recognition for an officer of junior rank. He served in several countries, including India, and travelled widely throughout Europe. The experience he gained helped him formulate his theories on the effective use of the cavalry arm, which he subsequently published in two books. His views and expertise were applauded by many in the army at a time when authors were still regarded within his profession with some suspicion.

Despite the controversy surrounding him and the influence of his cavalry studies, only one dedicated biography has been written about him, Hubert Moyse-Bartlett's *Nolan of Balaclava*, which has been of great use in writing this book. In consequence of this gap, Nolan's origins and career are obscure, and biographical details can be found only in related works restricted to brief and occasionally inaccurate summaries. Nolan's 'Crimean Journal', which provides further insight into his strongly held views, has only recently been made available to the public. Using this and other primary sources, I hope to provide a fresh look at Nolan and the early part of the Crimean War.

Having a considerable interest in military history, I have visited many battlefields including Agincourt, Crécy, Waterloo, the D-Day Beaches and Bastogne among others. Several people I have spoken to have mentioned how they felt a disturbing 'presence' at certain sites, particularly on the First World War battlefields of the Western Front. Until I visited Balaklava, I had never experienced this phenomenon. Indeed, I had commented on the absence of such feelings, judging myself insensitive and not at all prescient or superstitious. For example, when visiting the bridge over the River Côa in Portugal, where Craufurd's Light Division fought a controversial action against the French, I remarked on how pleasant the location was, which made it difficult to imagine a ferocious confrontation taking place there.

Balaklava was different. Having heard and read so much about the battle, I felt a sense of awe at actually visiting a place where such momentous events had taken place. Yet when we actually walked over the ground, and particularly on the floor of the valley itself, I felt distinctly uncomfortable. It was a beautiful day and, as I earnestly snapped away with my camera, I wondered why I felt that odd mixture of dread and excitement that one experiences when sensing danger. The valley itself looks unremarkable; with its fairly pleasant aspect and the fine weather, I had no reason to feel personally threatened; and yet I gained the distinct impression that something terrible had happened there – not being given to such feelings, I do not say this lightly. Certainly the reader will surmise that I had the benefit of foreknowledge, but in all honesty these sensations came as a complete surprise to me, particularly in the light of previous experience. The sites of the Malakoff, the Redan and the battlefield of Inkerman, which I also visited, all witnessed slaughter on a much greater scale than Balaklava; but I came away from the valley with an impression that I have not encountered before or since.

It is important to say a word or two about the interpretation of Russian words in this study. I have endeavoured to be consistent in using modern interpretations considered more akin to Russian usage – for example, Sevastopol rather than Sebastopol, Balaklava rather than Balaclava, Woronzov rather than Woronzoff, and so on. Some words I have left unaltered due to their repeated usage such as the 'Tchernaya' river rather than the more modern 'Chernaya'. With quotations, I have left the writers' original interpretations unaltered, according to common practice.

The battles of the Alma and Balaklava are of course included in this work, but, since this is essentially a biographical study, they are not covered in exhaustive detail and are mainly described from Nolan's perspective with comments on their relevance to his life and career.

During the writing of this work I have benefited from the help and advice of many people. Foremost among these are Pauline Buttery, Bert Godley and Stuart Hadaway who proof-read the manuscript in addition to Pen & Sword's own proof-readers who served me so well on my previous book. I am also grateful to Rupert Harding, my Commissioning Editor, for his help and advice during my second project for Pen & Sword. I would also like to thank Dr Douglas Austin for checking through the script using his wide knowledge of the Crimean War. In addition, I am a great admirer of his work for the Crimean War Research Society, of which I am a member.

I have used a number of libraries and archives and would like to thank the staff of the British Library, the National Newspaper Archive at Colindale, the Public Record Office/National Archives and the National Army Museum. As an ex-student, I am once again grateful to the University of Leicester and their library staff and would like to single out librarian David Charlton in particular for his assistance.

I have used some Austrian primary sources for this book and could not have done so but for the help of Renate Domanich of the Austrian State Archives who sought out Nolan's conduct list and other documents on my behalf. My German language skills are poor and the Austrian alphabet has been changed since the nineteenth century, so I feel obliged to Dr Scheer for her help in translating these documents. Without such assistance, I would not have been able to do justice to the Austrian section of this book.

There is no substitute for seeing the ground itself, and I would like to thank Holts Tours for the fantastic excursion they provided. I benefited greatly from the topographical and military knowledge of Colonel Peter Knox and Mr Brendan McDonagh while visiting Sevastopol, Balaklava, Inkerman and other sites. I would like to thank Anna Chernova of Sevastopol for showing me around and teaching me a great deal about the Russians and Ukrainians living in such an intriguing and fascinating city. Lieutenant Colonel Wade Russell deserves thanks for being an agreeable companion in what turned out to be quite an adventure during our travels. I also met Mr Alexander Sim on the tour, who has since provided me with useful advice about the British Army and great encouragement during this project.

Chapter 1

A Family Tradition

Louis Edward Nolan was both the son and grandson of a soldier. By the time of his birth in 1818 the army had already played a large role in the Nolan family's history and this choice of profession had become an established family tradition. The Nolan family originally hailed from Ireland, claiming to trace their heritage back to the O'Nuallain clan, whose leading members had been influential many years earlier in the service of the Princes of Foharta in County Carlow. It was a respected lineage in Ireland, though it lacked the prestige of former times.[1] Babington Nolan, Louis's grandfather, was a trooper in the 13th Light Dragoons. The 1790s saw him posted to the West Indies during the Revolutionary Wars. The climate made sickness and disease greater foes than anything man could devise; many more men were lost to yellow fever in the tropics than to enemy action. Already a widower, Babington Nolan was himself struck down by yellow fever in 1796 and died in St Domingo, leaving the young John Babington Nolan and his sister orphaned.

John guessed his age at this time to be 11 since like many of his class, he never learned his true date of birth. Fortunately, Colonel Francis Craig of the 13th Regiment had taken a liking to the children and they remained in the care of the army and were even given a bounty, a privilege usually offered only to the orphans of officers. In honour of his father, John began to use his second name in preference, and his benefactor ensured that 'young Babington' received a good education. Since the military life had been all he had ever really known, it came as no surprise that by the age of 17 he considered becoming a soldier.

During the early nineteenth century most officers' commissions could be bought or sold. The purchase system came about through the establishment's fear of violent rebellion and revolutionary upheaval. In the second half of the eighteenth century, both France and America experienced bloody revolutions, and Napoleon's resulting dictatorship proved that the fears of the old order were not empty paranoia. Charging large sums for commissions supposedly ensured that only those with a stake in the country could become officers and as such would make unlikely revolutionaries. Wages were also minimal, acting more as a retainer, and the expense of maintaining the kind of lifestyle demanded by most regiments ensured that only men of independent means could afford to be officers. The system was open to abuse and money often changed hands privately, especially when the more prestigious regiments were involved, and captaincies, majorities and colonelships often fetched prices far above the official government rate. In the hope of preventing promotion by purchase alone, officers were obliged to spend a certain period in each rank before being allowed to buy the next step up, but unscrupulous individuals could get around this by going on half pay. Half pay permitted an officer to sell his commission yet still remain on the army's books and receive half his salary. After waiting for the required period of time without actually performing any service, he could purchase the next rank and return to his regiment.[2] Some men remained on half pay for years, returning to the army only to find that they had forgotten their duties or that their knowledge was outdated.

However, deaths in the service through disease, injury or battle also allowed a man to gain a commission without purchase, though such promotions were not always confirmed by the army. If a man was the senior captain in the regiment, dictated by the time served in that rank, he might also gain a promotion if no one could be found to buy the commission in time. Exceptions were also made during the period when England was under threat of invasion during the Napoleonic Wars and badly in need of troops. If an individual transferred from the militia and brought a large number of volunteers with him, he could be awarded a commission as a reward.[3] Another exception was possible when an individual was considered a suitable candidate and had a number of respectable backers to recommend him. This would still have to be endorsed by the commander-in-chief since this form of patronage was intended to ensure that money was not the sole criterion for advancement and so allow talented individuals a method of entry.[4]

This was the manner in which Babington Nolan became an officer. He applied for a commission in 1803, at a time when England lay under the threat of French invasion by Napoleon, who had massed an army at Boulogne. The army was desperate for men and the 17-year-old had good references from Colonel Craig and other officers. He was gazetted as an ensign, the most junior officer rank, in the 61st Regiment of Foot on 9 July 1803. The regimental colonel was George Hewitt. He had been granted his commission under similar circumstances years before, so this demonstration of the power of patronage was not lost on the young officer. Staying with the 61st for only a short period, he transferred to the 70th Foot, a mostly Scottish regiment nicknamed the 'Glasgow Greys' which was about to be sent to the West Indies. Babington arrived at regimental headquarters in Antigua in 1804. It was a distant and dangerous posting with disease and climate both taking a terrible toll on the European troops garrisoning the empire. The high mortality rate soon enabled him to gain a lieutenancy, and his immediate superior, Captain Gerald de Courcy, was often absent on military business, which gave him frequent opportunities in the role of acting captain. Having enjoyed a close relationship with the army all his life, he soon fitted in well with the regiment and developed an increasing affection for the Scots.

French strategy against Britain meant that the regiment moved between garrisons as different areas came under threat and when the British seized the Danish fleet at Copenhagen in 1808, the 70th helped to occupy the two Danish-held islands of St John and St Thomas. At this time, Babington married a woman seven years his senior, whose maiden name is unrecorded but whose Christian name was Frances. The union was tragically cut short in the same year when she died at Walworth, probably from disease.[5] The 70th were called upon to take part in the attempt to wrest Guadeloupe from the French in 1810 – this was probably the only occasion that Babington was under fire during his military career. The operation was successful and the light company received a commendation for capturing artillery batteries dominating the anchorage of Grande Aîne. Though Babington was afflicted by sickness in the tropics on several occasions, suffering particularly in 1811, it was the high mortality rate and the disinclination that many had for service in the tropics that enabled him to gain a captaincy without purchase on 30 January 1812.

The British Army had been fighting a desperate war in the Iberian Peninsula at this time, and in 1813 the 70th were recalled to Scotland to spend the next three years garrisoned at Perth. There was a large barracks in the town with a depot and prisoner of war camp nearby. Up to 7,000 prisoners were imprisoned there from France, Holland and the German states. Babington was often called upon to help guard the POWs, who could be difficult to manage, and there were frequent escape attempts and occasional riots. There was also civil strife, because of discontent at the increasing pace of industrialization in Britain, and the regiment was called out on several occasions to suppress riots at Montrose and Dundee that year. With his increasing affinity for Scotland, Nolan was undismayed when left in command of the depot as the first battalion sailed to Canada, the 70th being stationed there to guard against American invasion.

Another reason for his contentment was his meeting with Eliza Ruddach in Perth. He was 27 and she was 34 years old. She lived in Rose Terrace, Perth and as a widow benefited from a pension of £200 per annum for life. Once again, he had fallen for an older woman, and they were married on 12 July 1813 at St John's Episcopal Church in the East Church Parish of Perth. Nolan wore his full-dress uniform for the occasion and many of the regiment attended the service, presided over by the Reverend H Henry.[6] Born Elizabeth Hartley in Holborn, England, in 1779, the bride was the daughter of George Hartley from an old English family. Her first husband had been a Scot named Andrew Macfarlane, whom she had married in 1801. She bore him three children, two of whom died in early childhood. The third, William Macfarlane, was born in 1806 and became Babington's oldest stepson.

When Macfarlane died suddenly, Eliza was swiftly remarried in 1810 to Charles Ruddach, aged 52. She moved back to Totteridge in England but retained the family home in Bloomsbury. The family owned land in the colonies, which included plantations in Jamaica and Tobago. Eliza had two children, George and Charlotte, the family habit being to name their offspring after family friends: on his birth in 1810, George was named after their local doctor, George Elsy. However, Charles became ill and died shortly after the birth of his daughter in 1811. His daughter followed him swiftly, dying of an illness in January 1813, aged only 2. Though he left their house in Keppel Street and its contents to his wife, his will specified that his youngest son should inherit his shares in the plantations along with his brother Alexander. When Alexander died on a voyage out to see the property, George Ruddach became the sole beneficiary.

Babington's and Eliza's courtship had been swift, both seizing upon the opportunity to further their positions in society with matrimony. Babington wanted to rise within the military and a wife would be of great assistance in the society circles he hoped to enter. Furthermore, as a widow she had inherited a considerable amount of money and property from her former husbands and thus enjoyed a regular income. Although she had been married twice, Eliza knew that she needed a husband to help and support her and the children, so the marriage was a practical arrangement as well as a love match, but it suited both partners. Babington Nolan now had a wife and two stepsons.

Over the next few years, he was kept very busy at Perth depot sending recruitment parties all over Great Britain. The Duke of Wellington was fighting his way across Spain at this time and urgently needed new recruits despite his incredible string of victories. Between 1813 and 1815 Babington claimed to have raised over 600 men to send to the colours. The War of 1812 against America was still raging also, and though the 70th had been posted to Lower Canada, where an American offensive was expected, most of the

FAMILY TREES

The Macfarlanes

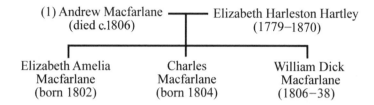

(1) Andrew Macfarlane ———— Elizabeth Harleston Hartley
(died c.1806)   (1779–1870)

Elizabeth Amelia   Charles   William Dick
Macfarlane   Macfarlane   Macfarlane
(born 1802)   (born 1804)   (1806–38)

The Ruddachs

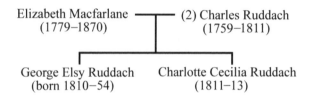

Elizabeth Macfarlane ———— (2) Charles Ruddach
(1779–1870)   (1759–1811)

George Elsy Ruddach   Charlotte Cecilia Ruddach
(born 1810–54)   (1811–13)

The Nolans

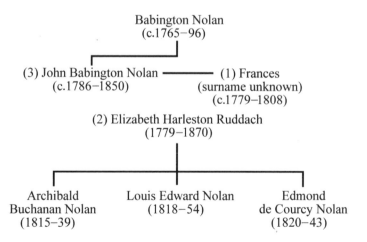

Babington Nolan
(c.1765–96)

(3) John Babington Nolan ———— (1) Frances
(c.1786–1850)   (surname unknown)
                                  (c.1779–1808)

(2) Elizabeth Harleston Ruddach
(1779–1870)

Archibald   Louis Edward Nolan   Edmond
Buchanan Nolan   (1818–54)   de Courcy Nolan
(1815–39)   (1820–43)

fighting took place along the Niagara frontier and around Lakes Ontario and Erie. It had been an unnecessary conflict that saw almost the entire eastern coast of America blockaded by the Royal Navy, and Washington was taken and sacked by the British Army. Both sides were relieved when a peace treaty was agreed in 1815, the British particularly anxious to resolve the conflict as Napoleon had returned from exile. Fortunately, his imperial ambitions were finally crushed during the Hundred Days' Campaign, culminating at the Battle of Waterloo that same year.

Hostilities had ceased by the time Babington Nolan was sent to join his regiment in Canada. Archibald Nolan had been born in 1815 and Eliza dutifully accompanied her husband with the entire family. Regimental headquarters were at Kingston in Upper Canada, but the family had to get used to an itinerant lifestyle as Nolan was posted to several garrisons over the next two years including Fort George, Drummonds Island, Amherstburg and York. With a family to support, Babington saw that there were opportunities in the New World and toyed with the idea of settling there permanently. With this in mind he purchased two vacant lots in the town of Markham, north of Toronto, which the family later referred to as 'Nolanville'. On 4 January 1818, while still stationed in Canada, in York County, Eliza gave birth to Louis Edward Nolan.

During his Canadian service Babington met Thomas Scott, brother of the famous Sir Walter Scott, and their shared interest in Scotland and the army ensured that they became friends. However, the appeal of Canada was waning for the Nolans, and with Eliza pregnant once more, they wished to return to Scotland. It was 1819, and after the disastrous series of wars that had blighted Europe, the government was keen to scale down the army. Though the family was reasonably well off, advancement without purchase in the army was unlikely, so Babington Nolan decided to sell his commission and go on half pay. Captain Thomas Read of the 4th West India Regiment agreed to exchange commissions with Babington, who benefited from the £300 difference between the two regiments. By 1820 the family had returned to Scotland.

With the birth of Edmond de Courcy Nolan, named after Major de Courcy, Babington now had four sons to support; and with his income reduced, the family moved into rooms at 79 Queen Street, Edinburgh, where Louis received his early schooling. Although Babington put himself forward for another placement, hundreds of officers were on half pay in Britain and even the unfashionable regiments had many applicants. Despite their contacts it seemed that prospects for the Nolans were bleak in Scotland, and so in 1829 they decided to move to Italy, where Babington's military skills might be of use and he had heard there were opportunities in the British Consulate. Louis was 11 years old when the family sailed for Italy. His half-brother William stayed in Scotland and eventually gained a commission in a Highland regiment with his stepfather's support.

They stayed briefly at Piacenza in the Duchy of Palma but soon moved to Milan. Italy was a divided nation at this time. The Vatican ruled over a separate papal state while the northern principalities had been fought over numerous times during the recent wars, with both France and Austria claiming sovereignty, though by the 1830s many Italians dreamed of independence. In Milan, Babington Nolan was introduced to William Money, the British Consul General. Money was an ex-naval officer who had seen considerable service with the East India Company. With Italy divided into eight states, he was obliged to run several consular centres, especially since Austrian fears of revolutionary activity increased restrictions on foreigners. The Austrian Empire was in decline, increasingly threatened by internal rebellion. To counter this, the Austrians resorted to repressive measures such as censorship of the press, police surveillance and the imprisonment of radicals. The rules were relaxed for British subjects, but they insisted on keeping track of them nonetheless. Any interference in local politics was strongly discouraged and the consulate was expected to monitor the activities of British expatriates and make certain they had the correct licences and visas. The British Consul General was expanding his responsibilities and therefore looked favourably on the application of an army officer.

Babington Nolan was offered an unofficial position in the new consulate in Milan on the understanding that though it might eventually become permanent, this was not guaranteed and he would receive no salary, only being allowed to retain some fees to pay for his expenses. While this was a meagre income, the chance to make influential contacts within the expatriate community and with the Austrians was an incentive. However, the government was annoyed by his unfortunate use of the title 'His Majesty's Vice-Consul in Milan' which he had no right to use, being only a consular agent. He was also foolish enough to use the rank of major before he was officially gazetted (it would be 1838 before he actually received this promotion). Forced to apologize, he rapidly discovered that the government imposed stricter protocols than the military.

For several years Babington Nolan performed his consular duties adequately until, in April 1834, Money returned home complaining of a cold and a stomach disorder, fell into a coma and died shortly afterwards. Perhaps assuming that someone had to take over immediately, as in the army, Babington Nolan acted swiftly, informing London:

> *I therefore consider it my duty to repair forthwith to Venice and take upon myself the charge. If the Vice Consul at Trieste approves of this measure on my arrival there I shall continue in the performance of the Consular duties there until I am favoured with further instructions from your department.*[7]

Babington had misjudged the situation. The need to replace Money was far from urgent and his own failure to observe official custom was poorly received. Mr Cazaly, his obvious successor in Italy, had more experience than Nolan, which resulted in a serious disagreement. Naturally, Babington's already tarnished reputation influenced government circles: the authorities insisted that the formalities must be observed. In addition to dealing with a stormy correspondence with Cazaly, they insisted that Babington return some unauthorized fees he had collected, much to his embarrassment. He was confirmed in his position as vice-consul, but taking over Money's role was out of the question.

Money was eventually replaced by Lieutenant Colonel Sir Thomas Sorrell. Any hopes Nolan may have entertained about forming a good relationship with an ex-army officer were soon dashed: Sorrell took his task very seriously and conducted a far-reaching investigation into consular practices, which revealed unflattering facts about Babington. He considered him a bad businessman and remarked on the fact that he had charged British subjects for unnecessary visas, which had caused complaints. He was over-enthusiastic about making introductions on the consulate's behalf with more regard to his own interests than the government's and, despite some useful military intelligence he had gathered, Sorrell recommended his removal from office.[8]

Such criticism could not have come at a worse time. In 1835 the Austrian Emperor Francis I died, leaving the throne to his son Ferdinand. The new emperor was popular with his subjects but suffered from epilepsy and displayed signs of mental illness. A regency council was established under Archduke Ludwig, which easily manipulated the impressionable monarch. It was dominated by the Archduke and the Ministers Prince Klemens Metternich and Count Kolowrat.[9] Metternich had played a leading political role in Napoleon's downfall and was a leading reactionary, but even his leadership was unlikely to quell the emerging nationalism spreading across Europe and the Austrian Empire. Baron von Hübner believed that many of the Austrian ruling classes were complacent about the widespread unrest and that even Metternich seemed paralyzed when it came to taking effective action:

> *the more I examine the situation in Italy, the more convinced I am that the game is up. One doesn't arrest a revolutionary by means of diplomatic notes or leaders in the Press that one reads. It's like trying to stop a steam-engine with a walking-stick.*[10]

With the region becoming increasingly unstable, Lord Palmerston had far more weighty matters on his mind than dealing with departmental squabbles. So Babington was removed from his position as the simplest way of solving a minor dispute. He was mortified, but his entreaties for reinstatement were futile.

Babington Nolan's career in both the military and the consular service had been unsatisfactory. He had not risen far in the army during a period when the war against France permitted even an officer of limited means to gain advancement through active service and, although a capable officer in an administrative capacity, his career had been steady but unremarkable. However, his consular service had revealed a different side to his character. A mixture of political naivety and unscrupulous ambition had seen him come dangerously close to impropriety. It remained to be seen just how much the young Louis would take after his father.

Chapter 2

Imperial Service

Although his own career was in a downward spiral, Babington Nolan was determined to ensure that his sons prospered. His stepson William Dick Macfarlane had already purchased a commission in the 42nd Foot in 1825 with the help of his patron, Dr William Dick, after whom he was named. He served with the regiment in Gibraltar and later, in 1832, transferred into the 92nd Highland Regiment of Foot with the rank of captain.[11] Yet it was his own troubled career and the need to provide for his other sons and stepsons that troubled Babington Nolan.

In his usual style, he petitioned Horse Guards (the headquarters of the British Army) in London for another appointment for himself and recommending his teenage sons for commissions. However, during peacetime the army had no pressing need for officers, and the majority of places were likely to be given to those with wealth and influence. Despite bombarding Lord Raglan, then Military Secretary, with letters and calling in all the favours he could from friends and associates, his attempts were met by bureaucratic indifference. He even suggested selling his own captaincy to William, then a lieutenant, which met with a curt refusal.

During his time in Italy, the Imperial Austrian Army had impressed Babington Nolan and, if entry into the British Army was blocked, service on the Continent was an attractive alternative. Having heard that the Austrians allowed foreign cadets in their military colleges, Babington bought a place for his stepson George Ruddach in 1826 with the K.k. Philip Prinz zu Hessen-Homburg 19, Infanterie-Regiment. George completed his training and later transferred to a cavalry regiment (K.k. Kaiser Franz 4, Uhlanen-Regiment) in 1829. He served with this lancer regiment until 1832 before resigning his commission.[12] George's experiences convinced Babington Nolan that a commission in the Austrian Army was the next best thing to a British commission for his other sons.

Archibald Nolan was multilingual, speaking Italian, German and French and, although Lord Hill showed some interest, he failed to secure him a commission despite his father's entreaties. In order to make him a more attractive candidate, Babington Nolan decided to enrol him in one of the

Austrian regimental cadet schools. Accordingly he wrote to Lord Hill:

> *that he may be the better prepared when called upon, I am entering him*
> *into a Military College near Vienna where the studies they pursue are*
> *much the same as in the Senior Department of the Royal Military*
> *College at Sandhurst, with the addition of practical field works and*
> *every other branch necessary to fit them for the Quartermaster General's*
> *Department.*[13]

In fact, British military training was still in its infancy and the Austrian colleges and academies were considered superior in many ways. In the British Army, the cavalry and infantry tended to conduct all training within the regiments themselves and only specialists such as engineers, artillery and staff officers received formal military education.

Having been frustrated at every turn by Horse Guards and seriously entertaining the idea of permanently retiring from the British Army, Babington decided to enter both Archibald and Louis into the Military Pioneer School at Tulln, near Vienna, where they were admitted as 'Achilles' and 'Ludwig' Nolan. Both were accepted as *ex-propriis* cadets in the K.k. Friedrich Wilhelm III, König von Preussen 10, Husaren-Regiment. At 14, Louis was older than many applicants and, since Archibald had just turned 17, he was lucky to be accepted.[14] Both took to the college with enthusiasm: Babington was so impressed that two years later he bought a place for Edmond Nolan at Tulln to serve in the K.k. Carl Albert König von Sardinien 5, Husaren-Regiment. Yet the personal register for Louis records that he entered the 10th Hussars rather than the 5th Hussars on 15 March 1832 as a voluntary cadet and that his father paid the *montur* of 80 florins and 49 kreuzer for his uniform, horse and equipment. It listed his place of birth as North America 1818 and recorded his religion as a Protestant.[15] It is interesting to note that, although an infantryman himself, Babington showed a marked preference for getting his sons into cavalry regiments which enjoyed senior status in the Austrian Army as in the British.

The Austrian Army had gained a great deal of experience during the Napoleonic Wars, with the Habsburgs joining six out of the seven coalitions formed against France by the allied powers. After the shocking defeats of 1805, the Austrian Archduke Charles, appointed Generalissimus, had pushed through a series of much needed reforms against serious bureaucratic opposition and resistance from the nobility. However, the Austrian Army never really matched Napoleon's vaunted Grande Armée, being slow moving and restricted by its style of fighting in large, dense formations. It fought at its best during the battles of Aspern-Essling and Wagram in 1809, when given room to manoeuvre on open Marchfeld plain near Vienna, but in more restrictive country it was regularly outclassed by the French.[16] The forces raised against Napoleon included well-trained and disciplined infantry and a large, well-equipped artillery arm. However, though the cavalry were well trained, they lacked sufficient horses to raise enough regiments against the French. By the 1830s, the Austrian Army still contained both heavy and light cavalry but their dragoon regiments were beginning to resemble a cross between the two. Kurassiers, Dragoons and Cheveauxlegers were officially classed as heavy horse intended for shock action in battle, while Hussars were classed as light cavalry intended primarily for raiding, scouting, outpost work and the pursuit of a fleeing enemy force.[17]

Hussar regiments in the Imperial Army were exclusively Hungarian and were renowned throughout Europe as the classic model for light cavalry. During the eighteenth century, impressed by the stylish uniform and panache of the Hungarian hussars, many Western European armies had adapted their light cavalry in emulation.[18] Their tight, colourful uniforms with fur-edged pelisses (a jacket worn attached to the shoulder for show rather than practical use) came to embody the dash and spirit of the cavalryman above all other types of horseman. The only other light cavalry were the uhlan (or lancer) regiments: these carried lances in addition to light sabres, had the distinctive squared Polish style *czapka* helmet and wore flamboyant uniforms rivalling the hussars.

Few regimes needed an efficient and professional army as much as the Austrian Habsburgs, whose empire was beset by internal strife as well as external enemies. The historian A J P Taylor accurately observed that 'The Habsburg Monarchy was the toughest organization in the history of modern Europe'.[19] Over the centuries they had withstood the Reformation, the Turks and the French under Louis XIV. After 1815 their union consisted of the Austrian Crown hereditary and Bohemian lands of the kingdoms of Galicia, Illyria and Dalmatia, the Hungarian kingdoms of Hungary and Croatia-Slavonia, the Grand Duchy of Transylvania and the Italian states of Lombardy-Venetia. Many believed that the Habsburgs' rule over this sprawling confederation of diverse nationalities and religions was tenuous and that her imperial days were numbered. Nevertheless, it had weathered a storm of hammer blows from Napoleon and eventually saw him deposed and exiled. The Imperial Army was apparently ideal for a young man seeking to gain military experience.

Austrian military schools and academies had a long history, dating back to 1717 when Prince Eugene of Savoy had founded an Academy of Engineers to train specialist troops such as artillery, and in 1769 the Empress Maria Theresa established the Military Academy at the Castle of Wiener Neustadt. These were the two premier military Hochschulens. There were also a number of regimental cadet schools at Ollmütz, Graz and Milan along with the Pioneer School at Tulln, which was considered second only to the two main academies. Despite the existence of these military schools, there was no established system for recruiting officers; candidates were usually drawn from the gentry, nobility, veterans of the wars, sons of soldiers and occasionally from promising non-commissioned officers who had risen from the ranks.[20]

Wiener Neustadt was still considered to give the finest military education available. Its graduates enjoyed an enhanced reputation with increased chance of promotion and a stronger likelihood of gaining entry into the top regiments. In addition, only their students automatically became officers upon graduation. However, the college had been resting on its laurels and in many ways no longer delivered the training it claimed to provide. The huge expense of training there discouraged many, and it had become the almost exclusive province of the sons of serving military officers in the higher ranks. Even the nobility had begun to desert Wiener Neustadt, considering its fees to be a waste of money in comparison with the benefits of the cadet schools.

An absurdly repressive system was imposed on the pupils with fraternization between the years forbidden and the boys kept in a state of almost total isolation from the outside world during term time. Their education was limited to a narrow field, with learning largely taught by rote. Even practical military training (such as riding) was poorly taught because of the restrictions imposed. Excessive punishments were commonplace and the only things in which the academy excelled were discipline, the instillation of self-confidence and loyalty to the empire.[21] Its reputation was such that six places in each regiment were usually held open for Wiener Neustadt graduates, but Joseph II had spoken strongly about putting the college 'on a more military footing' with the need to produce 'intelligent officers for the army'.[22] Joseph died, however, before his planned reforms could be implemented.

The Nolan boys were fortunate to benefit from a more liberal and modern education at Tulln. This cadet school was part of the '*Inhaber*' system, *Inhabers* being the 'colonel-proprietors' of each regiment. Although an *Inhaber* held equal status, the colonel of the regiment was usually a separate officer and *Inhabers* often performed few duties for the regiment itself. They were often of general rank or above with aristocratic and royal patrons being commonplace. The system was an echo of the seventeenth century when the king had been obliged to allow the nobility certain rights in order to persuade them to raise troops for the Crown. Though their powers had been slightly curtailed by the Hofskriegsrath (military council), they still wielded enormous influence and no cadet was accepted without the approval of the regimental proprietor. Although purchase was only officially permitted for the lowest ranks of the officer corps and promotion was ostensibly through merit, this was a system of direct patronage. Consequently the apparent social inclusivity of the cadet schools was deceptive:

> *The Austrian army is open to all: but its genius is, in the same sense in which the observation may be made of the British army as compared with the French, decidedly aristocratical. Both the crown and the proprietary colonels are inclined to give preference to the members of those families which with us would be understood to constitute the gentry; and it is the policy of the state not only to engage in its service members of its own highest nobility, but many princes likewise of the smaller reigning houses of Germany.[23]*

The reactionary attitudes of the establishment were exacerbated by recent unrest and so it exercised control over unpredictable men who could rise only through merit and whose loyalty to the Habsburgs was not beyond question. Without their proprietor's acceptance, a graduate would remain a cadet and live an unhappy existence, with his status falling between the ranks of officers and men, being despised by both and treated like a servant by his superiors.

The cadet schools cost less than the academies, but Babington Nolan was prepared to pay for his sons to enter the most prestigious arm of the service despite the increased cost of uniforms, weaponry, horse tack and mounts. The education Louis and his brothers received was varied and occasionally involved temporary transfer to other cadet schools in order to learn about the different arms of the service. Cadets were always expected to be in uniform and march in formation about the college, but the regime imposed was far less severe than the academies, and cadets were permitted a reasonable amount of freedom. Serving within the ranks like common soldiers was part of their instruction, enabling them to gain some insight into how the men were treated. However, as with most armies, the officer corps was not studious and great faith was placed in tradition, regulations and obedience; any suggestions of reform were treated with suspicion.[24]

The Austrian officer Freiherr Fenner von Fenneberg remarked that apart from learning the regulations, cadets' education consisted merely of 'situation drawing, terrain study, knowledge of weapons, history and geography'.[25] While it was true that the standard of teaching was unexceptional, the assumption that practical exposure to the subject would eventually teach by example over eight years of instruction had some merit. Good students would have the determination to learn under such circumstances if they applied themselves. However, Fenneberg was not the only critic of the system. Archduke Maximilian d'Este conducted an examination of the selection and training of officers in an effort to improve military efficiency. He had a poor view of cadets, commenting:

> *They are youths of twelve to eighteen, mainly those who were too lacking in talent, too slovenly and too wild to do well at school or were unable to hope to secure an honourable position in civilian life. The parents just say: 'the lad is fit for nothing, he will have to be a soldier'.[26]*

While this may have contained an element of truth, committed students are rare under any system, though there were notable exceptions. Louis Nolan proved to be one of these: few took as great an interest in their subjects as he did. Determined to succeed and wildly enthusiastic about the cavalry, he impressed his superiors and excelled in horsemanship. He valued the theories on the art of horsemanship and cavalry that he studied under Colonel Haas and later spoke of him as the best teacher he ever had.[27] He was also a keen reader and fascinated by military history. A great deal of time was taken up at the school in language instruction: since the empire they were to protect and police was multi-national this was unsurprising, but the Nolans had an advantage in that they were already multi-lingual. Louis's regiment was Hungarian, as were all the hussar regiments, so he was compelled to learn that language too.

In May 1835 both Archibald and Louis graduated from Tulln and were confirmed as subalterns in the 7th and 10th Hussar regiments. Although only 17, Louis gained this promotion one year early, probably on the recommendation of Prince Liechtenstein. Naturally, this was reliant on his instructor's reports, but the length of the course was under revision and Louis was not the only man to graduate a year early. Archibald Nolan did not enjoy Austrian service, resigning within a year, but Louis was determined to become a career soldier.

Life in the service was tough, especially in the garrisons along the military border regions around Croatia. Likewise, postings to northern Hungary and Galicia were unpopular with officers, who were obliged to spend months in isolated outposts and poor conditions. Regiments were often billeted over a wide area and they might be unable to socialize with their fellow officers for considerable intervals whilst living in villages where they only had a limited grasp of the language.[28] Garrison life could be boring and squalid enough to make even inspections something to look forward to since they involved contact with the rest of the regiment. Louis, or Ludwig as he was known, was stationed briefly in Hungary and on the Polish frontier as well as Austria itself.

In common with most European armies, training was often inadequate and marksmanship was neglected because of the high cost of ammunition. Only Great Britain, with her mercantile power, could afford to provide regular live-firing target practice at this time. In addition, expense precluded military manoeuvres being held on a large scale.[29] Although imperial service had its appeal, it was easy to see how Nolan, as a very keen officer eager to progress, began to be dissatisfied when he compared his army to that experienced by his stepbrother William, by then serving with the 92nd.

Louis became popular in the 10th Hussars, swiftly rising to become the senior lieutenant in the regiment; but the fact that he was a foreigner troubled him since Austrians or Hungarians were likely to get preferential treatment. Though it was true that promotion after the first rank was supposedly through merit alone, money or favours were often exchanged unofficially and although the Hofkriegsrath had tried to curb the power of the *Inhabers* many times they met with little success. Realistically, the practice was likely to continue in spite of any legislation passed. Another problem for Louis was that the army was full of the Austrian gentry and nobility and as von Fenneberg remarked, 'Nepotism rules here in its whole fearful power.'[30] As in Britain, patriotism and loyalty were virtues prized above all others: a man of Austrian or Hungarian birth with social connections was bound to have an advantage over a foreigner, however popular or able he might be.

Mark Boyd, a firm friend of Louis's family, recalled his talents and how they had impressed the Austrians when he wrote his memoirs some years after Nolan's death. He equated Louis's remarkable flair for languages with his musical ability as an accomplished violinist, flautist, piano player and singer. Babington once told him a tale about how Louis's colonel, Vincenz von Ezvik, showed off his protégé to the Grand Duke who was reviewing troops in Milan. Telling him that this officer was an accomplished linguist, he challenged the

Duke to guess his nationality after conversing with him and

> *His Imperial Highness first addressed Nolan in Hungarian, who replied with fluency and correctness. He then went to Polish (Nolan's regiment had been stationed on the borders of Poland), and here he was equally at home; Italian and German followed with the same result. Next came English, and lastly French. The Duke then said: 'Colonel, all you told me of this young officer is true: and it is only from his light hair and moustache that I see he is German.'* [31]

The Duke was therefore surprised when told of Louis's origins, since the English were hardly renowned for their grasp of languages. Interestingly, this brief description contrasts with the few depictions of Nolan that mostly show him as dark-haired.

An officer who excelled in his duties but who lacked money or social connections should have been able to rely on his *Conduitte Liste* (conduct list). Compiled by his superior officers, this document recorded strengths, weaknesses and potential for promotion. Technically, an officer could request to see the list and challenge anything it contained that he considered unfair. However, in practice this was rarely permitted and therefore this attempt to introduce promotion by merit was open to abuse. It was not unknown for an *Inhaber* to recommend a candidate for promotion purely on the basis of his conduct list, knowing the officer concerned only slightly and assuming that everything contained within it was legitimate. Officers had few avenues to complain if they believed they had been treated unfairly; they risked becoming unpopular in their regiment and alienating their *Inhaber* if they did so. Even when such complaints were successful, such troublemakers were often forced onto the pension list in consequence. [32]

Louis's conduct list reveals some interesting information and is mostly in the form of tables with brief entries describing his abilities, knowledge and character. It records how he served as a cadet for three years and two months, then a further three years and five months as a second lieutenant. His health was described as very good, his natural talents as many and his mind, or character, as 'ambitious and austere'. [33] However, considering the strict regime practised in Austrian service, the use of the word austere may not have been intended in a negative sense. Although it praises his German, French and English language skills, it remarks that he only spoke 'a little Hungarian', [34] which would have been a weakness in a Hungarian regiment. Nonetheless, this was a skill that would naturally improve given time.

Although the list praises his general appearance, his conduct on parade and knowledge of drill were classed as rather bad.[35] However, it remarks on his willingness to learn as far as horsemanship was concerned and classes him as a good rider. It is probable that the Pioneer School at Tulln marked him out as suitable for the cavalry early on, since the list states that he had no real training as a sapper. However, it does comment that he possessed some knowledge of military engineering but qualifies the remark with the intriguing aside that this was only 'like it was taught in the pioneer school',[36] implying that this was not as extensive as would be taught at the specialist engineering academy.

They were generally pleased with his behaviour and he was described as being popular within the regiment, polite to civilians and just and reasonable with other subalterns. He also maintained his quarters well, which was an asset since he was likely to be billeted under a variety of circumstances throughout the empire. A revealing part of the behaviour section for the Imperial Army is the list of potential lapses described under 'alcoholic, gambler, notorious debtor and quarreller'. Louis did not suffer from any of these vices according to this report. Rounding off this section, it is noted that he was always willing, enthusiastic and 'useful for duty', having clearly made a good general impression with his superiors.[37] The one stain on his record was his failure to attend military manoeuvres in 1837, but there was nothing in the report that would seriously harm his prospects for promotion.

Pay in the Austrian army varied according to whether the state was at war or peace, wartime pay naturally being higher. Expenses were huge and accommodation and preparation allowances (for travel) were often withheld. Man-servants were provided but the cost of uniforms and mounts could be ruinous. Pay was also deducted for taking leave of absence for anything over six weeks. For leave of up to a year, servants could be recalled unless retained at the officers' expense and no pay or allowances were permitted at all. Another expense was getting married within the service. This was officially discouraged: according to regulations, only one-sixth of the officer corps was permitted to marry. If a subaltern did marry, he would be obliged to pay a 'marriage settlement' to provide for his wife and orphans if he died within the service. Though this sounded like common sense, the amount was deliberately kept very high to discourage marriage, and consequentially couples often had a poor standard of living. Although there is no evidence that Louis wished to marry, the desire to do so eventually and bring up a family may have influenced his decision to leave the service.

During the 1830s Babington Nolan persisted in the campaign to get his sons commissions in the British Army, dividing his time between London, Edinburgh and Milan. Edmond Nolan left imperial service shortly after qualifying from Tulln and returned to London but, after his father's efforts fell through, returned to serve with his brother in the 10th Hussars for a year before resigning his commission. In 1837 his father was finally gazetted major in the 6th Foot, a regiment he never actually served with, and he retired that same year. Archibald finally despaired of entering the British Army and took up the management of the Ruddachs' Adelphi estate in Tobago. With emigration to the colonies on the increase, Archibald prospered for a while by opening a general store for the new colonists.[38]

Louis had proved by far the most committed Nolan in regard to military service. However, his conduct list recorded the fact that through 'his own guilt that he defaulted the year's *Concentrierung*'.[39] This was one of the high points of the military year in the imperial service, where large-scale manoeuvres took place. It was unusual for such a dedicated officer to miss it, but Nolan had some excuse. Taking leave of absence he had returned to London for the coronation of the young Queen Victoria, but failed to return in time. Nevertheless, it was one of the few really negative remarks his superiors made against him since these important manoeuvres were only held once a year.

Following the death of William IV that year, many in Europe hoped that the accession of the 18-year-old queen would usher in a new era thanks to her youth and extensive family connections on the Continent. In addition, she was unmarried and many hoped that an arranged union with one of the great royal European dynasties might forge a new alliance. Elaborate ceremonies had been planned, with Parliament voting £200,000 for the occasion – her predecessor had received only £50,000. In addition, the tradition of a procession to Westminster Abbey was being revived, even though this would cost £26,000 and had not taken place since 1761.

A host of military events were to take place before the coronation. The Queen attended a review of the Life Guards, Grenadier Guards and a detachment of Lancers in Windsor Park on 28 September 1837. She dressed in the 'Windsor uniform', dark blue with a red collar and cuffs, and enjoyed the spectacle, later writing: 'I saluted them by putting my hand to my cap like the officers do, and was much admired for my manner of doing it.'[40] Louis attended a similar review held in Hyde Park on 9 July 1838, though this was on a larger scale. Some 130,000 spectators witnessed the Queen inspecting her troops along with several complex military manoeuvres, live artillery firing, skirmishing, cavalry charges and musketry in the forms of volley, file and rapid fire. However, as *The Times* conceded, some spectators, Louis being amongst them, had seen demonstrations on a far grander scale:

> *but to many of the distinguished foreigners who have been in the habit of witnessing such vast assemblages of troops as those at the reviews of Toplitz and other places on the Continent, it would appear no doubt as only a grand review in miniature.*[41]

It must have passed through Louis's mind that he had missed an opportunity of taking part in the far larger *Concentrierung* for that year; but the Hyde Park event's smaller scale perhaps gave him a better view of the proceedings, which large numbers might have obscured.

Two large levées were held immediately prior to the coronation and while both were remarkable successes, one was unwisely held on 18 June, the anniversary of the Battle of Waterloo, which irritated the French Ambassador. A vast number of foreign dignitaries attended, including Victoria's uncle, the Duke of Saxe-Coburg, her half-brother and sister (Prince and Princess of Leningen) and the renowned Marshal Nicholas Jean Soult, who had fought against the British in the Iberian Peninsula.[42] Many were greatly impressed with the bearing and dignity of the new sovereign, the Duke of Wellington remarking loyally, 'She not merely filled her chair, she filled the room.'[43]

With so many royal German relatives and dignitaries present, many of the dances in the quadrilles were to German music, and a particular fuss was made over the Austrian Ambassador, Prince Esterhazy, and the Ambassador Extraordinary, Prince Schwarzenberg. At the second State Ball, Esterhazy wore cavalry uniform whilst introducing a number of Austrian officers:

> *The most magnificent uniform was that of Prince Esterhazy the Austrian Ambassador, it was a pelisse of dark crimson velvet, the sword belt thickly studded with diamonds, and the scabbard was also very profusely ornamented with diamonds; the hussar cap had several rows of pearls with a string of diamonds in the middle, finished with a very beautiful tassel set in brilliants. The Order of the Golden Fleece (suspended round the neck) and the . . . jewels of the other orders of knighthood worn by the Prince, were also set in diamonds and precious stones.*[44]

His entourage included Baron de Vrints Berberich, Count Thun, Count

Albrizze, Marquis Strozze, Lieutenant Kerr and the 20-year-old Lieutenant Louis Nolan of the 10th Hussars.[45] Immaculately turned out in full-dress uniform, though perhaps not as spectacularly turned out as his benefactor, Louis must have swelled with pride at the honour bestowed upon him. Quite how he had secured a place in this diplomatic mission is unclear, but it is not beyond the realm of possibility that Babington Nolan had called in a few favours for his son from his contacts in the Austrian government. Nolan must have exercised considerable charm to gain a place on the mission, though the fact that he was one of the few Englishmen in the service must have influenced his *Inhaber*'s decision. It would certainly further his career. Nevertheless, it is highly unlikely that his *Inhaber* would allow his participation, or that the ambassador would present him to foreign royalty, unless they placed great confidence in him.

The coronation was held on 28 June 1838 and proved to be a remarkable display of pageantry, with the military playing a large part. Westminster Abbey was decked out in crimson and gold, bands played patriotic music in all the London parks, a huge two-day fair was held in Hyde Park with numerous illuminations and firework displays. Although traditions were honoured, the establishment had also made new concessions such as permitting the members of the House of Commons to hail the sovereign in the same fashion as the Lords, who had done so for centuries, cheering her a full nine times after she was crowned.[46]

This display of patriotism may have influenced Louis, but it is likely that he had harboured desires to join the British Army for some time. Though he had benefited from his Austrian service, as a foreigner he would never be fully accepted; besides, the British had the best army in the world and their empire dominated world trade. At Horse Guards Louis secured an interview with Lord Fitzroy Somerset (the future Lord Raglan) and made a good impression. Meanwhile, Babington petitioned General Count Edouard von Clam-Gallas with a view to easing Louis's exit from Austrian service. Louis also wrote to Colonel von Ezvik requesting further leave and confiding that he intended to resign from the 10th if he could find a viable alternative.[47] However, learning from his brothers' mistakes, Louis would not resign until a British commission was confirmed.

Eventually, Somerset agreed to substitute Louis's name for Edmond's on the waiting list and, on the payment of £450 from his mother Eliza, he was sold the rank of ensign in the 37th Foot. However, Babington was determined to see that he gained some foreign service and this was transferred to the 30th and then the 4th Foot in rapid succession. The Nolans then changed their minds again after seeing the 15th Light Dragoons (a Hussar regiment) pass through Edinburgh. Its military bearing impressed them but it was also about to be posted to India and Babington knew that his son was a cavalryman at heart. He wrote to Somerset:

> *the interest of the Service would be forwarded by the humble efforts of an efficient officer, acquainted with the duties of the Field, and Riding School, he having had the advantage of assisting at cavalry manoeuvres on a very extended scale, where he had the honour to act, as Aide de Camp, on the personal Staff of his (Proprietor) Colonel, Field Marshall Lieutenant Baron Bretschneider, commanding the cavalry at the camps in the Austrian Lombardo-Veneto Territory in Italy with a force of nearly one hundred thousand men.[48]*

As chance would have it, Babington's old friend Sir Walter Scott (son of the author Sir Walter Scott and nephew to Thomas Scott) happened to be the Second Lieutenant Colonel in the regiment and added his recommendation. The Military Secretary, probably weary of the Nolans' incessant requests by this time, relented, but with the stipulation that Nolan accept the lower rank of cornet rather than his current Austrian rank.

The Nolans celebrated Louis's commission in the 15th Light Dragoons on 23 April 1839, though they suffered two bereavements in that year that dampened the celebrations. William Macfarlane died in Perth aged only 31 and Archibald succumbed to the climate in Tobago, dying on 30 August 1839. In addition, the Austrian Army was displeased that Louis had overstayed his leave and initially refused to accept his resignation. For a short time he held commissions in both armies, but after some deliberation the Hofkriegsrath had him struck off their rolls. It seemed that he had not followed the correct procedure after overstaying his leave in Scotland. Sickness was the official reason he gave for his already extended leave, and when he finally tendered his resignation he also forgot to write a *Quittirungs Revers*. This declaration not only formalized his resignation from the Imperial Army but also gave a commitment never to take up arms against the Habsburg Monarchy. His colonel remarked that this was probably through ignorance of the correct procedures and Nolan eventually asked his friend Lieutenant Esserich to write it for him, sign it in his stead with two witnesses, and to submit it to the regimental adjutant, Lieutenant Cluncsits.[49]

There was also a financial discrepancy involving his brother Edmond, who had left the army without paying his *equipirung*. This was a bill covering expenses for the care of his horses and payment of grooms amounting to 150 florins 56 kreutzer. As he had left the service and was beyond military jurisdiction, either Louis or Colonel Ezvik was obliged to honour the debt. The colonel, who had now retired, tried to get Louis or his family to send him the money, writing that several of the regiment's letters had been left unanswered. Though Louis received no formal rebuke or mark against his name, his actions were clearly considered to be poor form: it was an unfortunate way to end his service in the Austrian Army.

Chapter 3

Home and Abroad

Nolan was unusual in seeking service in India; many officers transferred regiment in order to avoid such postings. However, the Nolans were not wealthy, and the advice of his father, who had served in the colonies himself, probably influenced his decision. Furthermore, reputations could still be made in India despite the fact that the elite looked down upon such service. A significant faction within the military felt that the restrictions of the climate led to a drop in standards, such as infrequent drilling on account of the heat, and considered that soldiering in such an atmosphere bred laziness and ineptitude. In addition, experience gained in the incessant minor conflicts on the Indian subcontinent was viewed poorly in comparison to the effort required to defeat a modern European enemy. To some extent these attitudes were based on snobbery and ignorance; but these were not the only problems: prior to the opening of the Suez Canal (1869), the trip to India took several months; living expenses were high with the vast number of servants required to maintain an officer's lifestyle; and worst of all, sickness was rife among Europeans in India, resulting in a high mortality rate. All these factors made Indian service unpopular.

Nolan did not join the 15th immediately, though he had already incurred considerable expense in buying the 15th's dark blue uniform with gold braiding, scarlet pelisse and scarlet shako, which alone cost the equivalent of two years' pay in the regiment. By the time of his arrival at Maidstone the majority of the regiment had already left for India. Lieutenant Colonel Lovell Benjamin Badcock (who would later change his surname to Lovell) had embarked, as had Sir Walter Scott, who served as a 'secondary' colonel. Having two colonels was a peculiarity of Indian service since one colonel would often serve as a brigadier, consequently having little time for regimental duties, and the second colonel was necessary to act in his stead. Though the East India Company maintained studs in India, most cavalry regiments kept a troop at the Maidstone cavalry depot to train recruits, conduct advanced courses in horsemanship and occasionally provide remounts. The barracks there had been constructed during the Napoleonic wars:

A Depôt for the cavalry regiments serving in India was established in Maidstone in 1797, the barracks being constructed by John King, one of the magistrates of the borough, who contracted for the work. Horse and foot regiments frequently passed through the town, and their movements were attended with far more bustle than now.[50]

Captain George Key was left in command of the Maidstone troop, and upon discovering their common interests in cavalry and horsemanship, Nolan rapidly struck up a friendship with him. Having served in a foreign regiment for several years, Nolan must have found the transition to a regiment where he could speak his mother tongue relatively easy, and his adoption into the 15th went smoothly. As in his Austrian service, he was rarely referred to as Louis, most of his comrades preferring to anglicize his forename to 'Lewis'. Having served as a lieutenant in the Austrian Army, he possessed far more experience than was expected of his junior rank, and he rapidly drew attention for his skill and competence.

The regiment sailed in three troopships to Bombay, and Nolan was just in time to catch the last of these. The voyage on the *Malabar* was lengthy and arduous, sailing on 14 July and arriving in India on 9 November. The journey proved a trial for Louis; very soon after the regiment's arrival at Bangalore in southern India he fell ill. The difficulties Europeans had in adjusting to the Indian climate made this far from unusual. However, when Nolan appeared before a medical board they granted him a full two years' sick leave. Even allowing for the time of the return voyage this seems overly generous to modern eyes; but possibly Nolan contrived this to avoid as much Indian service as possible since he was already having difficulties in paying his servants and making obligatory purchases such as another new style of uniform. He left for England as soon as he was able, his leave dating from 26 March 1840.

Nolan's recovery was fairly swift and he returned to the depot in June 1841 well before his sick leave expired. His recent illness, personal preferences – or both – made home service appealing to Nolan, and certainly he took to duties at the depot with a will, despite having to take another short period of sick leave. He purchased a lieutenancy in June 1841 and, rather than return to the regiment in Bangalore, opted to take the riding masters' equitation course at Maidstone. It is sometimes claimed that Nolan rose through the ranks through his abilities alone, but in fact he purchased all his promotions. His interest in horsemanship had developed into something of an obsession, and in the company of men like Captain Key he was in his element. He took an active part in the social life at the officers' mess and attended Holy Trinity Church regularly with his fellow officers, though he does not appear to have held strong religious convictions.

Though the use of cavalry was gradually diminishing on the modern battlefield, the mounted arm still played a vital role in warfare. Their speed and mobility made them ideal as the eyes and ears of an army, providing reconnaissance, protection on the march, harassment of the enemy and swift warning of enemy action when the army was encamped. Though improvements in the accuracy and volume of fire that infantry and artillery could deliver lessened the cavalry's effectiveness in battle, when properly employed the cavalry were still formidable. It should also be remembered that against some colonial foes with firepower inferior to that of a modern army, the cavalry were far more effective, and between 1815 and 1914 colonial warfare was the main occupation of the British Army.

However, conditions at the depot were far from ideal. Seven cavalry regiments maintained a troop at Maidstone to support their regiments overseas, six being stationed in India and one in South Africa. At times more than 400 recruits were posted there; this led to overcrowded and unsanitary conditions. The drop in living standards meant indiscipline, and in consequence courts martial were regularly used.[51] One soldier commented:

> *The greatest source of annoyance to me was the bad ventilation and overcrowding of the barrack-rooms, three or four-and-twenty – sometimes more – men being crowded into rooms not large enough for half the number. I was always thankful for the reveille and when it was my turn for guard, as the oak floor of the guard-room was infinitely preferable to the close and noisome troop-room.*[52]

Officers enjoyed much better conditions. Although timber-framed like the rest of the barracks, the officers' mess was a large, three-storey building with brick chimneys and a slate roof. 'Flights of stairs divided it internally into three, and there were service wings to the rear. The officers had small, plain rooms with a fireplace in one corner and a built-in cupboard in the other, and they were issued with bedding, a table, bellows, fire irons and a chamber pot.'[53] The building was clad in white weatherboarding and, if spartan by a gentleman's standards, offered some comforts. It was one of only three such buildings constructed as officers' quarters in England, and Maidstone's is the only one to have survived to this day, as the *White Rabbit Inn*, while the others have long since been demolished. Nolan would have spent a considerable amount of time here although he may have maintained additional rooms in the town at various times.

The main purpose of the depot was to train recruits in basic horsemanship, instruct officers and NCOs in advanced equestrianism and acquire horses suitable for service abroad. Though remounts were also purchased in India, there never seemed to be enough and English thoroughbreds were considered the finest mounts available in any case. Horses had to be capable of surviving both the long voyage out to India and withstanding the rigours of the climate upon arrival. Selection was difficult; Nolan would later write of the depot's deficiencies, claiming that the standard of breaking-in horses and equipping them was poor.

Riding instruction was central to a cavalryman's training and teaching the correct 'military seat', or riding stance, was the foundation of this training. In previous years saddles and stirrups had been constructed so that a rider sat almost straight-legged as an aid to supporting the weight of armour and weaponry. Changes in military equipment led some to see this 'balance seat' as obsolete and unnecessary. Though many clung to the old method, new styles were being suggested with shorter stirrup lengths intended to produce a more relaxed and practical riding posture.[54] With the rider's knee bent at a greater angle, it was more comfortable and allowed greater use of the knees to control the horse. Nolan and Key were firmly in favour of such methods, but Captain Louis Meyer, the current riding master, believed in teaching the traditional 'high German' style of equitation, which led to numerous disagreements.

It was vital for a cavalryman to be able to ride in formation with his troop and not just as an individual rider. Depending on the size of the formation, the troop would conform to the movements of the squadron, which in turn would conform to the regiment. When riding as a brigade, regiments would follow the directions of a brigade commander. Moving as a body was difficult and lines had to be kept straight and correctly spaced in order to effect the twenty-one basic field movements, such as advancing, wheeling and retiring, without losing formation. In theory, regular drilling should make such movement virtually instinctive and on the battlefield a cavalry unit would be highly manoeuvrable and capable of swift changes of formation and direction. Officers rode in front and the men would follow their orders, which were conveyed either verbally or by a trumpeter. A well-trained horse would assist in these movements, as would the NCOs, who would be constantly watching for gaps in the line or riders falling out of formation. It was considered poor form for an officer to turn in the saddle to check if the men were conforming to his lead as it implied a lack of confidence. Therefore it was vital that all the participants knew what was expected of them. It took a great deal of patience and skill to produce a cavalry troop capable of performing complex manoeuvres. Therefore the army did its best to ensure that training continued after instruction at the depot, Queen's Regulations stating that

> *In order to give full effect to the approved system of Equitation which has been established throughout the Cavalry Service, the Commanding officers of Regiments are called upon, from time to time, to select certain Non-commissioned Officers and Soldiers, and to send them to the Riding Establishment at Maidstone, for the purpose of being practised in the Equitation Exercises, and of being rendered competent, on returning to their Regiments, to afford instruction . . .*[55]

Although this was fine in theory, many soldiers who trained at Maidstone believed that lack of time and resources prevented them from receiving adequate instruction. Firstly, the depot was too small and officers desperately tried to cope with its limitations in accommodation, storage and stabling. Therefore, the time available for teaching was curtailed. Secondly, as the non-commissioned officers were the backbone of the army, regiments were usually anxious for their return; this made time a restrictive factor – particularly so with regiments stationed in the colonies, where the high death rate made the swift return of NCOs paramount, occasionally to the detriment of their completing their courses. One major weakness that Nolan would later identify was the failure to teach sufficient horse-breaking techniques to sergeant trainees. After all, a poorly broken-in horse was a liability, especially on campaign.

Nevertheless, Nolan learned a great deal from the years he spent at the depot and found several like-minded officers with whom he discussed the role of the cavalry in modern warfare. British cavalry at this time was unique in Europe. This was partly due to Britain's enormous and ever-increasing empire, where the army faced colonial foes on a regular basis rather than European enemies. For example, while the difference between light and heavy cavalry was still distinct in most continental armies, the line between them in the British Army had become blurred, her small army meaning that regiments were often required to perform the services of both. Furthermore, although transporting horses by sea was always a difficult operation, the British needed to move their small army swiftly around the globe when trouble flared within the empire and were consequently more experienced at this than most nations.

To some extent weaponry determined the difference between light and heavy cavalry. The heavy cavalry carried a broad, straight blade about 35 inches long, which, though it had some benefits for thrusting, was generally clumsy in a mêlée but still capable of inflicting considerable damage through brute force. The light cavalry carried a light sabre 33 inches long, which was a much superior weapon but had its own defects. The 1796 pattern was considered a fine blade but suffered from a hilt that gave limited hand protection. The 1820 model improved on this with a 'half basket hilt', and the later 1853 version technically combined the merits of the two. Because of the expense, most cavalry regiments were still equipped with the 1820 model at the beginning of the Crimean War.

Opinions varied on how well swordsmanship was taught in the British cavalry. In an era of extravagant uniforms, when a soldierly appearance became an obsession, some experts believed that practical training suffered. For example, Robert Henderson, who was a sergeant-instructor at the depot commented: 'To burnish a sword-scabbard until one could shave in it was thought more of at Maidstone than dexterity in the use of the sword itself.'[56] Henderson was a man of considerable experience. He had initially joined the navy when the untimely death of his father rendered him destitute. He had been involved in a scheme to place Donna Maria on the throne of Portugal when in naval service and had joined the British Auxiliary Legion in Spain during the First Carlist War (1836–8). Rising to the rank of captain in the legion cavalry, he returned to Britain in the 1840s, unable to gain a commission in spite of his record. For a time he became a professional jockey but, after falling into debt, decided to join a cavalry regiment, where he soon gained promotion to the rank of sergeant.

Henderson came to know Nolan as well as their difference in rank would allow. He recorded that Nolan was one of the few who could hold his own in a fencing bout with him. He also remarked on his personality:

> *In a long and varied experience of men and things, I have never seen a gentleman whose thoroughly amiable temper, kindness of disposition, and really fascinating manner so completely won everybody he came into contact as Captain Nolan. He was a thorough soldier, as well as a finished gentleman. As regards horsemanship, he was a perfect enthusiast. There are many who soldier to live. Captain Nolan was a man who lived*

only to soldier. He had been in the Austrian service, and like most
Continental officers his manner to those in the ranks, while it forbade the
slightest approach to presumption, was so kind and winning that he was
beloved by everyone.[57]

Henderson was not the kind of man to bestow such praise lightly and it would have taken a great deal to impress such an experienced fighting man.

While officers could afford private tuition and had the time for private practice, the ranks were taught basic sword-fighting techniques. There were nine guards for the defence of both horse and rider, a circular parry, three points (or thrusts) and seven cuts for attack. Fencing experts debated endlessly over the merits of the point compared to the cut in combat. In a mêlée, a slashing cut was easier to deliver but was more likely to wound rather than kill as a blade had to be very sharp to cut deep and its effect could be lessened by clothing and accoutrements. A point was best delivered at speed, with the horse's momentum adding to its impact and penetration. Such thrusts were more likely to pierce organs, resulting in a greater chance of incapacitation or death, but this required greater skill to be effective. When facing enemy cavalry, recruits were also taught to aim blows at the opposing horseman's bridle with the intention of making the bit fall from the horse's mouth so as to render the enemy's mount difficult to control.[58]

Some regiments of the light cavalry also used the lance as their primary weapon. After an absence of over half a century, the lance had reappeared in Europe largely as a result of Napoleon's enthusiasm for the weapon when he observed its use by Arabs, Poles and Russians. He had introduced Polish lancers into his army and converted some French dragoon regiments into lancers when they proved successful. After encountering enemy lancers in the Iberian Peninsula and during the Waterloo campaign, the British cavalry readopted the lance, which they had not used since the English Civil War.

Initially, Horse Guards decided to introduce a troop of lancers into each regiment, but this idea was soon dropped in favour of having specific lancer regiments. Troopers would also carry swords as a secondary weapon and lancer officers would only carry the sword in order to make themselves more visible to the men. The length of the lance, varied at first, was soon standardized, and by 1829 measured 9ft 1inch and weighed 3lb 11oz. The shaft was constructed from ash but this would eventually change to bamboo. Both the point and butt were shod with sharpened steel and a loop roughly halfway along the shaft enabled a rider to hoop the weapon over his shoulder for ease of carrying. A small leather bucket, or holster, attached to the rider's stirrup also allowed the soldier to ease some of the weapon's weight when it was held in the vertical carry position.[59] All lancer regiments were classed as light cavalry and there was considerable debate over the effectiveness of the lance in comparison with the sword.

Though Nolan was interested in the practical aspects of horsemanship and weaponry, he was also concerned about the tactical and strategic roles of cavalry and what tasks they were capable of performing in warfare. Reconnaissance had always been vital: the Duke of Wellington had remarked, 'Why, I have spent all my life in trying to *guess what was at the other side of the hill*.'[60] With their ability to move rapidly, cavalry were the natural choice for a scouting force: the Duke prized cavalry for this far above their other functions. An army on the move needed protection while the infantry was strung out on the march and cavalry would guard their flanks and reconnoitre ahead, seeking natural obstacles that might impede the movement of the main body or discover enemy forces lying in ambush. In addition, they would seek intelligence of enemy strength and movements and try to prevent their counterparts doing the same. Skirmishing with enemy scouts attempting to perform the same duties could prevent the enemy gaining important intelligence, which occasionally proved tactically decisive. Foraging for supplies was also important, especially in climates where a sufficient water supply was paramount for the health and survival of an army, and it would be cavalry that mounted swift raids against enemy communications or supply bases. These duties were paramount for an army commander who needed to learn and receive such information quickly. No other arm could provide this in the same way as the cavalry.

When an army was stationary or encamped, it was also important to monitor enemy activity and mount guards to give prompt warning of any movements made against them. Cavalry were therefore required to provide picquets covering all aspects of approach to the army in bivouac. The picquets would in turn send out vedettes to observe the area they were guarding. Vedettes were two riders who would signal the picquet when they detected enemy action. A variety of signals existed to warn the picquet from a distance. For example, if both vedettes circled their horses to the right, the approach of enemy cavalry was indicated. If one rider circled right and the other circled left, a mixed force of cavalry and infantry was indicated, and so on. The picquet would then send riders to advise the camp that enemy action was in progress. A commander could not afford to be caught by surprise, and the cavalry provided the fastest warning system available.

It was outpost work such as this that saw the cavalry's main use of firearms. Officers and sergeants carried pistols; troopers, with the exception of lancers, carried a carbine (a shortened version of the infantry musket for use on horseback). Though repeating revolvers were beginning to come into use, pistols were very short-range weapons and carbines only enjoyed a slightly better range and accuracy. Naturally, even from a stationary horse firing would reduce their effectiveness even further and reloading in the saddle was a slow and difficult procedure. Discharging a firearm from the saddle when moving at trotting speed or more was an optimistic action if the user hoped to hit anything more than 15 feet away. As far as the cavalry were concerned, pistols were very much secondary weapons.

The charge is often considered the raison d'être of the cavalry, but this is misleading. This is not surprising, since many cavalrymen considered a successful charge to be the ultimate achievement that the cavalry arm could deliver on the battlefield. Nonetheless, an army could deal out far more damage using artillery or infantry fire and a poorly judged or mistimed charge could lead to significant losses for little gain. The excitement and spectacle of the cavalry thundering down upon an enemy had a certain romantic appeal, but charges were becoming increasingly rare because of their potential risk and wastefulness. Many believed that cavalry were far more useful to a commander in watching the flanks of his army, conducting reconnaissance or pursuing a routed foe than in seeking glory in attacks of questionable value.

Cavalry charges are often misrepresented in films as chaotic affairs with each cavalryman riding as fast as possible, dispersed in a ragged mob. In reality the charge was a much slower matter until the last moment, and the need to maintain close formation, even when under fire and suffering losses, was essential. In order to inflict maximum damage at the point of impact, cavalry needed to remain formed in a compact unit, both to punch through a line of infantry or opposing cavalry and to allow officers to maintain control over the men. After clashing with the enemy, a troop would need to reform, and if they were widely spread out this would be extremely difficult. Cavalry would advance relatively slowly until they were close to the intended target. This would assist the riders in keeping formation and ensure that last minute changes in direction had a better chance of success. Most importantly, an advance at the walk and then the trot did not tire the horses as much. If they had galloped the entire length of a charge, the horses would be blown (exhausted): this would sacrifice a mounted man's best asset on the battlefield, his mobility. Moyse-Bartlett wrote a fine description of a correctly delivered cavalry charge:

> *The regiment moved off, flanks steady, files dressing to the centre, knee to knee but never touching (Regulation distance was six inches). On the command 'Trot!' the pace was applied gradually, the line remaining steady. Some 200 yards from the point of impact came the order 'Gallop!' and at fifty yards the final command 'Charge!' Down came the long line of lances or swords from the 'carry' to the 'engage' . . .*[61]

There was discussion about whether a cavalry charge should be delivered in one or two ranks, since the second, or supporting rank, might career into the backs of the first when they had arrived at the point of impact and disrupt rather than assist their comrades.

A charge was often considered to be the epitome of martial spectacle and glory, and it was every cavalryman's dream to take part in a successful one. However, though the tight formation of riders presented an intimidating sight to the enemy, equally they provided an inviting target. The increasing use of conical bullets from 1823, and an improved system of ignition with the percussion cap from 1839, together with an increasing use of rifles with greater range and accuracy than the smoothbore musket, made the charge far more risky when facing infantry.[62] Improvements in artillery, always capable of inflicting bloody ruin on a body of horsemen, also made poorly judged charges extremely hazardous. They were best used in conjunction with other arms, especially when the enemy was weakened by sustained artillery or rifle fire. Likewise, an outflanked, disordered or unprepared enemy was a more inviting target; the charge excelled when used against a routed enemy.

The threat of a charge on the battlefield was highly effective in itself, especially when acting in conjunction with infantry or artillery. Infantry would form square when threatened by cavalry. They would stand in three ranks with the outer rank kneeling, bracing their muskets or rifles against the ground and presenting a hedge of bayonets against which a horse would probably baulk. The two ranks behind them would fire over the heads of the first, presenting an almost impregnable formation to horsemen, and squares were rarely broken by cavalry alone. However, the compressed square formation was a large target and infantry or artillery could weaken the square with their firepower, allowing the cavalry the opportunity to exploit their success when casualties and disruption had been inflicted. Likewise, the mere presence of cavalry and the perceived threat of a charge could intimidate an enemy into maintaining position since they were more vulnerable on the move. In such circumstances, the enemy would usually be obliged to bring up their own cavalry to counter the threat. After the technical improvements in other arms, a charge mounted against other cavalry had become the most effective use of this tactic.

Nolan immersed himself in his duties at the depot and did well in his six-months riding master course. His knowledge and zeal impressed many. Sergeant Franks of the 5th Dragoon Guards commented that he was a:

> *thorough gentleman in every respect. He had one peculiarity, however, a complete absence of anything in the shape of pride, and in all his intercourse with the Non-Commissioned Officers and men of the Classes he was as unpretending, and I may say as familiar as any of us. Some one has said that 'familiarity breeds contempt,' but in this case it bred a very deep and lasting feeling of esteem . . .* [63]

Discipline was maintained by keeping a certain distance between officers and men. Social status also dictated that gentlemen remained slightly aloof when speaking to those of a lower class, and those in the ranks were obliged to request an officer's permission to speak before addressing them directly. The authorities believed that excessive familiarity could lead to insubordination and the men taking liberties, but it seems that Nolan's evident enthusiasm made him a likeable officer and that he had a talent for being approachable whilst retaining respect. Obviously this was a difficult line to judge, but in the light of both Henderson's and Franks' accounts it seems that he was successful. The impressions that both men recorded of Nolan's character seem totally at odds with the description in his Austrian conduct list as 'ambitious and austere'. [64] Nolan was undeniably ambitious but austere is not a word that fits with either description, though it is likely that he had matured considerably since then.

Now the course was finished, the regiment required Nolan's services and there was no excuse to linger in Maidstone. He enjoyed a brief spell of leave and in October 1842 both he and the recently promoted Major Key took ship for India, arriving at Madras on 9 May 1843. Shortly after his arrival he heard that his brother Edmond, also in India for business purposes, had died, aged only 23. It was generally felt that, for Europeans, maintaining a rigorous level of fitness would help stave off sickness and reduce the risk of infection. Exercise routines were followed rigorously along with the practice of vigorous sports and hunting in order to further this aim. [65] Doubtless this helped to an extent, but both of his brothers had been young and physically active and had fallen prey to sickness as had so many of their countrymen throughout the British Empire.

The 15th were still stationed at Bangalore in southern India. After the fall of the Mahrattas the region had been relatively peaceful, but trouble was brewing in the north, especially in the Punjab. Although a succession of wars took place in the north, Louis failed to see active service during his eight years in India. He had just missed the disastrous First Afghan War (1838–42) and more conflicts were to follow. In 1843 the British campaigned in Sind, and Gwalior and (1843–5) saw the First Sikh War when the martial power of the Sikhs with their highly modern army was subdued with enormous difficulty and loss when they invaded British India. The period 1848–9 saw the Sikhs challenge the British once more and, following their defeat, the Punjab was finally annexed as part of the British Raj.

The shortage of regular troops such as the 15th was crucial because a British presence was required in the south as they were considered to be more reliable than the East India Company (EIC) forces. As one of the few Queen's cavalry regiments in southern India, the authorities wished to keep them there as a precaution. Although actual warfare forms only a fraction of a soldier's life, it is the ultimate test of his profession; and Louis was not the only one frustrated at being sidelined in this fashion.

Shortly after settling in at Bangalore, Nolan took several months' leave in the company of Major Key, and on 13 August 1844, soon after his return, he was appointed regimental riding master. Louis now had a reputation for expertise and, in addition to the equitation courses taken at Maidstone, he was widely read on the subject and frequently rode for pleasure and hunting purposes. In India he took every opportunity to hunt wild boar on horseback. Known as hog hunting or pig-sticking, the pursuit of these dangerous animals using a spear from the saddle was a great test of horsemanship and skill.

Bangalore was one of the more settled regions of the Indian subcontinent and after years of peace the countryside around the garrison had been heavily shot over, denying officers some of their favourite physical recreations. This was a transitional period in the history of the British Raj, and although some army wives were present it was before the period of the memsahibs when women had an increasing role and influence in Anglo-Indian society. During the earlier period of imperial expansion in India, Nolan could have taken an Indian wife without adverse comment, but this was now frowned upon. English women were beginning to travel there in greater numbers and families were even making an appearance, but the shortage of suitable women in Bangalore meant that his social life was limited. In any case, Louis's financial position was poor and he would not have been able to afford to marry at this point. It is possible that he took an Indian mistress like some officers, but there is no record of any women in Louis's life during this period. Consequently, Louis had more time to devote to his profession, and even his leisure time was largely taken up with related pursuits. From 1845 onwards he began to ride as a jockey at races held in Bangalore, Mysore and Madras; horse racing was extremely popular. It was also a chance to make money and, after several wins, Louis soon made a name for himself.

Louis intended to introduce radical changes to the training programme and selection of remounts as practised by his predecessor, Lieutenant Surnam, who had disliked the use of practice posts and leaping bars, largely because of the Indian climate. This kind of training resulted in frequent falls with occasional injuries to horses and riders; in India even minor wounds could fester and be exacerbated by the heat. This made such rigorous exercise a trial for men and animals, but Nolan felt that these were risks worth taking. He reintroduced these practices and also followed the principle of training riders as individuals before teaching formation riding at squad level.[66] Such experience was valued but was time-consuming and often rushed through or neglected. With his evident knowledge and outspoken manner, he managed to convince his superiors of its necessity and Key's promotion to the rank of colonel greatly assisted him in this; the job was also made far easier with the arrival of experienced men from Maidstone. As a result, his dedication, patience and skill soon produced results.

Nolan also appointed a rough-rider to each troop whom he would personally train to break in new horses. Such training within the regiment spared the time, expense and difficulty of sending men to Maidstone. He took great pains to ensure that saddles and stirrup lengths were appropriate for each man and horse in an attempt to produce a uniformity of seat and, although this was standard practice, his unusual diligence produced remarkable results. His new rough-riders were given the duty of checking that these tasks were carried out in his absence, and during the next few years the regiment's standard of equitation rose, justly bringing Nolan a reputation for excellence in his field.

This improvement in riding standards was evident when the regiment was inspected. Major General John Aitchison had become the commander of the Mysore Division in 1845 and inspected the 15th that year. A veteran of the Napoleonic Wars, Aitchison was known for his frequent clashes with subordinates and extremely high standards regarding discipline. His time in the command was controversial: there were frequent courts martial, including the notorious case of Dr James Mouat (regimental surgeon of the 15th) whose prosecution was widely considered unjustified. His reputation as a military martinet was such that his inspections were dreaded by officers and men alike, and it came as a surprise when Aitchison was sufficiently impressed by the appearance and horsemanship displayed by the regiment on parade that he took the time to view them in training. He later wrote:

> *Nolan's system of training horses and teaching riding is worthy of being more generally known. The seat of the men is more uniform and the hand light and firm, and as the hand and heel work together the horses in the ranks are steady to a degree I did not expect to see on a regiment mounted on entire horses.*[67]

Aitchison inspected the regiment on several occasions and even commanded them in person when they went on manoeuvres. The general was clearly won over by Nolan who, contrary to many of the myths about him, tended to get on well with his superiors. The good opinion of a general who was notoriously difficult to please was a considerable accolade.

Despite his success as riding master, Nolan wished to further his career and managed to gain a staff appointment. In January 1849 he joined the staff of General Sir George Berkeley, commander-in-chief in Madras, as an aide-de-camp. This was no small achievement: generals appointed only men they knew and trusted as aides, often resorting to open nepotism with the appointment of family or close friends. Consequently, generals were frequently pestered for lucrative positions by relations: Berkeley himself had two of his own sons on his staff.

Even in peacetime Louis was obliged to maintain at least three horses and buy several uniforms at ruinously high prices, as well as meeting the cost of socializing in high society. However, he knew that the potential boost to his career would be worth the expense and so he rapidly ingratiated himself with Sir George's two sons, Captain and Lieutenant Berkeley, who shared his love of horse racing. His responsibilities on the staff did not prevent him winning some renown, riding 'Waler Brigadier' at the Madras Spring Meeting that year.

The New Year brought the news that his father had died on 16 January 1850. After Babington's strenuous efforts to see his sons well placed, it must have broken his heart that most of them had predeceased him, although this may have been partially alleviated by Louis's success. But the length of the return journey made attending his father's funeral out of the question, and it is probable that by the time he had heard the news his father had already been buried.

General Berkeley decided to conduct a tour of inspections over his vast command in 1850. Louis accompanied him and found the means to purchase a captaincy on 8 March 1850, possibly benefiting from his father's will. The tour was also used to conduct an experiment which greatly interested him. For many years the merits of employing stallions for military use had been hotly debated in cavalry circles, some advocating the merits of geldings in preference. Stallions were believed to be intelligent, brave under fire, aggressive in the mêlée and possessed great stamina. In addition, with their impressive size and sleek coats, they were the best-looking horses, which added to the military spectacle on parade. However, stallions also ate prodigiously, which was a problem on campaign, when fodder was limited. They also had a tendency to fight each other, cause riding accidents, could not be used in conjunction with mares and often proved difficult to manage both in stables and when riding. Although their merits led to these factors being partly overlooked, they were unpopular with both officers and the ranks when it came to their use and maintenance.[68]

The use of mares was discounted because they were smaller and lacked stamina along with the fact that their presence in mixed studs led to obvious problems. Geldings became more docile after castration and were easier to ride and break into their duties. The main prejudice against their use had been their less impressive appearance, lack of aggression for battlefield purposes and a perceived lack of stamina in comparison to stallions.

However, the government disliked the use of stallions primarily because of their cost, both to buy and feed. Therefore a series of horse trials had been ordered by the Military Board in the 1850s and Berkeley's tour included one such test. A mixture of geldings and stallions would be employed and their merits would be carefully recorded and compared. Sir George took elements of the 15th and some Horse Artillery, with one squadron mounted on stallions and the other on castrated mounts. Nolan's opinion as an expert was sought, and, during the long tour, forced marches were conducted in addition to comparative tests of speed and endurance. The final results seemed to prove that geldings were the equal of stallions when it came to stamina and that other differences were unimportant for military purposes. At the end of the tour Sir George passed on his recommendations to the governor and it was decided that eventually all Madras cavalry would be mounted on geldings.

Although Nolan had gained considerable experience in India and a reputation for his knowledge of cavalry, he believed that prospects were far better back in England since he could ill afford the expenses of Indian service. His Indian reputation was a dubious recommendation as far as Horse Guards was concerned, and he needed to seek other ways of furthering his career. Several friends, including Colonel Key and Charles Berkeley, were returning on leave and so he decided to join them. On 16 January 1851 Louis appeared before an army medical board and obtained two years' sick leave. The board's decision was based on the 'special reasons' that Louis put before them – he had nothing physically wrong with him.[69] These reasons amounted to the fact that he wished to return home to seek further advancement. Joining Key's party in February he boarded the steamer *Hindostan* and embarked for home.

Chapter 4

The Cavalry Fanatic

Since Nolan's funds and influence within the service were limited, he needed to promote his worth in military circles. His expertise in equestrianism and the army were his main strengths, and friends agreed that he should use them to his advantage. His idea was to write a practical book that offered new theories on the arts of horsemanship in relation to the cavalry. As the horse was then the main form of transport, with which most men were familiar, his work would have to be carefully researched and accurate to be well received with such a readership; but he was confident of his abilities and prepared to meet the inevitable criticism. Few had written on the subject in recent times and a new look could be successful; indeed, a slightly controversial book would stand out and therefore serve his interests.

During the long return voyage, Nolan drew up plans for a tour of Europe in the company of Colonel Key. He had decided to write two books, the first a specialized examination of cavalry training, the second a more ambitious and general work examining cavalry warfare and all it entailed. He hoped that a tour of the Continent would add to his knowledge and provide interesting and little-known facts for an English readership.

Following a brief period in England, the pair set out on their grand tour, having made arrangements to meet as many equestrian experts as possible. Among the countries they visited were France, Russia, Sweden and Germany. Nolan was particularly impressed with the Swedish Horse Guards under the leadership of Count Stedingk. They performed most of their drill in virtual silence while maintaining near perfect formation. Intrigued by their claim to perform the charge at full speed, or at least the best speed of the slowest horse in the formation, Nolan rode with them and later wrote: 'This is one of the best regiments of foreign cavalry I have ever seen.'[70] Some authors confine themselves to theories based only on observation or the experiences of others, but Louis was prepared to put his ideas to the test.

Of all the experts he met, François Baucher impressed him the most. Baucher was widely respected in France and, after examining his methods, the French cavalry arm was contemplating adopting them. When they met in Paris, Louis found his theories so inspirational that he considered writing a straight

English translation of Baucher's book, but he wanted to offer more than this: the benefits of his own knowledge of British cavalry, which he had gained from Maidstone and India, were worthy of promotion too, and so, although he acknowledged and incorporated Baucher's *Méthode d'Équitation* into his theories, he meant to write a personal work.

Nolan returned to Maidstone in October 1852 long before his official period of absence had ended. Although he was still in the process of writing, the lure of practical soldiering was strong and it was sensible for him to maintain his skills and test his theories. However, he had no wish to return to India and he managed to obtain command of the regiment's depot troop. Because Major Meyer was the riding master, that position was unattainable for the foreseeable future. Meyer still held rigidly to his traditional methods, although Colonel Frederick Griffiths, the depot commandant, allowed some cautious experimentation.

The Duke of Wellington died on 14 September 1852. While his political career had not matched his military achievements, his influence had been enormous, particularly within the army; many felt that Britain had lost 'the father of the country' with his passing. In his later years his traditionalist influence at Horse Guards had stifled military innovations such as rifled firearms, but, as a commander, his methods and example inspired generations of soldiers and his influence far outlived him. Parliament granted him a state funeral, a distinction usually reserved for royalty, and he was to be buried in St Paul's Cathedral in a spectacular show of military pageantry. Every regiment in the army was to be represented in the funeral cortège, and Nolan was given the honour of leading a small contingent for the 15th Light Dragoons, a regimental sergeant major, one corporal and six private soldiers. There could be no mistakes on such an important occasion and so his selection for the role was an honour.

London was unused to such a vast military spectacle, with eight cavalry squadrons, three batteries of artillery and over 3,000 infantrymen in the procession with more lining its route.[71] Over a million people turned out to watch the cortège. St Paul's was full despite the fact that 14 November 1852 was a particularly cold and wet day. Nolan's troop performed their funerary duties well, but on the return journey to Maidstone a minor calamity occurred when one of the horses bolted down a particularly steep hill.[72] Three men were hospitalized, one with a broken leg, but all concerned were relieved that the accident had not occurred earlier in London.

After this display of national grief the publication in 1852 of Nolan's first book, *The Training of Cavalry Remount Horses*, came as a welcome distraction. Nolan acknowledged his debt to Baucher as follows:

> *Everywhere I found that Monsieur Baucher's new Méthode had excited much attention, and not a little jealousy, amongst the followers of the old system. Books and pamphlets have been published, trying to turn into ridicule the bold intruder who, in two months, brings his horses to do what years could not accomplish in the old school.*[73]

Nolan ensured that a French translation of his book was soon on the market. Dedicated to Lieutenant General Sir George Berkeley, the work began by quoting letters from three serving army officers advocating the new system of equitation. These were John Aitchison, Major General Lovell and George Key. Louis had served under all three officers, and Key in particular was a firm friend, so these endorsements were perhaps a little biased. However, Aitchison was the kind of man who would never give a recommendation unless he firmly believed in it and Nolan was aware that his association with these officers was public knowledge.

The book is a slim volume with sixty-one pages of text along with illustrative panels. Its small size was probably deliberate since it appears to be intended for swift consultation and could easily be carried in the field. However, although it has a lengthy contents page with breakdowns for each chapter, an index might have been useful for this kind of practical work. The clear black and white images, particularly those depicting a rider performing manoeuvres, are practical and useful to anyone trying to emulate Louis's proposed system. It is more than possible that he modelled for the artist who drew these illustrations as they bear a striking resemblance to the few pictures available of him – and he was the kind of expert who believed in demonstrating concepts in person.

The book is a highly specialized work aimed specifically at cavalry officers and goes into considerable detail regarding the use of the snaffle, the bit, the spurs and reins. The paces of walk, trot and canter are covered along with specific manoeuvres that Nolan favoured, such as pirouettes and reining back. He also included passages on the gradual acclimatization of horses to gunfire, the rattling of accoutrements and the beating of drums in battle. The whole book is laid out in a very concise and informative style. It was written with a clear view to practical instruction but it is certainly not the kind of book a non-professional, casual reader would find of interest.

One of the more controversial aspects of Baucher's theory was his use of bending lessons to teach the horse certain movements. Nolan fully endorsed their use and insisted that they could be performed both standing and from the saddle. In the early stages these consisted of using the reins and bit to control the horse's head and neck movements since all the horse's directive motion originated from there.[74] Slow, repetitive exercises would be performed to accustom the horse to their use and make them appear natural. In the early stages this was not easy:

> *A young horse generally attempts to resist the bit, either by bending his neck to one side or other, setting his jaw against it, carrying his nose high up, or low down. We must, therefore render him manageable by bending him to the right, left, and 'up and down', that is, teaching him to bring his head home, and to arch his neck on the reins being felt . . .*[75]

In theory, these repetitive exercises would swiftly make accepting the rider's direction second nature to the horse and thus shortened the initial training process. Nolan admitted that on occasion it might require 'the whole strength of a man's arm to make them obey',[76] but emphasized that this only occurred in the first stages and that time and persistence would rapidly pay off. However, 'It is of the utmost importance that the horse never be allowed to take the initiative. *Always oppose the raising of the horse's head – always lower your hands and bring it down.*'[77]

Bending lessons manipulating the horse's head and neck would soon bring the horse to obey without excessive use of the whip or other punishments. Indeed, Nolan was very much against the use of force to correct horses, believing in 'punishment never being inflicted on a young horse, except for decided restiveness, and downright vice. Even in that case, your object only being to oblige him to go forward, you will, the moment he moves on, treat him kindly.'[78] He argued that pain taught only fear and a horse that feared its rider could not be relied upon in battle. The promise of a reward was a far better incentive, and bending exercises should be used until 'the horse yields and opens his mouth to the slightest feeling of the reins.'[79] Afterwards, when more sophisticated manoeuvres were attempted, similar bending exercises would be applied to the shoulders and haunches.

These methods seemed to produce results. Baucher had certainly used them on the Continent with some success, although the French cavalry eventually declined to adopt them. What seemed to impress most observers was the short time it took to instruct horses in this form of equitation. Nolan later summarized his methods for early horse-breaking in his second book:

1. The horse is gently used, the progress is gradual but certain.
2. For a few days he is ridden on the snaffle with a loose rein, at a walk and a trot; then ridden a few days more to steady him at a trot.
3. He is then bitted, and a few simple lessons teach him to yield to the feeling of the rein and the pressure of the leg.
4. Next he is collected and got in hand, not by pulling and sawing at his mouth, but by gradually pressing him with the leg till he raises himself off the bit and gathers himself up at a walk, when he can be collected and put together to any extent required, by the judicious use of the spur. As all this is done at the halt or at a walk, the horse undergoes no fatigue.
5. Reining back then perfects the horse in the use of his limbs and in unqualified obedience to the rider's hand and leg. This once attained, a few lessons will teach the animal to canter, change leg, passage and pirouette, and the horse becomes a perfect charger in a very short time, without having in any way suffered from his breaking – indeed, without having been once tired or overworked during the whole of his education; and from his mouth having been gently dealt with, it remains fresh and good, instead of being hard and callous.[80]

He claimed to have used these methods with a variety of horses including English thoroughbreds, Arab, Cape, Persian, Australian and Indian horse breeds with notable success.

One manoeuvre that Nolan favoured was the pirouette. This allowed for rapid change of direction from an almost standing start conferring great advantages in a mêlée. The key to this was to teach the horse to keep his rear legs virtually still and pivot using his forelegs and haunches. This allowed the benefits of 'the most useful "Air of the Manège" for a cavalry soldier; for, when engaged sword in hand with an enemy, he can turn his horse right, and left, and about, in an instant, and thus gain the advantage over his antagonist.'[81] Nolan believed that the power to control his mount was the single most important skill a cavalryman could possess. Even an exceptional swordsman would find it difficult to counter an opponent who, though outclassed with a blade, had superior control of his mount.

Reining back was of even greater importance. Bringing a horse from speed to a swift halt was an essential skill. Nolan believed that this was best performed by the rider gripping tightly with both legs in combination with rearward movement of his reins.[82] He believed that leg and knee pressure were even more important than skilled use of the reins. The use of diagrams to illustrate these manoeuvres made his instructions far more understandable and was a facility that many books of the period lacked. Another asset was the question and answer section Nolan provided as a shortened explanation of his new system. To some Victorian readers this may have appeared overly simplistic, but it helped explain a lengthy concept.

Nolan's second book was a very different kind of study. Published the following year, it covered a broad range of subjects including the history of cavalry, its tactical use on the battlefield, horsemanship, training and equipment. Aware that many of his theories were controversial, in the preface he outlined his belief that his notions should prove useful to the service and pointed out the scarcity of recent books dealing solely with the cavalry. It was far more accessible and readable than his previous book. The first few chapters dealt with the history of cavalry from ancient times up to the 1850s. Nolan managed to condense these centuries of conflict in a neat, concise manner and picked out numerous cavalry commanders whom he felt were the most skilled and successful for their time. Foremost among these in his opinion were Oliver Cromwell, Seydlizt and François Kellerman. They were also the most relevant to modern warfare and he used colourful references to historical examples to illustrate his points.

The book then goes into great descriptive detail about cavalry and Nolan's suggestions for improving what he believed to be the foremost arm of the service. As a serving cavalry officer, he was honest enough to admit his bias and also that the significant leaps forward in military technology had limited the use of the mounted arm on the battlefield. Notwithstanding, he went on to elaborate how his theories, if implemented, might remedy this situation. Early in the book he outlined the general problems regarding the use of cavalry, which had not changed for centuries:

> *Of all arms, cavalry is the most difficult to handle in the field. It cannot engage an enemy except where the ground is favourable. It is always dependent on the condition of its horses. It is easily dispersed, and it easily gets out of hand. However brave and intrinsically good, it is of no use without good officers.*[83]

Yet cavalry were of great use off the battlefield by keeping the army secure from unexpected attacks, protecting it on the march, finding its supplies, exploiting a victory and covering its retreat in the event of a disaster. In short, 'Cavalry ought to be at once the eye, the feeler and the feeder of an army.'[84] He also believed that large bodies of cavalry were not necessarily an advantage since excessive numbers made them difficult to handle and deploy; he cited numerous instances of Spanish mismanagement of their unwieldy and overlarge cavalry arm during the Peninsular War. On the battlefield such difficulties could lead to confusion and the disruption of other arms, while large numbers of horses consumed huge amounts of provisions. He argued that smaller contingents, kept well in hand, were far more effective. Above all he believed cavalry excelled as a highly mobile, aggressive force but that they had little role to play in defensive warfare, whose passive nature was alien to the spirit of the mounted soldier.

When examining the difference between light and heavy cavalry Nolan clearly favoured the former. If heavy cavalry had to be retained, Nolan believed that the idea of large men mounted on large horses was a mistake. Overweighting, as he had emphasized in his previous book, greatly reduced a cavalryman's effectiveness. Strong heavy horses were ideal for heavy cavalry but it did not follow that their riders needed to be of great stature. In order to bear the weight of weaponry and accoutrements, shorter, lighter men were preferable. The armour worn by some heavy cavalry added to this weight and although breastplates offered some protection against swords in a mêlée, their use against firearms was limited:

> *At some experiments made in England, a Minié ball passed through an earthen breastwork three feet thick, and killed a soldier standing behind it, smashing his skull to pieces! What sort of cuirass would resist such a bullet?*[85]

Furthermore, such armour only protected the chest, back and stomach. Nolan argued that a cavalryman's arms were in greater need of protection. If either arm were disabled, the rider would lose the use of either his weapon or his bridle, leaving him at the mercy of his assailant. Although he considered most armour a useless encumbrance, surely some kind of gauntlet would be preferable if armour had to be worn. He included an illustration giving his impression of the kind of gauntlet he had in mind. Such armour would weigh considerably less than a cuirass and every ounce saved improved the horseman's greatest asset – his mobility.

Believing that speed and mobility counted for more in a mêlée than swordsmanship, he cited numerous examples from the past of light cavalry overcoming heavy cavalry when they were matched against each other. Nolan revealed how the Hungarian 10th Hussars (his former regiment) defeated enemy cuirassiers in the recent Magyar War (1848–9) at the Battle of Tétény. A former comrade who fought there concurred with many of his theories: 'I quite agree with you that the strength, and lasting qualities of the horse, make the cavalry soldier formidable . . . therefore, the animal should not be made to carry any unnecessary weight . . .'.[86] He added that the type of cavalry and their horses were not as significant as the men's determination to succeed, being accustomed to victory, having confidence in their leader and timing the charge correctly. Despite his varied experience, Nolan had never been in combat at this point, but he made great efforts to consult those who had and recorded their observations.

Louis was not alone in his reservations about heavy cavalry. To retain an arm intended primarily for battle but of limited use in other cavalry roles was an expensive luxury. Though light and heavy cavalry were becoming increasingly similar in the British Army, some believed that combining the two to form one type of cavalry soldier would be preferable. The Duke of Wellington was well known for his scathing remarks about the performance of his cavalry during the Peninsular War, at least in their battlefield role. However, the climate and geography of the Iberian Peninsula made cavalry a difficult arm to use effectively and, while Wellington wished to increase the size of his cavalry division, he acknowledged that the difficulty of maintaining horses meant that he had to make do with an undersized contingent. It was hard enough for light cavalry to perform the varied tasks he demanded of them and the heavy cavalry, who needed more fodder, were of dubious value. He demonstrated this view by sending his heavy cavalry regiments to the rear when he led the army over the Pyrenees into southern France.[87]

Weaponry was of great interest to Nolan. The sword was the cavalryman's primary arm and he favoured it above all others. He admitted that the lance had some value for intimidation, but emphasized that since it took speed to use effectively it was nearly useless in a mêlée where it took far more effort to wield than a sword. It was only truly effective at the first shock of impact; his experiences while hunting wild boar in India had reinforced this belief. Riders often commented that when the boar was cornered and they struck at it from a standing mount, even razor-sharp spear points tended to bounce off its thick hide. He also heard accounts when talking to veterans of the Sikh Wars such as his friend Captain Morris, then with the 16th Lancers. Riders claimed that the lance lacked penetrative power, being easily deflected by armour or heavy clothing, but 'I could tell them a better reason: it was because those who failed did not know that it requires speed to drive a lance home, and that it must be carried into the object by the horse.'[88]

Lancers were also vulnerable to being shot down by enemy picquets during outpost work. The weight and difficulty of handling a lance made the additional weight of a carbine impractical and, even with pistols, they were easily outmatched. The sword was a far better, universal weapon he argued and, though it lacked the reach of the lance, it was better in the mêlée. After initial contact a lancer was at a considerable disadvantage once a swordsman got past his point, necessitating that he back off before delivering another thrust or resort to using the shaft of the weapon. Lances could be discarded and swords drawn after the first clash but the time taken to do this could leave the rider open to attack. Nolan preferred to do without them altogether. He made little mention of the use of the lance against infantrymen where the length of the lance meant that even if a soldier threw himself flat on the ground a lancer could reach him. However, a rifle with a bayonet had a considerable reach and an infantryman lacked the difficulty of wielding his weapon from the saddle. In this kind of contest what the sword lost in terms of length it gained in terms of manoeuvrability.

Yet there were also problems with British cavalry swords. The cutting power of the sabre, with its slightly curved blade, was generally favoured over the straighter blades of the heavy cavalry; but despite several attempts to improve matters with a succession of different sword models, many believed them to be inferior weapons. One contemporary writer commented that while infantry weapons had progressed:

> in the cavalry, how different is the case! The sword, their peculiar weapon, is actually not near as good as it was two hundred years ago . . . Even in half the pawnbrokers' shops you will find Andrew Farrara blades, with which the modern sword might be almost cut in two without injury to the edge of the former.[89]

Nolan believed the problem was not so much the kind of sword used but how sharp the blade was kept. Since so much emphasis was given to the appearance of cavalry and martial display that metal sword scabbards were used which looked fantastic when polished and emitted an impressive metallic rasping sound when drawn. The practical problem with this was that the scraping effect of metal on metal dulled the sword's edge slightly every time it was drawn from the scabbard. Naturally, a sharp sword was preferable in combat, but sharpening blades was time-consuming and not always possible in large numbers when on campaign. Subsequently Nolan remarked that some cavalrymen during the Sikh Wars had even favoured the pistol since they had so little confidence in their swords.

During General Berkeley's tour, Nolan had enquired about the recent combat between the Nizam of Hyderabad's irregular horsemen and the Rohillas. The Rohillas had been soundly defeated and, reading a doctor's report on the treatment of the wounded, he discovered numerous instances of decapitations and hands or limbs severed by single blows during the mêlée: 'I was astounded. Were these men giants, to lop off limbs thus wholesale?'[90] The effect of such terrible wounds upon enemy morale had been obvious. Mystified he investigated and recorded one exchange with one of the Nizam's men:

> I said, 'How do you strike with your swords to cut off men's limbs?' 'Strike hard, Sir!' said the old trooper. 'Yes, of course; but how do you teach the men to use their swords in that particular way?' (drawing it). 'We never teach them any way, Sir: a sharp sword will cut in anyone's hand.'[91]

In fact there was no mystery: the swords used were usually discarded British blades that had been given different hilts, sharpened to a high degree and – the real difference – kept in wooden scabbards to keep them sharp. They were rarely drawn except in action and the blows dealt with them often resulted in instant death or incapacitation. The wooden or leather scabbards gave better protection than metal scabbards, which often snapped or bent if stressed, sometimes chipping or breaking the sword blades. Even if slightly bent, the scabbard might prevent the blade being withdrawn. Wooden scabbards tended to bend further with rough treatment and would not blunt a blade so badly when it was drawn. Metal scabbards also tended to rattle and make a great deal of noise, a problem when scouting or on patrol. Nolan argued earnestly for the British to adopt wooden scabbards, at least in the field, as they were far more practical. Following a debate over cavalry weaponry and uniforms in *The Times*, one cavalry officer wrote:

there is not a single soldier who wears a steel scabbard to his sword that would not give his head to get rid of it, for it not only is a most troublesome thing to clean, but also in a very considerable degree blunts the edge of the sword, and, when bent . . . prevents the sword being drawn. In proof of this I need only cite the late Captain Nolan, whose opinion on these points is universally respected . . .[92]

Another extravagance that Nolan had little time for were the elaborate and impractical uniforms currently in use: 'we have too much frippery – too much toggery – too much weight in things worse than useless. To a cavalry soldier every ounce is of consequence!'[93] Since cavalry duties often included riding through rough country, woodland, fording rivers and sleeping rough or under canvas a more practical uniform was called for on active service. It need not be inelegant, he conceded, but it should be tough, warm on the lower half of the body and looser on the upper half allowing unrestricted arm movement. The tight, constrictive uniforms of the cavalry, whose design owed more to fashion than practicality, may have looked dashing but were prone to damage and offered little protection against the elements.

Regarding firearms, Nolan had little time for pistols. To train a man to stand and take careful aim and give him the expertise to use a pistol accurately at much beyond 25 yards requires a great deal of time, even with modern weapons. Although revolvers were beginning to make an appearance by the 1850s they were still inherently inaccurate and outranged by carbines and rifles, and a man using one from a moving horse would rarely hit anything beyond very close range. Pistols had some use in the mêlée, but since most of those available were single shot weapons, a sword had obvious advantages at such close quarters. The main use for cavalry firearms was for outpost work, and here Nolan favoured rifled carbines above all else, remarking that their main use would either be by dismounted men or from a standing mount.

Since the horse was the cavalryman's greatest asset, the art of horsemanship was covered in considerable detail in Nolan's second book. Referring to his observations when travelling on the Continent and in India, he considered the English to be superlative riders who were second to none: 'Left to his own free natural seat, and the Englishman beats the world in a ride after the hounds and a run across country.'[94] Like many military theorists, Nolan believed that fox-hunting was ideal practice for cavalry warfare. There is much to the theory that fox-hunting in England and boar-hunting in India not only improved riding skill by taking the pursuit over all kinds of ground at speed but also taught the ability to predict and interpret the lie of the land. The urgency and need to outwit a quarry also taught the ability to make swift decisions, occasionally at a gallop, which was always an asset in a cavalry commander. The savage nature of these blood sports also honed the spirit of aggression necessary for a warrior.[95] Therefore Nolan disapproved of the fact that, since the seventeenth century, the military had copied continental riding styles in line with military fashion. Paradoxically, the military instructed their officers to ride in one fashion while most men rode in the older, more natural style for recreation. He believed that military riding standards had suffered since Cromwell's Ironsides rode to war in exactly the same way that they rode across country.

As we have seen, many cavalrymen favoured the 'balance seat' for military riding, which originated in the age of heavily armoured horsemen. When combatants either jousting or in the field were almost entirely covered in plate and chain mail armour it was necessary to counter this weight by lengthening the stirrups to give the rider a more upright stance. In this way the weight could be evenly distributed without unbalancing the rider. Changes in armour and weaponry meant that this was no longer necessary. Nolan advocated a far more relaxed military seat with shorter stirrups producing a more natural riding posture. This was far less rigid and allowed the rider to have his knees slightly bent and closer in towards the horse which, allied with a good saddle, permitted him greater control. Knowing the value of illustration as a demonstration aid, his book contained two paintings of the military seat as it should be and the current mode of practice. The fact that the style Nolan favoured depicted an Austrian cavalryman and the old-fashioned balance seat illustration depicted a British Hussar was not lost upon his readership, some of whom would later remark that this was an implied criticism of Meyer at Maidstone Depot.[96]

In breaking horses Nolan commented that a horse's education never finished and that additional instruction and preventing horses from forming bad habits was an endless task. Even when Baucher modified his views after receiving a storm of criticism, Nolan stood by his system of equitation. For example, Baucher's 'bending exercises' for horses had been derided as unnecessarily painful for the horse and the theorist admitted that perhaps he had been slightly overzealous in their application but nevertheless believed in their potential benefits. Seizing upon this admission, some critics dismissed Baucher's theories out of hand.

The backbone of Nolan's system was to teach horses with a firm yet gentle manner. In a humorous slight on the old methods employed by traditional officers he suggested, 'Write up in golden letters . . . in every riding-school and in every stable: "HORSES ARE TAUGHT NOT BY HARSHNESS BUT BY GENTLENESS." Where the officers are classical, the golden rule may be given in Xenophon's Greek, as well as in English.'[97] However, there was good reason for this attitude: many instructors used the whip to excess along with other unnecessarily cruel methods in the hope that these would produce blind obedience. Instead, they rendered the horses nervous and fearful.

Describing the principles of Baucher's system in detail, he praised the idea that recruits were taken from the riding school to the field as soon as possible and that such methods emphasized practical military riding over the demands of the parade ground. For example, many instructors declined to teach the half pirouette, believing that teaching both the horse and rider to perform this turn took too long. Nolan disagreed, pointing out that Baucher claimed to teach it in a matter of months. It could make all the difference for tactical manoeuvring since a cavalryman always wishes to present his right side (covered by his sword) to his enemy while seeking his opponent's weaker left side.[98] Although he admitted that Baucher's theories were not perfect, he had personally achieved great results with over a hundred horses, teaching them to be capable of pulling up swiftly from speed and of turning quickly for the mêlée and skirmishing.

Nolan's cavalry book also contained several chapters on drill, the intervals he recommended and their uses in the field. To illustrate his points, he compared and contrasted continental practice with the methods employed in Great Britain, constantly reiterating the point that dressing and formation must be maintained for the arm to be of any use as an offensive unit. Stressing that officers must be knowledgeable about the correct riding pace for each manoeuvre, he believed that the men would conform naturally to their example if they possessed confidence in their leaders. The only way to achieve this was by incessant drilling until the movements required became almost second nature.

Regarding intervals, Nolan believed that small units with sufficient gaps between them were the key to the effective use of cavalry. He disapproved of the large, unwieldy double squadrons employed in the Austrian Army. Such formations often contained 300 men or more, and, according to Louis's experience, the press of so many riders was constrictive:

> *I have ridden in these Austrian divisions, and the pressure of the horses was often so great as to lift me, with my horse, off the ground, occasioning*

great pain, and making one and all quite helpless. A few resolute
horsemen dashing in on such a mass would throw it into utter confusion.[99]

He believed that combining squadrons in this manner was folly, and he
revealed how most European cavalry employed an interval of between 4 to 12
yards between cavalry units. Such intervals allowed injured troopers or
riderless horses to retire more easily, and, should one squadron be defeated,
they could retreat without disrupting the neighbouring unit. He favoured small
troops of twenty-five files as the key unit, led by a captain with two subalterns
on the flanks. A 12-yard interval would be preferable between other troops:
anything less ran the risk of throwing the flank of a neighbouring unit into
confusion if a troop should retreat since terrified horses instinctively clustered
together and their fear was infectious. He argued that small units were far easier
to control and, though large units impressed the enemy, their effectiveness was
questionable.

Nolan thought that field movements should be simplified with the
knowledge that, once a cavalry manoeuvre had begun, it was nearly impossible
to stop. This was particularly true of cavalry charges. Throughout his book,
Nolan emphasized that a cavalry leader should be capable of making swift
decisions and that there was no place for hesitation. However, circumstances
could change rapidly on the battlefield, and he argued that cavalry should be
taught to pivot to the right or left in order to change direction whether in
column or line. Though keeping the dressing straight and maintaining
formation was important, he believed that the introduction of a simplified
method of pivoting should be introduced and made proposals for this.

Knowing that shouted orders and even trumpet and bugle calls were
difficult to hear over the din of battle he proposed a simple solution. If a
change of direction was needed whilst the unit was on the move, two troop
markers would gallop out on the flanks of the central unit, raising their swords
vertically to make themselves conspicuous. The officers in front would also
raise their swords high and indicate the change in direction desired to the troop
markers who would point where the commander wanted to lead them. As the
unit changed direction, the flankers would fall back into formation. It was
imperative that the cavalry should reach the correct destination, overriding all
other considerations:

In the advance in line, the direction of the advance is the important point,
and not the perfect alignment of the squadrons. So long as every horse's

head is turned straight towards the point of attack, it really matters little whether one squadron be or not be a few horses' lengths in advance or in rear of the line . . . Keep your alignment as perfect or as neat as you can, but do not make sacrifices to obtain the end, and, above all, think of your direction.[100]

This is a simplification of Nolan's lengthy examination of this issue. But he argued that his conclusions provided a common sense solution to a complex problem that had constantly blighted cavalry commanders through the ages. He also acknowledged that once a certain pace had been reached, it was nearly impossible to correct a mistake whatever the method employed. With horses moving at walking or marching pace a correction was possible, but at trotting speed or above the unit was committed. Furthermore, as cavalrymen rode almost knee to knee in the charge, the necessity of sufficient intervals was paramount if the direction was changed, as illustrated by his previous example of the chaotic disruption he had experienced in constrictive Austrian formations. At Balaklava the difficulties of changing direction once a manoeuvre was in progress would be demonstrated with devastating effect during the Charge of the Light Brigade.

Nolan explored cavalry tactics at great length, making many acute observations on current practice. He favoured attacking in one line rather than two, repeating his point that the second line might be disordered by fugitives if the first were defeated and that they might career into the backs of the first while they were engaged in a mêlée. He preferred attacking in echelons if the line were too long. The advantage of this, he proposed, was that different units could offer mutual support if necessary and, as long as the correct intervals were employed, a defeated unit could withdraw without causing confusion.

Throughout his study he emphasized that cavalry could overcome nearly anything on the battlefield but only when used in the correct fashion. Of the three arms, fighting other cavalry was perhaps the hardest task in his opinion. The swift movement of cavalry meant a commander had to keep his wits about him and be prepared to counter enemy moves with very little warning. Using many military examples, he commented that just as infantry bayonet charges were rare in the infantry, cavalry were reluctant to enter a close quarter fight knowing the random nature of the initial clash. He pointed out that either horseman would be aware that one, or even both riders, might be brought down if the two met at speed. Once again, he rated horsemanship over swordsmanship for survival when cavalry charged one another. He admitted that they were best employed in conjunction with other arms and his view that cavalry could effectively charge infantry squares or artillery batteries has often been taken out of context, but he emphasized the need to prepare such attacks with the concentrated fire of infantry or artillery. Though surprise or a retreating enemy could also be factors, he believed that the magical formula of combined arms was always the key to success.

With artillery, he argued that advancing with relatively few men in skirmishing order was preferable since artillery would be less effective against a dispersed force. They would only increase to charging speed when within range of case shot, and Nolan pointed out that the moment when guns were limbering up was the ideal time to act against artillery. Whenever possible they should also be approached on the flank. As always, the timing of a charge was everything. He also stated that damaging the guns was often more practical than trying to hold them:

> *If, after getting into the battery, they see a superior force of the enemy coming to the rescue, they should endeavour to do as much damage to the battery as possible by cutting down the drivers, severing the traces, etc., and then trust to the speed of their horses for safety.*[101]

The best way to render cannon inoperable was to hammer a nail into the touch-hole and then saw it off so that the weapon could not be fired. However, this required long, thick nails about $3/8$ of an inch wide, and hammers. This was known as 'spiking the guns', but Nolan never mentions its use and does not recommend carrying the necessary items, perhaps because of their weight and the fact that they were used relatively rarely. Although aware of the great risks cavalry incurred when attacking artillery, because of the large target a man and horse presented, he also stressed the great value that this arm had on the battlefield. Artillery was expensive, deadly and often decisive, and so it was worth making strenuous efforts against it whenever possible.

When threatened, infantry would form a square that many believed was almost invulnerable to cavalry attack. While admitting that improvements in infantry weapons had made the task more difficult, Nolan argued that determined cavalry could always break an infantry square if they approached it correctly. He gave many examples of infantry squares being overcome by cavalry in previous wars. Acknowledging that there were even more examples demonstrating the exact opposite, he countered with the theory that such charges were not pressed home correctly. Though a horse and rider were easy targets at close range, Nolan pointed out that the mount's head and neck largely protected the rider and that horses were capable of withstanding horrific damage without being killed instantly. He maintained that determined riders attacking a square on at least two sides should always achieve their objective and that the horses alone were capable of breaking the square formation:

> *The infantry soldier can only try and aim his bayonet at the horse's breast, and let him spit himself like a wild boar. In this case he must hit the heart to kill him, for any other wound would be quite useless at the moment; and even reaching the horse's heart cannot save him; for . . . with his great weight and the impulse of speed, will dash the whole rank to the ground in his fall.*[102]

This was controversial since it clearly called for the sacrifice of men and horses in order to bring about success, and conventional military wisdom said that all the advantages were with the infantry. The usual outcome was dictated by the fact that infantry fire inflicted enough losses to break the cavalry's morale and so cause chaos by disrupting their formation. In the knowledge of this, cavalry rarely tried to press a charge home through their own choice, though it was in fact possible. Nevertheless, Louis clearly stressed that it *could* be done under the right circumstances; and he was not the only one to think so. During the 1830s two officers conducted a debate about the effectiveness of cavalry in the *United Service Journal* under the pseudonyms 'J.M.' and 'Vindex'. Whilst questioning the claim that breaking squares was easy, Vindex admitted that it was possible when the infantry's 'order has been severely shaken by the fire of cannon, when they have not had time to complete their formation, when a general movement of retreat . . . compels them to keep in motion towards the rear.'[103] Nolan also conceded that cavalry had a far greater chance of success in similar circumstances.

Nolan covered virtually every aspect of cavalry warfare and included sections on the march, the bivouac, outpost work and skirmishing. Patrolling and reconnaissance were vital duties which he summarised thus:

> *Patrols should constantly push forward to front and flanks to feel for the enemy, search the side-roads, farm-houses, woods, etc. etc., and look into any place likely to conceal troops. Always secure your flanks before entering defiles, by taking possession of the heights or other commanding positions, near them.*[104]

No other arm matched the cavalry for this purpose, and he frequently reminded the reader how seeking knowledge while preventing the enemy from gathering counter intelligence was often crucial on campaign.

He also gave practical advice on the selection, planning and protection of an army's encampment and cavalry in particular. The cavalry needed to be in a position with open views where they could spot enemy movement and send rapid support to threatened areas when needed. Ideally, it should allow easy communication from flank to flank, front and rear. Wood and water should be in plentiful supply, and the camp should be laid out so that troops could rapidly get under arms swiftly. Though of lesser importance, he gave plans for peacetime encampment and provided sketches and maps to illustrate his points.

Nolan considered there was great room for improvement in cavalry skirmishing. He gave examples such as cavalry vedettes during the Peninsular War exchanging carbine fire for days with no casualties being inflicted on either side. He ridiculed the practice of riding in circles to confuse the enemy's aim and stopping periodically to return fire. Firing from the saddle, even with the horse standing still, was inaccurate. Skirmishing with carbines made an enemy keep his distance but he believed that, if the enemy persisted, the skirmishers should charge with sword in hand and decide the matter rather than waste ammunition during indecisive exchanges of fire.

However, tales of how the Sikhs skirmished in the 1840s had impressed him. Acting in teams of two, one man remained saddled to protect his partner whilst the other dismounted and fired his carbine on foot for greater accuracy. It was difficult to counter:

> *if you charged they proved more formidable with these dismounted men amongst them than when they were all in the saddle. If you rode at the dismounted man, the mounted trooper would interpose, and, while you were engaged with him, the man on foot would quickly shoot you down, or knock over your horse.*[105]

After hearing such accounts from Captain Morris among others, Nolan argued strongly for the British to adopt the practice. Using a firearm on foot was always going to be more effective, and with mounted protection such skirmishers would be difficult to drive off without calling up reinforcements or adopting similar tactics. In the event that reinforcements were called out, the skirmishers would have managed to occupy a larger body of men at the risk of only a few men. The enemy would be distracted from other tasks and their horses potentially tired out by countering what amounted to a nuisance rather than a serious threat.

Nolan finished his second book with an appendix detailing a long-term project he had been working on. After their visit to Holland, Colonel Key bought a Dutch cavalry saddle to assist him in his experiments at Maidstone. The current model used by British cavalry was known as the hussar saddle and based on a pattern used by the Prussian Ziethen Hussars. It had been in use since 1796 and had been officially authorized in 1805. Nolan considered it too high, forcing a rider to raise his thighs and restricting the use of the lower leg. It fitted well with the balance seat mode of riding, which explained its time in the service, but he believed it slightly unstable and prone to shifting position, one of the primary causes of sore backs for the horses. He earnestly believed that the cavalry deserved a better model.

To this end he made careful notes of all the different saddles he had used in India and Europe, and, with the assistance of David Johnson, saddler sergeant at the depot, worked hard on producing a new cavalry saddle. Incorporating ideas from the Danish model they joined the hind fork to the sideboards and shortened the sideboards themselves in order to lengthen the seat. The front fork was constructed with a peak and long points at Johnson's suggestion, and with the use of blocked leather it resembled a hunting saddle as much as a military model. This was quite deliberate and in keeping with Nolan's theories on hunting and adapting the riding style to the more relaxed stance of recreational horsemanship.

The hussar model employed thick padding on the sideboards, which Nolan considered unnecessary and prone to excessive rubbing against the horse causing soreness. In India he had often used a *numnah*, or felt saddlecloth, in preference to the folded blanket in use by the British. This he also recommended. In addition, he reduced the sideboard padding to narrow strips of felt, which reduced rubbing, was less restrictive, cooler for the horse and absorbed more of the perspiration that was another cause of rubbing. He also considered the shabraque (a kind of saddle cloth) a troublesome and impractical adornment mainly for show and pointed out that this could also overheat a horse's back. If it had to be worn, he continued, 'it should be made of cloth, not water-proofed. Water-proofed cloth is less durable, and confines the heat to the horse's back.'[106]

He also included a number of minor improvements in buckles and straps designed to reduce the weight and improve comfort for the mount. He designed a new bridle capable of swift removal for feeding purposes: 'The bit, bridoon, and their head-stalls, are provided with hooks and links, by which means the bits can be slipped out of the horse's mouth, for the purposes of feeding without taking the bridle off the horse's head.'[107] Knowing that a description of such technical matters was rarely sufficient, Nolan included illustrations of both saddle and bridle.

The resulting saddle and accoutrements were a marked improvement on the model currently in use, and in April 1853 the Duke of Cambridge, as inspector general of cavalry, attended a test of Nolan's saddle in Maidstone. The army were impressed and eventually commissioned Messrs Robert Gibson and Co to begin producing a new model for the cavalry. Admittedly they had added some modifications of their own, but it was essentially the work of Nolan and Johnson, whom Nolan credited in his book.[108] The saddle was tested by the Mounted Staff Corps in the Crimea and was adopted by the British Army in 1856. The Universal Wood Arch Pattern design, as it became known, owed a great deal to Nolan's work and would be used extensively for the next thirty years and unofficially for some time afterwards. It became commonly known as 'Nolan's saddle'. As a practical, long lasting innovation it was a considerable achievement.

The reaction to *The Training of Cavalry Remount Horses* was muted. This was unsurprising as it was a highly specialized work, aimed at a specific readership. It was also, as Nolan openly admitted, building on the theories of another, whose controversial methods were well known on the Continent. Nevertheless, as a well researched and useful study it achieved some recognition for Nolan within equestrian circles and the cavalry. Nolan's publishers, W Clowes and Sons, helped promote the work and numerous adverts appeared in the press during 1853, particularly in *The Times*, leading to respectable sales.

His second book had a much warmer reception. The *Illustrated London News* carried a lengthy review remarking, 'In no branch of our military armament is reform more needed than the cavalry, which has for a period beyond the memory of living men been given up to the control of foreign martinets, and Royal tailors.'[109] Although this periodical enjoyed poking fun at the establishment, clearly delighting in Nolan's criticism of military tradition, it gave a detailed account of his work. It was accompanied by three drawings of the 'Hottentot' method of carrying a gun on horseback, along with close copies of the military seats contained in the book. The review itself could scarcely have been more favourable, applauding the author for writing a much needed work, praising his knowledge, enthusiasm and common sense approach. Using lengthy quotations from the book, the writer recommended it unreservedly to civilians as well as the military as a readable and informative volume.

The Times also allocated considerable column space to another complimentary review. Commenting that Nolan was well known in the service, the reviewer deferred to Nolan's experience and approved of his theories in every case. He agreed that the lance was a dubious weapon and that heavy cavalry should be maintained only if 'the weight should be in the horse, not the rider.'[110] The argument that the Hungarian Hussars comprised mostly small men was one of the points that convinced the reviewer. Even Nolan's arguments on the cavalry's capability to break infantry squares drew praise. Citing his observation that maddened horses appeared fearless and almost unstoppable, the reviewer remarked that 'we are inclined to believe that a horse at full speed is one of the most awful "missiles" known in warfare. A horse will go on for some distance, maintaining its speed, even if it has received its death-wound.'[111] The review ended with a firm endorsement of Nolan's work.

Nevertheless, some of his theories drew criticism. Having seen the review, one light cavalryman wrote in to *The Times* saying 'I was struck with your idea of cavalry being resistless, which is so contrary to the general opinion.'[112] In his view the way that cavalry were trained would in itself prevent horses from pressing such an attack home. On a brigade field day, charging an infantry square was a regular exercise but, when within a dozen yards, the orders 'Right troop threes right, left troop threes left' would be given and each troop would wheel to the rear to make room for the next squadron. Therefore in practice the horses never actually made contact with the square. He argued that, being accustomed to this manoeuvre, the horses were likely to repeat it in the field despite the efforts of their riders. Some change in training would be necessary before Nolan's theories had a chance of working:

> *you cannot practice riding over infantry. Of course not, but could there not be some straw men made for use in every cavalry barrack to practice riding them down? At any rate, it is certain that so long as cavalry horses are practised not to face a square they will not break one.*[113]

Nolan's theory that cavalry could overthrow infantry squares with relative ease was always going to be one of his more controversial ideas, but it is notable that this criticism came from a fellow cavalry officer and a light cavalryman at that.

Cavalry: Its History and Tactics was generally well received over the next few decades as an important, even ground-breaking, work. Colonel Beamish, who wrote several military texts, gave it his general approval in 1855, but lamented the fact that Nolan had made inferences against Major Meyer. Although these were subtle enough to fall far short of actual insults, his illustrations captioned 'The military seat as it ought to be' for his own recommendation and 'The military seat as it is' were clearly a slight on his rival's well-known preference. In addition, Nolan was also openly criticizing current practice at Maidstone Cavalry Depot, an establishment of some repute. This was not the act of a gentleman. Beamish also ridiculed the riding posture suggested by Nolan, believing it to be far too relaxed for military purposes and more applicable for sporting use.[114]

Indeed, the balance seat still had its admirers well into the next century. While not referring to Nolan specifically, Lieutenant Colonel French criticized the tendency to adopt 'crouched' riding stances as ungainly and detrimental to controlling the rider's mount. He recalled a sergeant major at Canterbury riding school crying out 'I can't 'ave you a-setting like a broody 'en!'[115] when a rider adopted a similar posture. He argued that:

> *The natural seat on a horse is best demonstrated by a man riding bareback, for then he instinctively positions his body and legs so as to enable him to acquire balance, apply a firm grip, and exercise control. Riding bareback, the short, crouch seat would be impossible to maintain; from which it follows that it can only be adopted by artificial means, namely saddles, stirrup irons, and preposterously short leathers.*[116]

Even by the 1950s, when French was writing, equestrian experts debated the merits of various seats, although with the horse superseded by the tank, the military argument had long since become academic.

Although the contemporary reaction in the press was generally favourable, many in the military considered Nolan, as a junior officer, to be rather headstrong even to write a book on tactics, let alone a controversial one. Many of his ideas went against traditional methods of long standing, and the army could be very reactionary when it came to reform. The idea that Nolan was impertinent merely for having put forward his own opinions was a common attitude in some quarters and the modern view is far more forgiving. One contemporary writer, commenting on the later events at Balaklava, described him as an 'author of a book on cavalry tactics, in which faith in the power of that arm was carried to extremes'.[117] His views on attacking infantry were perhaps the most controversial, and the fact that he had not seen action at the time of writing was unhelpful in this regard.

The book was well written and popular and some critical army officers were undoubtedly jealous of his success. Nonetheless, he was a soldier of considerable experience, having served twenty-five years in two armies. When the fact that he possessed considerable knowledge and expertise became more generally known, some of his critics relented. Few would question its instructive value for the military regardless of Louis's occasional over enthusiasm for his arm of the service. Yet despite what people thought of his book, its popularity brought his name to prominence and one dominating trait in Nolan's character was undoubtedly his ambition.

Yet other contemporary reactions were favourable. When the book *British Cavalry* appeared in 1858, the author quoted at great length from Nolan's work. The writer was Captain Valentine Baker, who was clearly impressed with Nolan's ideas. His only real reservation was Nolan's insistence that the troop should be the basic operational unit. Whilst he agreed that exercising control over a troop was easier compared with larger formations, he considered it too small to be effective and that dividing a large formation, such as a brigade, into so many individual sections could lead to confusion. Yet he fully approved of the majority of his ideas, especially regarding uniforms and weaponry.

The second book was also well received in America. Major General G B McClellan, author of *European Cavalry in 1860*, considered Nolan's book the only English volume worthy of note, basing most of his work on continental cavalry. The fact that he favoured Austrian cavalry in particular is probably significant, since Nolan used examples from the Austrian Army extensively. Another American writer, Dr J Roemer, formerly of the Dutch cavalry, praised Nolan for his keen observations and for exposing the shortcomings of his nation's cavalry. However, like Beamish, he felt that Meyer had been subjected to unfair criticism and strongly disagreed with Nolan that heavy cavalry were a thing of the past.[118]

Writing in the 1870s, Denison broadly approved of Nolan, referring to his work several times. However, he derided previous European writers for their preference for the sword over all other weapons. Firearms, he argued, had come to dominate the battlefield:

> *in close fighting, the revolver's bullet cannot be warded off like a sword or a lance thrust. If it strikes, the wound is severe. It does not require the speed or weight of the horse to give it impetus, as does the lance, or the*

perfect training of the charger, which is necessary for an effective use of the sabre when mounted.[119]

Denison echoes Nolan's arguments on the use of lances and the need for skilled horsemanship over and above good swordsmanship. Yet, had Nolan lived to see the wars of the next two decades, it would have been interesting to see his reaction to the improvements and increasing use of revolvers and whether he would have altered his views in consequence. However, Denison was writing in the 1870s with the recent examples of the American Civil War and the Franco-Prussian War to prove his point. The revolver had only just begun to make an appearance on the battlefield at the time of the Crimean War, and its use was almost exclusively confined to officers who bought them privately. Despite Denison's arguments, cavalry swords continued to be used during the First World War and beyond, though admittedly their use was diminishing.

It is clear that Nolan had spent considerable time and effort in writing both his books. The first is a sober, thoughtful and practical work intended primarily for those with prior knowledge of the subject. Yet even after 150 years his second book still reads well as a comprehensive examination of cavalry aimed at a wide readership. Although a writer's personality is not always evident in his work, neither of these books gives the impression of someone who is reckless, hot-headed or impatient. In fact, precisely the opposite conclusion can be drawn, as they are obviously the result of long-term and careful study. Nolan writes with the utter conviction of an expert, which can appear arrogant, but modesty was hardly a common trait in Victorian cavalry officers and it should be borne in mind that Nolan wished to provoke a reaction to his work. Yet he was clearly someone who watched and listened shrewdly, and, with what was to follow, this is worth keeping in mind.

Chapter 5

The Crimean War

The Crimean War was an unusual conflict and should have been avoided by diplomatic means. It was known more appropriately during the 1850s as the 'Russian War' since the Crimea was only one theatre of operations with important naval and land actions taking place in the Balkans, the Baltic Sea, White Sea and Pacific Ocean. However, the famous events that took place there and common usage have ensured that the conflict will always be known by this name. British involvement in the Crimea lasted for only two years, but the harsh lessons learned in the fight against Russia forced the government to re-evaluate the organization of the armed forces. Following a long period of relative peace in Europe, a jingoistic public greeted the outbreak of war with unseemly enthusiasm. The Crimean campaign began with a series of dramatic actions that included three major battles in the latter half of 1854. Journalists, photographers and artists who travelled out to see things at first hand, recorded how the war subsequently became bogged down in the ruinous siege of Sevastopol, noted for the squalid conditions endured by both sides and for huge loss of life. They brought the sober reality of war back home to the public in a way it had not experienced before and this, along with innovations in weaponry, steamships and the use of railways, made it a transitional conflict between old and new. In many ways it was the first truly modern war.

The origins of the war included a dispute over religious rights in the Holy Land. Much of the Middle East was under the sway of the Turkish Ottoman Empire, which allowed Christians access to the holy sites in Jerusalem. For many years custody of the Holy Sepulchre and other shrines had been disputed between the Roman Catholic and the Greek Orthodox Churches. Citing an old agreement, the French persuaded the Sublime Porte (the Turkish government) to give control of the holy sites to the Roman Catholics; Orthodox Russia was outraged. In 1852 Tsar Nicholas I of Russia applied diplomatic pressure on Sultan Abd-el-Mejid to return the keys of the Sepulchre to the Greek Church. Russian ambassadors used this issue as a pretext to champion the rights of Christian subjects in the Balkans, demanding concessions such as the withdrawal of Turkish troops from Montenegro. At an informal meeting at Tsarskoe Seloe, Nicholas made his views on Turkey very plain:

> *Look here, we have a sick man on our hands – a seriously sick man. It would, to be frank with you, be a great tragedy if one of these days he should leave us, especially before any of the necessary arrangements have been made . . .*[120]

As an Islamic state, Turkey had little interest in squabbles between Christian sects but deeply resented interference in their domestic affairs. While the Turks were prepared to compromise, Prince Menshikov, as Russian Ambassador in Constantinople (Istanbul), wished to formalize the agreement: he 'demanded that a convention should be signed between the sultan and the tsar, securing to the Greek subjects of Turkey their privileges, and accepting Russia as a guarantee for seeing those privileges perpetually secured.'[121] Religious disputes were one thing, but assuming control of Turkish subjects was out of the question. Intimidated by Russian pressure, the Porte sought the assistance of Great Britain and France to counter this aggression. Though France swiftly sent a fleet to the Dardanelles, Britain was initially reluctant to get involved, although a British fleet was eventually despatched. It took a Russian invasion of the Danubian principalities of Moldavia and Wallachia to stir Prime Minister Lord Aberdeen into real action.

The invasion of Moldavia and Wallachia drew almost universal condemnation in Europe, particularly from Austria, since this brought Russian troops directly into her area of influence. The Austrians rapidly reinforced their garrisons in the region, thereby heightening political tensions. Indeed, many Russian diplomats showed rare foresight in believing that the Turkish question would eventually be resolved in Vienna. Since the eighteenth century Russia had entertained hopes of seizing Constantinople, and Tsar Alexander I had made this intention plain negotiating with Napoleon at Tilsit in 1807. By the 1850s the Ottoman Empire was crumbling and Tsar Nicholas was openly talking about its demise and dividing its territories among the European powers. However, most continental nations feared the westward spread of Russian influence and possession of Constantinople would allow her access to the Mediterranean, improving Russian commerce and extending the reach of her armed forces to an unacceptable degree.

Some believed that Nicholas was persuaded, by the actions of vocal British peace parties and the beneficent aims of the Great Exhibition in 1851, that Britain was either complacent or preparing to relinquish her empire.[122] Many Russian diplomats believed that Britain would either back down over the

Map 1: From Constantinople to the Crimea

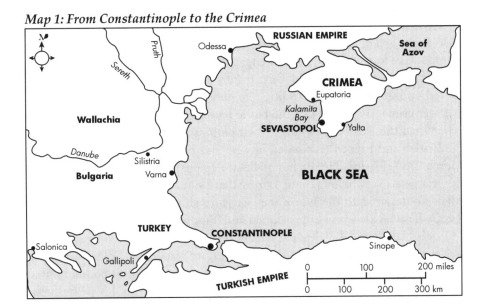

dispute or even help them dismember Turkish possessions if Britain benefited from the fall of the sultan. After all, Turkey was Islamic, while both Britain and Russia were Christian states. However, Russian aggression was denounced in both houses of Parliament, Lord Palmerston stating that the Porte was one of the most liberal regimes in Europe as far as religious toleration was concerned and predictions of its demise were premature. In addition, Russia was not only opposed to the British free trade policy but imposed harsh religious restrictions on her own subjects, which for Palmerston made the moral side of this argument quite clear.[123]

The Russians were in fact eager to resolve the matter by arbitration. It was evident that they had misjudged the situation and they deemed Turkey so weak that her empire would soon fragment with or without external pressure. The Russian geographical position made them relatively secure from attack and they could afford to await developments as far as Constantinople was concerned.[124] However, they were now at war with Turkey, and increasing attempts to dislodge them from the Danubian provinces compelled them to act. On 30 November 1853 Admiral Nakhimov led an attack against a Turkish squadron moored at Sinope. Against six Russian ships of the line, the Turkish force of seven frigates, a sloop, a steamer and some troop transports could not hope to win the action. Nonetheless, they put up stout resistance. For the first time Russians used explosive shells in action, which proved devastatingly effective, destroying all the enemy ships but one and even setting areas of the port alight when bombarding the shore batteries. At least 4,000 Turkish seamen were lost in this one-sided engagement.[125]

Events at Sinope provoked Britain into declaring war on Russia. Already stirred up into anti-Russian feeling, the public was outraged at what was seen as a war crime, though in fact the battle had been a perfectly legitimate act of war. When the Russians withdrew their ambassadors from London and Paris, the British and French responded in kind and both countries declared war in March 1854, joining Turkey in an alliance against Russia. Public support for the war was overwhelming and Lord Stuart summarized the views of many when he declared to the house that 'censure should be directed against the Tsar, whose reckless and unprincipled ambition has caused this necessity.'[126]

Louis Napoleon III of France, having recently seized power in a *coup d'état*, was anxious to gain favour in Europe and restore respect for French arms after the loss of the Napoleonic Wars. The war provided him with both a military opportunity and the chance to gain support in Britain for his new regime. Palmerston had made an unusual prediction in 1833 in proclaiming grandly to the Commons that 'France and England could command the peace of Europe; for France and England together would never make an unjust war.'[127] Whether the cause was just was open to debate, but, for once, the two nations did indeed stand united.

Although in 1855 Sardinia joined the alliance, in 1854 the armies of three nations were set against Russia. As the emperor of an already vast empire, Tsar Nicholas I was keen to expand Russian influence even farther. He was also devoted to the military: considering himself more a soldier than a ruler, he habitually wore uniform and had appointed the majority of his advisors from within the army. Known for his eccentricity, he ran his household in military fashion and by royal standards lived relatively frugally. Interested in all classes and aspects of society, he often walked unescorted around St Petersburg carrying out surprise inspections and passing judgements as a completely absolutist monarch.[128] His enthusiasm for the army was such that during the 1828 Turkish war in the Balkans he briefly assumed command. However, the demands of fighting a campaign combined with running affairs of state proved too much, and after a short period he was obliged to relinquish control. A stern disciplinarian, he was nicknamed 'Nicholas the Flogger'[129] by his troops and firmly believed that emulating the Prussian Army was the way forward.

However, to take the Tsar's interest as indicative of Russian military might was deceptive. In many ways his army was burdened with obsolete equipment, outmoded tactics and was officered by disinterested and uninspired commanders. One of the reasons for this was the perpetual fear of violent rebellion in Russian society. The vast majority of Russian subjects were serfs who as virtual slaves had few rights and were grossly mistreated by the landowners. Contact with the West during the Napoleonic Wars had made many of the small middle and upper classes question the values of their society and demand reform. During Nicholas's accession to the throne in 1825 the Decembrist Revolt had broken out, the main conspirators being army officers with Freemasonry associations who led their regiments into open rebellion.[130]

The revolt, though swiftly crushed, alarmed an establishment already fearful of rebellion into repressing intellectualism and personal initiative within the army command, in favour of unquestioning loyalty and obedience. One consequence of this policy was the lack of an effective general staff in the Russian Army. It was an unpopular posting, actively discouraged by some high-ranking officers; in consequence many generals went to war relying largely on their own personal abilities for planning and organization. There were exceptions, such as General Diebitch and Prince Gorchakov who insisted on forming proper staffs, but most general officers were forced to do without them.[131]

The Russian Army was huge but largely conscript-based. Young men were taken from their families and obliged in most line regiments to serve a twenty-five year period in the army. Since most recruits were serfs, they were generally poorly educated and treated like overgrown children by their officers. By 1831 around 80,000 conscripts were being pressed into the army every year, the vast size of the empire meaning that a large force was necessary to garrison its territories effectively. The Russian logistics system was poor but even a good supply administration would have had difficulty with the great distances involved. Despite the army's size, Nicholas was forced to impose compulsory levies six times to reinforce his army in the Crimea between 1852 and 1854.[132]

Although most Russian corps contained rifle regiments, the bulk of the infantry were still armed with cumbersome 12lb smoothbore muskets that had changed little since the Napoleonic Wars. Firing a .700-inch spherical ball, its effective range was barely 150 yards even when fired en masse by men in line. Except for guard regiments, which received muskets with percussion locks, many still had old-fashioned flintlock firing mechanisms. With the short range and slow firing rate of the musket, Russian infantry tactics relied on the use of dense, unwieldy columns for attack with an emphasis on closing with the enemy to decide the matter with the bayonet. The few rifle regiments available were largely equipped with the 1843 model Littikhsky rifle, which was muzzle-loading and had an accurate range of between 400 to 500 yards. Most line regiments possessed a skirmishing company of riflemen, but the introduction of new weapons was proceeding very slowly and many were poorly constructed, badly maintained and unreliable.

In the Russian Army both infantry and cavalry were extensively drilled, with an overemphasis on ceremonial and parade-ground duties. Russian horse consisted of heavy and light cavalry, the light cavalry being well equipped; hussars and uhlans carried carbines in addition to sabres and lances. Russian cuirassiers were armed only with swords and regular cavalry were taught to manoeuvre largely in dense formations. Their horses were rarely exercised to perform beyond their usual parade-ground functions and were predominantly small and unfit. In addition, they were often weighed down with excessive equipment and, due to their lack of stamina, huge numbers of horses died on campaign.[133]

Cossack light cavalry were generally more effective than their regular counterparts in everything other than shock action. Originally recruited from the frontier regions when the Tsars employed them to guard their borders, they had a tradition of military service, training their men almost exclusively as warriors. Cossacks fought intelligently and would never risk losses unless there was prospect of serious gain. As irregulars they rarely fought in formation and seldom stood to receive a charge by regular cavalry, but they excelled in scouting, raiding, skirmishing and harassing a retreating enemy.

The artillery was considered an elite arm within the Russian Army. Its officers were well educated and most benefited from cadet school training. It was organized in both light and heavy batteries, which were usually attached to infantry or cavalry brigades. Don Cossack light horse batteries were also attached to each corps. The majority of their guns were brass muzzle-loaders, fired by the outdated slow match, but they were well disciplined, efficient and capable of producing rapid concentrated fire. Effective range was usually between 900 and 1,000 yards. The standard arm of light batteries were 6lb and 9lb guns, whereas heavy batteries might field 12lb and 18lb guns. Round shot and case shot were the most common forms of ammunition, with shrapnel shells mostly the province of heavy batteries.[134] At this period artillery was by far the most professional arm of the Russian Army.

However, on the whole Russia was going to war with an ill-equipped, outdated army reliant on conscripted serfs for the bulk of its manpower.

Although it was one of the largest armies in the world, it was hidebound in tradition and the education and initiative of its officer class had been stifled through fear of internal dissent and rebellion. Its artillery was relatively efficient but Russian cavalry capability was uncertain for an arm that had been starved of money, practical training and resources. Although its infantry was dependable and tenacious in defence, Russia's offensive capability against a modern army was questionable.

In contrast, the Turkish standing army theoretically consisted of 700,000 men. In reality the figure was much lower than this, but the sultan commanded the allegiance of roughly two million Muslims and, given time, could produce a formidable force. Turkish infantry were generally brave soldiers with considerable powers of endurance and experience of combat from suppressing frequent revolts within the Ottoman Empire. Turkey could call upon troops from Egypt, Tunis and other dependencies whose effectiveness varied considerably. Once more great stress was placed on ceremonial duty, while practical training was lacking. The majority of Turkish soldiers were illiterate and the officer corps lacked the professionalism of most European armies. One major weakness was an almost total lack of administration and supply systems; Britain and France would be required to assist the Turks with this.

The Turkish commander-in-chief was Michael Lattas, a Croatian mercenary who had adopted the name of Omar Pasha after converting to Islam. He proved very agreeable to most allied commanders, being eager to secure their effective cooperation, but, although a soldier of great capability, he was handicapped by an inefficient administrative system and the frequent attempts of rivals to supplant him. In addition both the sultan and the Porte pestered him with constant attempts to interfere in the running of his army and liaison with the Allies. Despite this, he was one of the best commanders in the allied force.[135] Though Turkey was ostensibly fighting a defensive war, Omar Pasha was well aware that the sultan saw the conflict as an excuse to move northwards into the Balkans and seize further territory.

Captain Thompson of the 10th Hussars spent some time as an observer with the Turks as they fought the Russians along the Danube. In his opinion the Turkish rank and file were good soldiers but their officer corps was decidedly inferior. With the disdain of his class he remarked: 'Up to the rank of Captain inclusive they are usually raised from the ranks, and are in no respect whatever superior to the privates from amongst whom they have been chosen.'[136] He went on to say that such officers, while undoubtedly experienced men, were largely illiterate and treated contemptuously by the higher ranks as their social inferiors. Thompson believed that most Turkish officers above the rank of captain owed their positions to political or family influence and generally lacked military experience. Partially to compensate for this, the Turks hired many foreign mercenaries from Poland, Hungary and the Balkans, many of whom had converted to Islam.

The Turkish cavalry was generally of poor quality, lacking both horses and equipment. Cavalry was an expensive arm to maintain, and the Porte's reluctance to spend money on the military lay at the root of Turkish inefficiency. However, the artillery was well drilled and effective, but its main drawback was an armoury consisting of a bewildering variety of cannons in various calibres and models. Potentially this could confuse the gunners in action and made ammunition supply very difficult.[137]

The Turks also possessed large bodies of irregular troops such as Spahis, Bedouins and Bashi-Bazouks. These were often employed in a role similar to that of the Russian Cossacks, for suppressing internal revolts and guarding frontiers. They were highly effective for scouting and general harassment of the enemy, but in common with many irregulars they were prone to looting and indiscipline. In spite of their problems, the Turkish Army was a formidable force that had proved a match for the Russians on several occasions. One of the Turks' main motivations for seeking allies in the coming conflict was the sheer number of Russians likely to be facing them in the event of a major war.

Marshal Leroy de Saint Arnaud was put in command of the French forces: his support of Napoleon III's new administration influenced the appointment as much as his military ability. As a gambler, debtor and womanizer, he had been forced to leave France during his early military career, which had begun in 1816. He served with the French Foreign Legion, seeing considerable action in Algeria and was multi-lingual, which was a bonus in an allied force. Though experienced in colonial campaigning, he was unused to commanding troops above corps level, though this was not unusual in the four armies at the start of the conflict. Following years of excess with women and wine, St Arnaud was not in the best of health. Napoleon III had appointed Colonel Trochu to his staff in an attempt to make up for his deficiencies.[138] Though several senior appointments were influenced by the political reliability of the officers, the restoration of the Napoleonic regime had done away with the Bourbon purchase system and reintroduced promotion by merit. This made for a more professional and capable officer corps, which looked to modern conflicts like those in Algeria for their inspiration.

The French Army was just beginning to introduce rifles in the infantry to replace percussion-fired muskets. In addition to the Minié rifle they were introducing the Snider rifle, which loaded from the breech. This imparted a considerable advantage since it was the only weapon in the war that could be easily and swiftly reloaded when lying down. As veterans of Algeria, many French infantrymen had seen extensive combat and were used to hard campaigning. At the outset of the war, the French Army was perhaps the most professional and experienced land force to enter the conflict.

The French artillery was on a par with the British in terms of efficiency, but, despite its reputation for excellence, the French were sending fewer cavalry, providing a small brigade comprising squadrons from the 1st and 4th Chasseurs d'Afrique for the campaign. However, the French possessed the best commissariat of any army during the war, although British efforts would eventually better it in some areas. This had been developed in the Armée d'Afrique over twenty years of conflict in Algeria: this army had rapidly determined that the key to successful fighting lay in swift movement and the efficient supply of food, water and ammunition.[139] The difficult Algerian climate had rapidly taught them that undernourished and poorly supplied soldiers were ineffective.

The British Army had suffered from significant neglect during the long period of peace following Napoleon's downfall. In 1853 an exercise camp had been conducted at Chobham under Lord Seaton. This was the largest concentration of troops outside Ireland convened since 1815, with three brigades of infantry, one brigade of cavalry, artillery, engineers and a pontoon section assembled for manoeuvres. Most generals were totally inexperienced in manoeuvring such large bodies of men, and the exercises revealed many deficiencies. This applied to the artillery in particular with many gunners and drivers having insufficient knowledge of their duties to form an effective battery.[140] Although Viscount Hardinge introduced some initiatives, many commented on the lack of a commissariat corps, which had been largely disbanded after the Napoleonic Wars because of peacetime economies. Since the army's main duties were taken up with small colonial wars, Parliament felt justified in cutting back on logistics; few predicted a large-scale European war in the near future. The short-sighted policy resulted in great suffering for the troops in the Crimea.

The war caught the infantry in the process of rearmament. Debate over updating the army's main weapon from the smoothbore musket to the rifle had been going on for years, but the French Minié rifle was gradually being issued. This new arm was designed in 1847 by Captain Minié. It fired a cylindro-conoidal bullet rather than a musket ball, which possessed greater stability in flight since it engaged the rifling in the barrel and imparted spin to the projectile. Though its firing rate was relatively slow, at about three rounds per minute, its accurate range was between 400 and 600 yards, which far outdistanced the musket. Whilst other models such as the Enfield Rifled Musket were under consideration, most authorities considered adopting the Minié to be a major step forward, though infantry tactics were only beginning to adapt to these new improvements in weaponry. Even so, many regiments went to war carrying a large proportion of muskets that Hardinge was desperately trying to replace. For example, one guards' brigade possessed 200 Miniés and 650 muskets when they set sail for Turkey.[141] By the end of the war, the introduction of either the Minié or the Enfield was nearly universal in the British Army.

The force sent out to Turkey, and subsequently to the Crimea, became known as the Army of the East. It consisted of one cavalry and five infantry divisions, along with artillery, engineers and other specialists. Initially fielding around 26,000 men, the French were always the senior partners in the alliance, sending over 30,000 men at the outset of the campaign and eventually outnumbering the British contingent by two to one.[142] With the need to maintain troops in the Balkans area, the Turks sent only around 7,000 men to the Crimea in the early stages of the war.

The make-up of the British high command in the Crimea was controversial both during and after the conflict. Accusations of mishandling and incompetence abounded, and the personalities of some of those involved are relevant to Nolan's eventual fate. Unlike their French Allies, who possessed numbers of young officers fresh from Africa, virtually all the officers of general rank were over 50 and few had seen recent active service. Though the army possessed many officers who had fought in colonial wars, the disdain Horse Guards felt for such experience ensured that many deserving men were held back, a fact exacerbated by the antiquated purchase system. Nonetheless, it should be borne in mind that after nearly forty years of peace on the Continent, nobody was available with recent relevant fighting experience.

Lord Fitzroy Somerset Raglan, aged 66, was appointed commander-in-chief of the Army of the East. He was elderly for such a senior position and in failing health. A highly experienced officer, he had served throughout the Peninsular War in Portugal and Spain and lost his right arm at Waterloo. However, his knowledge was largely confined to staff work as the Duke of Wellington's military secretary and, although he had closely observed the Great Duke at work, he had not commanded large bodies of troops in person. Well versed in administration on the staff, he spoke good French and was known for his calm demeanour and ability for resolving disputes. Although popular at all levels in the army, his amiability was a weakness as a commander since when a firm hand was required his desire to compromise led to problems.

General Richard Airey would later prove a controversial appointment. Aged 51, he had lived an unusual life, building his own house in the Canadian wilderness whilst overseeing his family estates and business there. Prior to the war, he had been military secretary to Lord Hardinge and had initially been given command of a brigade on the expedition. Sent out in command of the 1st Infantry Brigade, he was eventually persuaded by Raglan to accept the appointment of quartermaster general, whose main duty was running the general staff.[143] Possessing unusual energy for a man in his early fifties, Raglan relied heavily on Airey's abilities and advice throughout the campaign.

The British cavalry division sent out to the Crimea comprised two five-regiment brigades of light and heavy cavalry. Initially this amounted to about 1,250 men in each brigade, but they were under strength and likely to be massively outnumbered by the Russian horse. Lieutenant General George Bingham, 3rd Earl of Lucan, was the divisional commander for the cavalry. An overbearing, suspicious and disagreeable man, Lord Lucan was notorious for his repressive management of his estates in Ireland during the Potato Famine of the 1840s, with large-scale evictions. Despite his long experience as a soldier, he had seen action only once, in the Balkans, ironically with the Russians on General Worontzov's staff.[144] The Russians generally acknowledged him to be an efficient officer and a brave man. Prone to perfectionism, ill-tempered and a stern disciplinarian, Lucan operated on the assumption that he was going to be disliked and conducted his relationships accordingly.

The Light Brigade was under the command of General James Brudenell, 7th Earl of Cardigan. Though a committed soldier, he had never been to war and was well known for his scandalous behaviour both with women and in frequent disagreements with his subordinates. One such incident led to Lord Cardigan being relieved from command, something almost unheard of in a peacetime army.[145] He was known for his conservative nature, prejudice against 'Indian' officers (officers who had served in India) and unswerving belief in rules and tradition. Although popular with the rank and file, many of his officers disliked him and his fanatical imposition of discipline had drawn severe criticism on several occasions. Worst of all, he detested his brother-in-law, Lord Lucan, who returned his scorn with equal enthusiasm, and the pair continued their feud during the campaign. This fact alone makes one question the wisdom of the decision to let him serve directly under Lord Lucan.

Major General Sir James Scarlett commanded the Heavy Brigade. At 55, Scarlett was florid-faced, white-haired and wore impressive military style moustaches, leading many to believe him to be an officer of vast experience whereas in fact he had never seen active campaigning. Nevertheless, he chose Colonel Beatson and Lieutenant Alexander Elliott (who had dropped a rank in order to serve in the Crimea) as ADCs, both having served out in India.[146] Enormously popular with the men for his bluff, hearty character, Scarlett knew his limitations and was intelligent enough to appoint competent men to assist him, much to the chagrin of some commanders who had refused appointments to 'Indian' officers.

The Army of the East set sail for Turkey with rather vague political instructions. Their primary objective was to protect Turkish interests and defend Constantinople. Yet even at the beginning of the war, the British Cabinet were considering taking the offensive. The difficulty was that although the Russian Empire was vast, the choice of a realistic strategic objective of sufficient importance was a problem. Though naval operations would take place in the Baltic, major Russian cities such as St Petersburg and Moscow were beyond easy reach. Previous attempts to penetrate the Russian hinterland by powers such as Sweden and France had met with disaster, and the Allies had no wish for a repetition. However, the port of Sevastopol, home to the Russian Black Sea Fleet, lay within striking distance of Turkey. From the outset strategists wondered if seizing this port might persuade the Russians to consider a negotiated peace.

Chapter 6

Horse-Dealing with the Bedouin

Louis Nolan was anxious to go to war. He had no wish to return to his regiment in India and judged that the way to promotion lay in staff work, especially in the kind of European war that Horse Guards valued so much. His writing brought his name to the attention of the Duke of Newcastle, Secretary of State for War and the Colonies, who needed an officer with equestrian skills and knowledge. Transporting horses by sea was a difficult and dangerous operation that resulted in the deaths of expensive animals and damaged the health of those that survived. As the voyage to Turkey lasted many weeks, Newcastle wished to find as many horses as possible nearer the region of conflict, to reduce such losses.

There had already been some embarrassing questions raised in Parliament: Lord Cardigan had questioned government transport policy in the House of Lords, saying that the superior speed of steamships made them more suitable for the cavalry than the infantry: 'the delay and inconvenience of conveying horses by sailing vessels was very great, and was also accompanied with much risk to the horses themselves'.[147] Replying for the government, the duke commented that most of the steamships available were in private hands; the expense of chartering vessels for the infantry was already considerable and proving a great inconvenience for the shipping companies concerned. Furthermore, relatively few steam vessels were equipped for loading and shipping horses or artillery, and so considerable adaptation was necessary. As Cardigan was a cavalry officer he did not mention that the demands of modern war made the transport of infantry a greater priority. The matter was raised again by General Wyndam in the same month and answered in similar fashion.[148]

Newcastle was therefore eager to find officers with relevant experience, knowledge of breeds and a buyer's eye for horseflesh. Aware of Nolan's books and reputation, he petitioned Raglan to give him a place on the staff: 'I find that a steamer leaves Marseilles for Constantinople . . . Will it be possible for Captain Nolan to go by that boat to purchase horses for the Army?'[149] Raglan consented: a place was found for Nolan as an aide-de-camp on the staff of Brigadier General Richard Airey.

Ordered up from Maidstone, Louis was ushered into an interview with Newcastle, who soon decided that he had picked the right man for the job. His initial instructions were to find and purchase remounts for the cavalry and artillery in Turkey. He would be provided with the necessary funds, though the army was having difficulty resolving its shortcomings in the commissariat. Mr William Filder had been brought out of retirement as commissary general at the age of 64. With the commissariat in such disarray, his appointment was far from ideal as the task would require great energy and persistence, but, having served in the Peninsular War, he was one of the few men available with experience of large-scale operations. Accordingly, Filder wrote to the assistant commissary in Constantinople to see that money could be made available on Nolan's arrival.

Nolan was now transferred to the staff and went on half pay with the 15th Hussars. Only six of the fifteen years he had served with the regiment had been spent in India; five had been spent on home service and a full four years had been spent on leave. It was two weeks prior to the declaration of war and, travelling via Paris, he was given letters of introduction by the British Ambassador and, accompanied by his half-brother George Ruddach, boarded the steamship *Thabor* at Marseilles for Constantinople. He was keen to get there quickly before French agents beat him to it.

Upon arrival at the Turkish capital, Louis rapidly made the acquaintance of Mr Skene, the Vice-Consul, who provided him with introductions and made arrangements for him to travel up to the front to view Turkish regiments outfitted for war. At times during his mission he would also enjoy the assistance of Mr Wilkinson, the veterinary surgeon for the 2nd Life Guards.[150] Omar Pasha had established his headquarters at Shumla and had already taken the war to the Russians, crossing the Danube in several places and achieving some success against the invaders. He received Nolan cordially and permitted him to review some of his regiments, particularly the irregulars that Nolan showed an express interest in meeting.

Nolan was not overly impressed with what he saw. He did not think the Turkish irregulars capable of withstanding a charge by regular cavalry and found their horses to be rather small, at an average height of 14 hands 1 inch. Nonetheless, he placed an order for 250 such horses at £16 a head, despite his reservations. He judged them sufficient for the artillery but the cavalry would require something better: English horses regularly reached between 14.5 and 16 hands in height. He believed English thoroughbreds to be the best horses in the world: 'No horse can compare with the English, no horse is more easily broken in to anything and everything, and there is no quality in which the English horse does not excel, no performance in which he cannot beat all competition.'[151]

Many equestrian experts would have agreed with him, and the style of horse bred for fox-hunting had become particularly valued for military purposes. The sport of riding to hounds had changed in the eighteenth century with the introduction of faster dogs. Consequently, horses needed to be swifter to keep the pace, whilst carrying large men and regularly jumping hedges or fences. Though it was true that campaign conditions meant that such horses could rarely be provided with sufficient fodder, they were highly effective in the charge if a reasonable diet could be maintained. However, failure to do so meant that they were prone to fatigue and vulnerable to exposure.[152] In this respect Turkish horses possessed a marked advantage. They were hardy animals capable of withstanding considerable deprivation and fatigue.

Nolan decided to expand the remit of his mission and provided some military intelligence gleaned from the Turks in his report to Raglan. However, this drew no reaction, although Raglan agreed to consider Nolan's proposal of a trip to Syria. Nolan claimed that there were better prospects for buying horses there. In addition, he asked that his half-brother, Captain George Ruddach, might accompany him on the proposed trip as an assistant. After all, his mission in Turkey was a failure, since the commissariat was unwilling to pay the prices Nolan had agreed, refusing to pay more than £5 a head for baggage animals. Luckily the Turkish contractor defaulted on the delivery of the horses, sparing him even more embarrassment.

By April the first British troops were landing near Gallipoli, joining French troops already assembling there. In the event of a serious Russian invasion, the Allies were uncertain of being able to reinforce Turkish positions on the Danube in time and considered deploying in a defensive line before Constantinople, cutting off the peninsula at its narrowest point. When Lord Raglan stepped ashore, one of the first officers to greet him was Captain Nolan. Surprisingly, the failure of his mission was actually useful to the commander-in-chief. The Duke of Newcastle had been praising the merits of irregular cavalry in Turkish and Russian service and was pressing him to recruit a similar force. Raglan disliked the idea, arguing that such troops were undisciplined, prone to looting and had little use beyond scouting. Nolan's view that the irregulars in Turkish service were both poorly mounted and decidedly inferior to conventional cavalry was therefore well received. If Newcastle's expert considered them second rate, he could hardly keep pressuring Raglan into compliance.

This probably influenced Raglan into approving Nolan's request, upon his assurance of better results, for a Syrian expedition. Captain Calthorpe, Raglan's nephew and one of his ADCs, addressed Nolan. He was interested to speak to someone who had been in the country six weeks and recorded that Louis had been able to purchase only between thirty and forty horses, finding it nearly impossible to find mounts of an appropriate size. He told him that horses suitable for the cavalry were difficult to come by but baggage animals were in plentiful supply. The Turks were having problems, because of their reliance on promissory notes and bills of sales and the British policy of paying in cash on the spot brought results. Louis told Calthorpe that he could have bought up to 1,000 such animals but that he lacked the authority to do so. By 5 May, Calthorpe wrote that Filder still had only seventy to eighty baggage mules, though he predicted the army would require at least 3,000 for his commissariat. Nolan made a good impression on Calthorpe, who noted that he:

> *is very highly thought of by the authorities. He has written a book on Cavalry which I have read with much interest; and although some of his ideas are perhaps rather extravagant, still there is much worth remembering, and which will be useful to know when in the field.*[153]

Over the next few weeks, as more troops began to arrive, Calthorpe echoed previous criticisms of the government's decision not to provide steamships for the horses sent out to Turkey. For example, when most of the artillery for the 1st Division arrived on 5 May, Calthorpe observed that they had lost 27 horses out of the 340 they had set out with. In addition, following a journey that usually took between sixty and seventy days by sail, a number of officers had lost their personal mounts and many of the surviving horses were sick: 'It is a very bad policy of the Government sending out the cavalry and artillery in sailing transports: many horses die on the voyage, and almost all arrive in bad condition, and are not fit for service for some time after they are landed.'[154]

Filder arranged to provide funds for Nolan's mission, though the lack of a sufficient commissariat in Turkey meant that he had to deal through Hanson and Co, a private company. Louis's stepbrother died after falling sick in Constantinople on 11 May, so Captain John Thompson of the 10th Hussars was appointed by Raglan to accompany him. Thompson had made the journey to Turkey in 1853 and spent some time as an observer with the Turkish Army at Widdin and Kalafat before returning to Constantinople. As an experienced officer with some knowledge of equestrian matters, he was an ideal choice for the expedition. Shortly after the war he wrote long accounts of his experiences in Turkey and Syria but never referred to Nolan by name. Though it is tempting to link this discretion with the furore surrounding Nolan's death, it should be borne in mind that the unassuming Thompson also omitted his own name from these accounts and was only positively identified through army records of these expeditions.

Thompson had been with the Turkish Army for some months and saw action along the frontier. Although he considered the horses of the Turkish regulars to be 'mere butchers' ponies',[155] the irregulars seemed to be better mounted. He was involved in one skirmish: the Russian Cossacks charged them in a compact body of around 200 men, an unusual occurrence for Cossacks. To his disdain, the Bashi-Bazouks fled in some disorder. Thompson frequently praised the courage of the Turkish soldiers and could not account for this sudden reverse: 'Nor could any excuse be found for them on the score of being ill mounted, for their horses, though according to English ideas, mere ponies in size, were compact, active, high-bred, and highly-broken.'[156]

The two officers were authorized to spend up to £30 each on cavalry horses with an initial fund of £300 to draw upon, which was later increased. However, they were forbidden to make purchases without reference to the British Consulate and the lack of administrative support in Constantinople forced them to postpone their travel arrangements. Thompson remarked on these frustrating delays and recorded that they only boarded *The Emperor*, bound for Alexandretta, on 9 May after two days of bureaucratic confusion. Recalling the squalid conditions in the capital and in Widdin, he found the travel arrangements on board a modern ship a refreshing change. With a mixture of relief and disgust, he recalled that the Turkish batteries failed either to challenge or fire upon the ship as they set out.[157]

When they stopped briefly at Alexandretta, consular officials informed them that Turkish agents had already swept much of northern Syria for army horses and they would need to search further afield. Sailing onward to Beirut, Mr Angelo Peterlini, an Italian horse-dealer, joined their party on 14 May to act as interpreter and stud groom. After consulting the authorities they decided to set off overland through Lebanon to Damascus on horses bought in Beirut. If they failed to find sufficient horses in the Syrian capital, they intended to make contact with Bedouin tribes in the hinterland, who, Peterlini assured them, raised some of the best horses in the country. Thompson recorded his vivid impressions of the lands they travelled through, which ranged from mountainous and hilly territory through to rough scrubland, fertile grassy plains and desert. Though good horses could be raised here, the party could tell that the climate meant they would never rival those found in England or Ireland.

Damascus was a disappointment to Thompson, who had been brought up on tales of the East from childhood. Known as one of the world's oldest cities and located at the meeting point of several caravan routes, it had a long history of commerce. The Romans had made it the capital of Syria for this reason and some of its bazaars and markets had been in use for thousands of years.[158] He thought it beautiful in parts but hardly the magnificent city he had expected. He had heard tales of the famed Damascus blades, whose western reputation hailed back to the Crusades, but was disappointed to find that most offered him were cheap copies and that the genuine article was just as rare there as elsewhere. The city had its squalid side: he recorded that fleas abounded and that different districts varied enormously in upkeep and cleanliness. As soon as the party arrived a black Syrian greyhound that accompanied them was set upon: 'Every street in Damascus swarms with curs, and all the curs in the street were on him at once, with a tumult of yelling and barking.'[159] The vigorous use of riding crops did little to defend their pet and the party were forced to ride over several of his attackers before they were left in peace.

Thompson had a poor opinion of the Turks, but disliked the Syrians even more. His account abounds with numerous references to the deceitfulness he encountered in his dealings with the Bedouin tribes, and he found city-dwellers little better: 'the proverb of their countrymen, which says that every Damascene is a scoundrel'.[160] However, they were well received by the governor, who treated them respectfully and allowed them the use of a barracks yard to view horses. They stayed at the Hôtel de Palmyre and, since their arrival had aroused considerable interest, many dealers brought their horses directly to the street outside. Directing them to the barracks Nolan and Thompson found their new base of operations to be a hindrance since none of the dealers would go there despite promises to do so. Upon enquiry they discovered that the Turks often press-ganged men into joining their army and in consequence an invitation to meet at any military establishment was viewed with deep suspicion by the locals, who feared forced conscription or the seizure of their property.

Undaunted, the two officers decided to follow local custom: 'we made a practice of pouncing at once upon such horses as were brought to us; examining and trying them in front of the hotel door, and throwing the whole street into an uproar.'[161] This was inconvenient but in reality they had little choice. The governor must have been aware of the circumstances that made a barracks an unsuitable place for buying horses, but, as the old Arab saying went, 'Your friend is he who tells you the truth, not he who agrees with everything you say.'[162] Yet it would have been unwise to request the use of another building from the governor since refusing the barracks might be taken as an insult. The Arab love of horses and mere inquisitiveness at the sight of foreigners drew large numbers of spectators who were nearly impossible to discourage; and in this chaotic atmosphere the pair made the best of a bad situation.

One of their best contacts proved to be Kalesh Bey, a Turk who tried to sell them his own horses and find other dealers in the market. Though he proved useful, Thompson wryly remarked: 'The modes in which he tried to swindle us were various. He did not succeed.'[163] Nolan and Thompson were both experienced with horseflesh and the local knowledge of Peterlini helped them to avoid most tricks and swindles. Nonetheless, they did not find horses in sufficient quantity or quality for their purposes and they decided to travel further. On 21 May, accompanied by a small, irregular Turkish escort and a consular representative to oversee their finances, along with dealers and servants, they left the city to contact Bedouin tribes in the desert.

They reached their first camp at Merj Kotrani, close to the camps of the Wulad-Ali, a Bedouin tribe of the Anazeh. Word of their arrival spread rapidly and horses were soon brought to their camp in large numbers. Thompson wrote: 'The horses are small, not rising in general above fourteen hands one inch; but they are fine, and have great power and size for their height.'[164] These were the best by far that he had seen in the east and the stallions were particularly beautiful:

> *looking like horses in a picture; the limbs flat, broad, and powerful, deep*
> *below the knee, small and fine about the fetlock, of a cleanness and beauty*
> *of outline enough alone to stamp blood on their possessor; the neck light,*
> *but yet arched; the flanks closely ribbed up; the tail carried out with a*
> *sweep like the curve of a palm branch; and the small head terminating in*
> *large nostrils always snorting and neighing.*[165]

The most common colour was dark nutmeg grey, which he remembered as being commonplace in Arab horses brought out to India. Bay, chestnut, brown and light grey verging on white were also common, but black was very rare in the desert.

Out in the desert they had ample room to ride and were able to test or see demonstrations of hundreds of horses. Yet these were far from perfect: 'The horses brought to us, handsome as they were, showed an amount of blemish –

chiefly consisting of curbs and enlargements of the knee and fetlock, and not perhaps, in the majority of instances, amounting to unsoundness of a disabling nature – which surprised me.'[166] Thompson believed that the reason for this was probably a result of the Arab style of horsemanship, which discouraged unnecessary exercise. Breeding horses mostly for sale, owners were reluctant to push them too hard for fear of injury and loss of value. Therefore they rarely rode them at more than a walk and proved very reluctant to display their wares riding at a gallop.

Those Bedouin who could afford it bought Turkish saddles and equipment that were generally of poor quality compared with European models. However, Thompson believed their use of smaller bits and the gentle treatment of their horses gave them greater control over their mounts than British cavalrymen gained using a heavier bit. Generally Arab riders tended to have more empathy with their horses, to the detriment of handling their mounts in battle: 'The Englishman seems unable to command that instantaneous and willing obedience which tell in single combat, and which make the horse to the rider as the boxer's legs are to a boxer.'[167] Though he believed that the Englishman was unmatched in riding headlong over the countryside he was generally impressed with Syrian horsemanship. This line of thought had much in common with Nolan's writing and it is likely that they discussed equestrian subjects intensely during their travels. Nevertheless, the Bedouin failure to press horses to great physical exertions and their subsequent lack of exercise was a weakness for the military horse market since they 'were plainly incapable of any great exertion, from an over fatness produced by the grass-feeding which they get at that time of the year, combined with the practice of never putting them out of a walk. In the winter, we were told, they are fed on barley and camel's milk.'[168] Though this may have been an overreaction, it could explain the mixed reception they received when the horses arrived in Turkey. Yet the army was desperate for remounts and, as the Bedouin proverb ran, 'When horses are scarce, you saddle dogs!'[169]

Thompson also saw large amounts of Turcoman horses brought into camp; he considered these very inferior to Arab horses. Although generally larger, they were 'heavy and clumsy, with coarse heads, staring coats, very drooping hindquarters, legs long in the shank, and coarse, dragging, ill-carried tails'.[170] Unlike the Arabs, the Turcomans brought geldings for sale, but even these were unsuited for military purposes.

The officers struck up a friendship with Sheikh Mohammed Doukhy, who assisted them in procuring horses and taught them a great deal about the

Bedouin. The only horses offered them were young stallions, and he did not recall seeing a single gelding in their possession. Although he frequently saw mares ridden, the Bedouin refused to sell them. With their long tradition of horse breeding they viewed them 'as a source of national wealth, . . . public opinion having set itself so strongly against letting the breed fall into other hands by selling them, that no individual ventures to do so.'[171] Indeed, Arab horses had been bred in the desert for centuries. Their pedigrees were carefully recorded and the Bedouin naturally wished to preserve their monopoly. English thoroughbreds actually originated from Arab horses sold to the English in the seventeenth century, but the better climate and fodder found in the British Isles produced larger, stronger horses with increased stamina, better looks and greater speed.[172]

One problem the party encountered was the refusal of the Bedouin to accept bills or banker's drafts as payment. Although they had been assured by the Turkish authorities that this would not be a problem, they were forced to carry large sums of money. Even with this incentive, Thompson found the Bedouin difficult to deal with, recording that they would barter for great lengths of time on the flimsiest of pretexts in the hope of getting a better price. Carrying large sums added to their anxieties over the trip and they had to increase the number of their armed escort to ensure the party's safety in the wilderness.

Thompson recalled occasional squabbles and at least one fight breaking out around their tent and theft was a constant problem. Nosebags and headstalls were often stolen when the horses were picketed along with frequent petty thefts around the camp. When they took their leave on 16 June a large group of Bedouin rushed the camp as the tents were being struck, making off with numerous belongings, safe in the knowledge that the escort were preoccupied with managing the horses. Thompson was blunt about their hosts: 'To sum up, the Anazeh are bores, thieves, beggars, swindlers, and extortioners (sic) of the most shameless nature, and if they possess, in any but their relations to their horses, any good quality whatever, certainly never showed it to me.'[173]

Travelling in caravan back towards Beirut, the party surprised a hyena from cover and the officers and some of the escort gave chase for sport. Returning slowly towards the caravan they were dismayed to be informed that the rear baggage had been set upon by tribesmen. Hurrying back with swords and pistols drawn, they were relieved to find that these men belonged to their host Mohammed Doukhy and Thompson wrote of his relief that the sheikh was not shot by mistake as they rode up.

The expedition led a string of one hundred horses out of the desert.

Seventy-two had been purchased from the Anazeh, others came from the Wulad Ali, Rowallas, Serhan and Beni Sakhr tribes. They had made two private purchases, one of which commanded the highest price of £71 and 17 shillings. The highest price paid for horses destined for the army was £50 and the average horse went for £34 according to Thompson's figures. They tried to select the largest and oldest of the mounts on offer with the average height at 14 hands 1.5 inches and usually aged between 4 and 5 years. Many younger horses had been on the market but were rejected as they rarely reached the necessary size and strength for army remounts. Of the different breeds available, they had mostly encountered Kahailans but the less numerous Soklawye were the most highly esteemed in the desert.[174]

While Thompson returned to Beirut with the desert horses, Nolan returned to Damascus in order to pick up the purchases they had made there and search for last-minute bargains. At Beirut the steamship *Trent* was waiting to transport them back to Turkey. This vessel had already been used to transport British cavalry to Varna, and he was pleased to see that the ship was specifically equipped for horses, having a wide deck to accommodate them and paddle-box boats with broad boarding planks for loading. The artillery had furnished some of their gunners and team handlers to assist with loading.

Yet they had 292 horses and 7 mules to put aboard from a flat shoreline with no pier or adequate landing place. Therefore the horses had to climb up the boarding planks at a steep angle. The surf was relatively gentle but this walkway heaved up and down nonetheless, and only a few horses traversed it without complaint. Most of the stallions proved totally unwilling to climb the ramp and Thompson had to use brute force. He had the gunners tie one long rope around the horse's head, which men in the loading boats hauled upon. This only made the horse kneel down, using its rear legs to resist. After further experimentation, two other ropes were then tied to the horse's forelegs, pulling them from under him and forcing him down on his haunches. Disabled in this fashion and unable to kick, two gunners would push him from behind and three or four men pulling and pushing manhandled the horse onto the plank. Once there, the horses tended to stand and rush up the plank as their only way of escape. Some panicked and bounded off into the surf and the whole process had to be repeated.

Once on deck, the stallions proceeded to bite, kick and resist all attempts to calm them. The horses were hobbled in Syrian fashion to prevent them moving about and at this stage Thompson felt obliged to:

*punch and shove him into his place, the closer the better to his neighbour;
tie his head down tight to the railing that surrounds the deck; wedge
horses in all round quite tight; give way with the tow boats, and away
you go, as pretty a little pandemonium of impotent wrath and ferocity as
need be.*[175]

It must have been a difficult and chaotic operation, yet the artillerymen told him that these horses had given them far less trouble than the loading of their troop horses back in England. Thompson was not a cruel man, but extreme methods were required to persuade animals to do something inherently against their nature. With the army desperate for remounts, there was also no time to find a better system. Though Peterlini assisted in the loading operation before taking his leave, it is likely that Nolan arrived during the latter stages of loading after spending a few days in the capital. The Turkish shore proved just as difficult as the Syrian coast for unloading and Nolan lost one of his own horses in the rough surf as they struggled to get the animals ashore.

Opinions varied over the quality of their horses. Other missions had been sent out and Raglan was more impressed at the results of Lieutenant King's buying expedition to Tunis, who brought back ninety horses. However, most observers considered the Syrian horses to be good remounts, though Raglan remarked on their small size; also, the condition of the horses had probably suffered after being packed in cramped conditions on deck during the voyage. It had to be said that the horses were not very different from those they encountered in Turkey, particularly as the Turks had bought many of their mounts from Syria in the first place. However, Lord Lucan made several cutting remarks about their quality, to Nolan's disgust. After conducting a difficult and occasionally dangerous search for Arab horses it came as no surprise that he was sensitive to such criticism.

The situation had now changed. The Turks were doing better on the frontier than expected, and when Omar Pasha met Raglan and St Arnaud he requested that they march to support his forces. Both commanders were reluctant to do so, because of the scarcity of supplies in Bulgaria, which had already been scoured by the Turks. Yet they were keen to demonstrate their support and their armies were already suffering from disease and deprivation in the south. They agreed to move some troops up to Varna around 50 miles from Omar Pasha's headquarters in Shumla. Raglan was eager to give the soldiers something to do following weeks of inactivity. In the cavalry, the antics of Cardigan and Lucan were already proving a trial to him. Insisting that he was accountable only to

Raglan himself, Cardigan failed to inform Lucan of his actions, thus contravening military rules and etiquette. Justly enraged, Lucan protested to Raglan and vented his frustrations upon his subordinates. With the army lacking in transport, supplying the troops was already a major problem and sending the advanced force to Varna only added to Raglan's difficulties. Having to resolve petty disputes between his senior commanders was the last thing he needed.

Meanwhile the Russians mounted an offensive over the Danube and invested the fortress of Silistria. The siege went badly for them, with the Turks putting up stout resistance and mounting effective sallies on several occasions. The Light Division under Sir George Brown began to arrive at the port of Varna at the end of May. The French had preceded them with one of their divisions and despite Turkish efforts to supply them with wagons and baggage animals, the supply situation was a nightmare with even more troops expected as the Allies had agreed to concentrate their main force there. Although Varna could be supplied by sea, Filder argued that he needed at least 14,000 baggage animals to support the troops camping further inland, and at present the commissariat had only a few hundred.

The Light Division moved towards Devna and, since the 1st Division were about to arrive at Varna, set up camp at the village of Aladyn. Although the site seemed perfect, the area was notorious among the locals for disease. The weather became increasingly hot and areas of the Varna valley were swampy; this exacerbated the situation and, with much of the water undrinkable and the troops having insufficient tents and no shelter for their horses, cholera struck rapidly. Before long, men were dying in large numbers.

The allied camp around Varna grew to over 40,000 British and French troops. As the area was clearly unsuitable for a prolonged stay, the troops were eager to get moving. The news that the Russians had lifted the siege of Silistria on 23 June was therefore received with mixed feelings. Despite the heroism of its garrison and the inspiration provided by some influential British military advisers, the fortress had come very close to falling, suffering considerable damage. Yet the Russians had other reasons to withdraw. After securing Prussian support, the Austrian Army had mobilized troops along the Transylvanian frontier, and the Russians feared a coalition of four allied armies against them. Also, the arrival of the Anglo–French navies saw Russia lose control over the Black Sea, making the only source of supply for their army a difficult route over the Caucasus Mountains. This change in the strategic situation made a Russian withdrawal almost inevitable.

It appeared that the Russians were retreating and that the war might be over before it had started for the British and French. However, the situation was uncertain. Since he had insufficient cavalry, Omar Pasha asked the British to follow the Russians and determine their intentions. Raglan ordered Cardigan to take two squadrons from the Light Brigade towards Silistria and locate the nearest enemy troops. The Turks had been fighting for nearly a year now and the British were keen prove their mettle, but Cardigan, knowing the nature of the land he was likely to experience, was reluctant to act. He took two squadrons of cavalry from the 8th Hussars and the 13th Light Dragoons along with a detachment of Turkish troops comprising around 200 men in total. The potential area they were to scout covered around 1,000 square miles of virtual wilderness. They had to travel light taking only three days' rations, no extra clothing and only one tent for Cardigan himself. As he recorded:

> *We might have come at any moment upon the Russian army; upon the Russian outposts. We travelled over the country, which I may call a perfectly wild desert, for a distance of 300 miles . . . and marched 120 miles without ever seeing a human being. There was not a single house in state of repair or that was inhabited along this route, nor was there an animal to be seen . . .*[176]

Blindingly hot during the day on the dusty plains, it was also bitterly cold at night. Wishing to get the dreadful business over as quickly as possible, Cardigan pressed the column hard, riding from sunrise to sunset, the force walking their mounts or riding for fourteen hours at a time.

Their rations soon ran low and forage was extremely scarce; the area had been ravaged by the Bashi-Bazouks. Scouting along the southern bank of the Danube, they rode northwards until they encountered a large Russian force encamped on the far bank. A Turkish officer was sent over under a flag of truce and the Russian General Lüders was intrigued at his first sight of British cavalry as the two commanders surveyed each other across the river by telescope. No further action was taken and, following an exchange of formalities, the British column began their return march after resting one day.

The Light Brigade had already been dismayed at the bedraggled state of the dispatch riders Cardigan sent back to record his progress and, when the column returned after seventeen days in the wilderness, they were in a poor state. At least five horses had died and seventy-five were unable to bear their riders. The men had also suffered and carts had to be sent out to carry some of them back into camp. Fanny Duberly, wife of Captain Henry Duberly 8th

Hussars, saw the return of the patrol:

> *I was riding out in the evening when the stragglers came in; and a piteous*
> *sight it was – men on foot, driving and goading on their wretched,*
> *wretched horses, three or four of which could hardly stir. There seems to*
> *have been much unnecessary suffering, a cruel parade of death, more pain*
> *inflicted than good derived; but I suppose these sad sights are merely*
> *casualties of war...*[177]

Aged 57, Cardigan had a weak chest and was often in a poor state of health, which had been aggravated by the reconnaissance mission. Raglan wrote to him saying: 'I hope that the fatigue that you and the squadrons have undergone in obtaining the information will not prove injurious to your health and that of the officers and men under your orders.'[178] Though some said he had exceeded his orders and taken too long over the mission, Cardigan had achieved his aim of finding the position of the nearest enemy unit and determining that they were in a state of retreat.

A further, much smaller, patrol of twelve mounted artillerymen and an officer set out into the same region four days afterwards and, since they took a string of baggage animals equipped with supplies, they fared much better and provided more detailed intelligence. However, it should be borne in mind that Cardigan's findings had enabled them to adapt to local circumstances and had revealed that enemy opposition was unlikely to be encountered, making the expedition of the smaller unit possible. Furthermore, when St Arnaud later decided to press the Russian withdrawal with the French 1st Division supported by a large number of Bashi-Bazouk irregulars, they encountered enormous hardship in the same area, suffering considerable losses.[179]

Nolan was said to have been a vocal critic of the 'Sore Back Reconnaissance' as it came to be known.[180] However, he was far from being alone in this: many observers were highly critical of Cardigan's performance. Yet the rough terrain and lack of forage meant that immense difficulties were inevitable and Cardigan's commanders would, or should, have been aware of this. Bearing this in mind, it is difficult to believe that others would have fared much better under the circumstances, and in a classic light cavalry role he had fulfilled his orders despite considerable difficulties. Though valuable horses had been ruined or lost, it may have been a necessary evil and it made the results of Nolan's horse-buying mission even more precious to the army.

Chapter 7

A Galloper for the QMG

Rejoining the staff at Devna, Nolan found the Army of the East in a sorry state, suffering from disease, heat and poor rations. Inactivity was affecting discipline and the army needed to regain its sense of purpose. The Russians were withdrawing from Bulgaria, Moldavia and Wallachia, having made an agreement with Turkey and Austria, to leave on condition that neither Britain nor France occupied those territories. The British fleet dominated the Black Sea, ranging along the coastline and bombarding Odessa on one occasion, but it seemed that Russia had abandoned her imperial ambitions for the present and peace was in sight. However, the British Government wanted to secure a favourable settlement, which required negotiation from a position of strength. Furthermore, after sending troops to the region at great expense, some effort ought to be made to deter future Russian aggression. The Duke of Newcastle reminded Raglan:

> it may become essential for the attainment of objects of the War that some operations of an offensive character should be undertaken by the Allied Armies. No blow which could be struck would be so effective for this purpose as the taking of Sebastopol.[181]

This port was the most important naval base on the Black Sea and its loss would greatly limit the Russian capacity for waging war in the area. Since the army was already in the region, taking Sevastopol was far more practical than attempting large-scale landings in the Baltic theatre, which risked dragging Britain into a protracted war. The idea had already been adopted by the newspapers, and the British War Cabinet was firmly in favour. The French reluctantly agreed to mount a joint expedition and the Turks supported any plan likely to weaken Russian influence in the Black Sea.

Yet both Raglan and St Arnaud were dissatisfied with their new objective. Despite the government urging them to seek intelligence, the distance and inaccessibility of the Crimea made this impractical. Very little was known about the port's defences, Russian military strength or the region itself. Estimates of troop numbers varied wildly between 45,000 and 140,000 Russian soldiers stationed in the area.[182] The logistical difficulties involved in an amphibious invasion would be immense and an artillery train capable of bombarding a strongly fortified city would take time to assemble and ship across the Black Sea. Furthermore, the Allies would be reliant on the sea for supply, and establishing a bridgehead would be difficult if they encountered resistance on the coastline. After that the Allies would have to find, maintain and defend landing points for re-supply. It was a daunting task, but the politicians had set their hearts on it and Raglan had little choice but to obey or risk being recalled.

Nolan soon adjusted to his role as a staff officer for Airey and was provided with a batman from the 33rd Foot, his former servant having been reassigned. Quartermaster General Lord De Ros fell sick and was invalided back to England and, to Louis's delight, Airey was appointed to take his place. Since his departure from England had been rushed, Louis had not had time to buy the frock-coat and cocked hat appropriate for his new position, nevertheless, this was a major step upwards.[183] Airey's main duties concerned quartering, encamping and managing the army on the march, but he had become a firm friend of Raglan's and soon took on a much greater role. Airey was a thoughtful, capable man who refused to be rushed into decisions and Raglan came to rely upon him to the extent that he almost became the de facto second in command. Although this angered many senior officers, it favoured Louis, who thus became privy to the workings of the army high command.

Military education in England was still in its infancy and training in staff work was rare. Engineers and artillery officers, as some of the most highly trained men in the service, were generally excluded from staff work because of their value elsewhere and, although Sandhurst carried out some limited instruction in staff work, opinions over its necessity varied. Colonel G W Prosser, one of their leading lecturers, commented: 'nothing but actual experience would bring out the real staff officer.'[184] However, attitudes were beginning to change; staff officers were increasingly required to assess rough country, roads and buildings for military purposes along with finding adequate camp sites for large bodies of men. Indeed, Nolan had suggested improvements for staff training in his writing, pointing out that the Austrian Army was years ahead with their training programme.

Fortunately, his experience as a staff officer in India stood in his favour as did his abilities, and good riders were always valued on the staff. Louis had a talent for ingratiating himself with his superiors and got along well with General Airey. From a family that had only recently become middle class,

Louis needed to be an opportunist and had developed a skill for making friends in the right places. He was his father's son in this respect, the only difference being that he was far more successful at winning people over than Babington had ever been. However, staff work in the forthcoming campaign was confusingly divided over too many departments, with the offices of the Adjutant General, the Quartermaster General, the Commissary General, the Master of the Ordnance and the Admiralty all playing a part.[185]

Now that the Crimea had been established as their destination, staff officers were kept extremely busy during the planning stages. The British were sending 30,000 infantry in five divisions – the 1st, 2nd, 3rd, 4th and Light Divisions. In addition, 1,240 cavalry were embarking along with 2,192 artillerymen and 54 guns. The French were initially sending a force of around 24,000 men with 70 guns, while the Turks provided a smaller contingent of around 5,000 men.[186] For the British, 3,379 horses for the staff, cavalry and artillery would have to be ferried over the Black Sea. The enormous scale of the operation meant that the Heavy Brigade would have to be carried over in a second wave as there were not enough ships capable of carrying all the army's horses simultaneously. In the first stage of the invasion, the British would have to rely on the Light Brigade alone, with about 900 men. Calthorpe wrote about hoisting the horses aboard ship, commenting that they had 'no little difficulty putting the slings on to already frightened horses. I never saw anything like the pluck of the blue-jackets: they hauled about the horses in a manner that no groom or batman would dare do.'[187] The heavy guns of the siege train would follow after the Allies had established themselves ashore.

Louis had begun to keep a journal, no doubt with the intention of writing a book about his experiences at a later date. Calling the invasion a 'hazardous enterprise' he commented on the uncertainty of the high command even after disembarkation from Varna on 5 September: 'many attempts were made even after we had set sail to turn the expedition from its course'.[188] Although eager to see action, he recorded his own misgivings: 'To judge of the risks of this enterprise we must consider the total absence of all intelligence regarding the country we were about to invade.'[189] Many shared this view and the staff and the commissariat realized how much faith they were placing in being able to adapt to local circumstances.

The vast size of the invasion fleet deterred any Russian naval interference, and so they arrived off the Crimean coast without mishap. Naval reconnaissance revealed that Sevastopol was relatively quiet, but there seemed to be a strong naval presence and Russian ships had been deliberately sunk to block the harbour. The port's defences looked very strong, with stone constructed forts covering the harbour mouth, making a seaborne attack unlikely to succeed. However, the Allies had always believed that an assault from the land would be necessary and they proceeded along the coastline towards the small fishing town of Eupatoria. They chose Kalamita Bay to disembark and began landing troops on 14 September. Eupatoria fell without resistance as there were only invalids and militia within the town.

With the threat of Russian interference, great efforts were made to make the landings as fast as possible. Some 326 boats had been brought for landing men along with twenty-four horse and gun flats, but the infantry were given priority. The surf was rough and some men were lost when boats capsized during the landings. The army had also brought cholera and dysentery with them and their problems were exacerbated by the incessant rain in the night. Although tents had been brought, they were buried so deeply amidst the supplies that their unloading was delayed.

Cossack patrols observed the operation from a distance. Sir George Brown and Airey, along with their staffs, were some of the first to land. In their anxiety to reconnoitre, the Cossacks came close to capturing the two senior officers but were discouraged with little difficulty. Many, including Calthorpe, were baffled that the Russians had not tried to intervene since they could have caused serious disruption on the beaches. Though he believed that the fleet's guns covering the shoreline would have seen off any serious opposition, the enemy had missed an opportunity nonetheless. A small number of cavalry had been set ashore and staff officers were rapidly sent out to scout the surrounding villages and farmsteads with orders to seek food and water in particular. Nolan personally requisitioned a Russian supply column of wagons manned by civilian drivers.[190]

Mrs Duberly had accompanied her husband to the Crimea against Lord Lucan's orders and, going ashore the next day, remarked on the apparent mismanagement: 'The landing of the horses is difficult and dangerous. Such men as were disembarked yesterday were lying all exposed to the torrents of rain which fell during the night. How it did rain! In consequence, an order has been issued to disembark *the tents*.'[191] The French and Turks had already landed their tents along with large amounts of supplies, much to British chagrin.

Duberly recorded how anxious Lord Cardigan was to get ashore and come to grips with the enemy. Both Lucan and Cardigan were present and, in the absence of the Heavy Brigade, Lucan was trying to exert his influence over Cardigan's command even more than usual. It was a sorry and unnecessary

Map 2: The Battle of The Alma

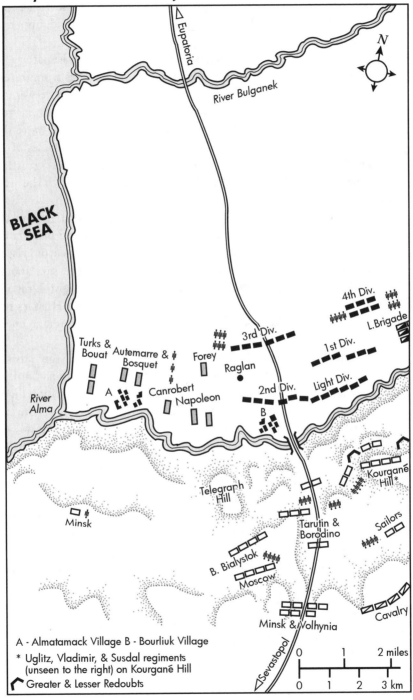

N

River Bulganek

Eupatoria

BLACK
SEA

4th Div.

L.Brigade

3rd Div.

Turks &
Bouat

Autemarre &
Bosquet

Forey

1st Div.

Raglan

2nd Div.

Light Div.

River
Alma

A

Canrobert

Napoleon

B

Kourgané
Hill *

Telegraph
Hill

Minsk

Tarutin &
Borodino

Sailors

B. Bialystok

Moscow

Minsk & Volhynia

Cavalry

A - Almatamack Village B - Bourliuk Village

* Uglitz, Vladimir, & Susdal regiments
(unseen to the right) on Kourgané Hill

Greater & Lesser Redoubts

Sevastopol

0		1		2 miles

| 0 | 1 | 2 | | 3 km |

state of affairs, as Calthorpe indicated: 'Of the two Generals of cavalry, I fear I cannot say they are popular, although both are said by some to be good soldiers . . . Active service shall decide. Both have violent and imperious tempers, so if they don't clash 'tis passing strange.'[192]

There was no sense in delaying matters. Leaving a garrison in Eupatoria, the Allies marched on Sevastopol. Kalamita Bay was around 35 miles from the city, but there were four rivers between them and their objective. These were the Bulganek, Alma, Katcha and Belbek. With effective modern land drainage in the Crimea, all these rivers have dried out and most are now little more than streams, but in 1854 they could all have presented serious obstacles if the Russians had chosen to defend them. Inland, the country, largely grassland with occasional gentle ridges and hills, was perfect for cavalry. With the sea as their supply line, the Allies marched south down the coast with the cavalry screening and protecting the main force. Raglan gave specific instructions that the Light Brigade's main duties were to scout, find supplies and prevent any enemy ambush along the march. With only 900 men they were to avoid risking losses in any unnecessary clashes with the enemy. The 11th Hussars and the 13th Light Dragoons rode in the vanguard with the 4th Light Dragoons bringing up the rear of the force. The 17th Lancers and the 8th Hussars rode on the left flank, this landward side being where Raglan most feared an enemy assault.

As they approached the Bulganek river, the cavalry in the advance encountered the enemy in some numbers for the first time. Raglan had ordered Cardigan to cross the small river and scout the other side in preparation for the main body crossing and, although Cossack scouts had been a continual presence watching from a distance and gradually falling back, they now came across a large body of these irregulars drawn up in skirmish order in a shallow valley just beyond the Bulganek. Cardigan advanced slowly and sent out skirmishers. The Cossacks began to fire carbines from the saddle and a brief exchange began, lasting for around twenty minutes.

Lord Lucan, who had been riding with the 17th on the flank, now rode up and began to argue with his brother-in-law over the next course of action. Observing the situation from higher ground to their rear, Raglan could see that the Russians had fallen back through the valley almost to the ridge about 2 miles from the river. A large force lay just out of the British cavalry's sight over the brow of the hill. This was a mixed Russian unit of nearly 6,000 men. Fearing that his cavalry might be drawn into a trap if they charged the Cossacks, he sent Airey forward just as preparations for an attack were in progress. While Airey conferred with Lucan, Louis rode to join the skirmish line. Corporal Powell of the 13th Light Dragoons saw him arrive: 'Up gallops the brave and daring Captain Nolan, and says to Adjutant Irwin in my hearing, "The Russians are dam'd bad shots;" the bullets were then flying over us; we were quite close to each other; Captain Nolan, as cool as a cucumber, dismounted, looks round his horse, remounts and rejoins Lord Raglan.'[193] Informing Lucan of what lay ahead of him, Airey persuaded him to withdraw. Nolan wrote:

> *At this time Ld. L. & Ld. C. had an animated controversy as to what should be done, Lord Cardigan wishing to ascend the height & charge the Enemy whilst Lord L. wished the Troops to retire. The discussion was cut short by an order from Lord Raglan to retire. This was done by alternate squadrons amidst the yells & shouting of the Russian horsemen who's skirmishers opened fire on ours, but their fire was not returned our men retiring leisurely across the Plain.*[194]

It was clearly the wisest course of action, but with the Light Division now over the river and the 2nd Division in the process of crossing, the cavalry felt humiliated by falling back before an apparently small body of Russians and the infantry found their discomfiture rather amusing. Being on the staff, Louis must have understood the reasoning behind the commander-in-chief's decision but clearly would have preferred a more aggressive course of action. Despite exchanging fire for twenty minutes, no casualties had been suffered on either side, giving credence to Louis's theories about firing carbines from the saddle. Yet in their first proper engagement of the war, the cavalrymen's blood was up and they were loath to retreat: 'I was with the skirmishers and spoke to the men . . . returning in the face of the Cossacks when a fine strapping Dragn. riding beside me said, It is a thousand pities Sir they would not let us dash at these miserable fellows & knock them over. It is too bad to go back before such rabble.'[195]

The Russian cavalry now advanced, supported by their own horse artillery, which opened fire on the retiring British cavalry. Now that British horse artillery had come up, a brief exchange took place: 'Our horse artillery came up and returned the fire making them limber up & go off & the Russian Cavalry coming on till they came within range of one of our horse batteries, which soon induced them to skulk off . . . The loss on our side was 4 men wounded & 6 or 8 horses killed. The Russians hovered for some time on our left flank then retired in the night.'[196]

After this incident, Lord Lucan gained the nickname 'Lord Look-on' in reference to his supposed timidity. The cavalry had avoided serious casualties by a whisker but had suffered a blow to their pride. With the benefit of hindsight, this seems unfair since, in addition to Lucan being bound by orders, Cardigan's four squadrons could have been badly cut up or even destroyed had they chased the Cossacks over the summit into the jaws of a Russian trap. Nolan is often said to have been the instigator of Lucan's new nickname but there is no evidence to support this, although his dislike of his divisional commander makes it a tempting supposition. Cavalry were of vital importance in this unknown country and Raglan was understandably reluctant to risk them when they were under strength and vastly outnumbered by their enemy counterparts. This action confirmed his belief that he needed to keep this arm firmly in hand.

The Russians rapidly fell back across the Alma river and the Allies halted as scouts brought the news of a well-prepared Russian position before them. The land from the north sloped down towards the Alma, which was narrow and shallow in most places. The valley was dotted with several small villages and occasional vineyards. On the far bank, the land climbed upward into a range of hills that steepened considerably towards the coast and the river mouth. The Russians considered the causeway road to be the best route up into the hills and had dug two strong, earth artillery redoubts towards the summit of Kourgané Hill to cover the small bridge and the area around the road. The long slope up to the redoubts was not excessively steep and therefore ideal for the artillery's round shot to use its bouncing, ricochet effect to the full. Russian artillerymen had prepared the ground, planting range markers to assist the gunners' aim in this killing ground.

Menshikov placed his main strength in and around the redoubts, but considered the hills and cliffs towards the sea steep enough to discourage any serious assault, placing only a small detachment to monitor the vicinity. His infantry manned the heights on both sides of the road and he positioned his cavalry on his right flank, prepared to sweep down through the river valley on the Allied left if things went his way. Menshikov had been castrated by a Turkish round shot during previous conflict with Turkey, which had made him a bitterly angry man with an understandable grudge against the Turks. He considered the defensive position along the Alma to be extremely strong and confidently anticipated stopping the Allied advance in its tracks or delaying them for several days if not weeks.

The Allied commanders conferred over the best course of attack that night. The British would assault the main Russian position and the redoubts, occupying their main body: St Arnaud believed that the French and Turks, attacking nearer the coast were capable of scaling the steep hills and cliffs and, when these were carried, could then roll up the Russian flank. They would be supported in this manoeuvre by the guns of the fleet, which had shadowed the march and now lay anchored at the river mouth. Raglan believed that St Arnaud was over optimistic over the chances of his flank attack succeeding but characteristically was too diplomatic to say so.[197] He agreed to give the French as much support as they needed while he would assail the heights before him, identifying the redoubts as the key to the Russian position. He placed the cavalry on his left to guard against any flanking movement by the enemy.

The Allies spent much of the morning of 20 September manoeuvring into position, and both armies began to advance in column. Coming under cannon fire, the British altered their forward formations into lines two–men deep to reduce casualties. Looking down into the valley before them, the Russians were impressed at the scale and spectacle of the French advance but judged the British lines to be flimsy in comparison with their own large formations. The guns of the fleet had begun to pound the seaward flank and Calthorpe recorded the cannon shot that opened the battle being fired at 1.30 pm:

> *About two minutes after the first shot was fired the Russians set light to the village of Bourlick, and in a few minutes it was in a blaze. Large quantities of hay and straw had been collected for the purpose . . . so that it burnt most fiercely. Indeed I think they rather overdid it, for before we advanced the greater portion of the village was reduced to ashes.*[198]

The Russians hoped that firing the villages on the southern bank would obscure their positions from Allied artillery and confuse and break up their infantry as they advanced on the river. However, Nolan observed that until the artillery could be brought closer, they could not match the Russian guns: 'Our artillery . . . in the early part of the action was of little use as it could do nothing against the heavy guns of the enemy at long range . . .'[199] Sir John Brown's Light Division was spread along a mile front heading for the Kourgané Hill aiming to take the Little and Great Redoubts while De Lacy Evans's 2nd Division advanced towards Bourliuk and the bridge. At first the Russian cannon fire had little effect on the oncoming infantry but, as the barrels warmed and the gunners found the range, men began to fall, as Private Gowing of the 7th Royal Fusiliers later recorded:

> *As soon as the enemy's round shot came hopping along, we simply did the*
> *polite – opened out and allowed them to pass on . . . As we kept on*
> *advancing, we had to move our pins to get out of their way. Presently they*
> *began to pitch their shot and shell right amongst us, and our men began to*
> *fall. I know that I felt horribly sick – a cold shivering running through*
> *my veins – and I must acknowledge that I felt very uncomfortable . . .* [200]

At this stage the British began to change formation and the troops lay down to limit casualties. The lines kept advancing and lying down in stages in their march to the river, which slowed their progress. The 1st Division, under the Duke of Cambridge, brought up the rear in support but began to lag behind.

Meanwhile the French attack was doing well. Bosquet's division scaled the heights with little opposition and were able to manhandle twelve cannons up the steep slopes. Menshikov was shocked at the French success, having deemed this flank almost unassailable. He had placed his headquarters on Kourgané Hill but now rushed over to stem this threat with eight battalions of infantry. Yet the French were slow to exploit Bosquet's success and the 1st and 3rd Divisions under Canrobert and Prince Napoleon made slow progress struggling up the slopes. The Russian guns opened a heavy fire on the French 3rd Division and effectively stalled its progress in climbing the Telegraph Heights.

Raglan was frustrated at the lack of progress his divisions were making. The advance had slowed to a crawl, with most of the forward battalions lying prone to avoid the cannon fire. He sent Nolan down to order them to renew the attack: the lines rose and marched down towards the river as the shot fell amongst them. As the Light Division reached the Alma, they plunged across. In some places they did this without difficulty but where other parts of the river were deeper the men had to hold their arms and ammunition above their heads to keep them dry as they waded across up to their armpits. The ridge of the far bank gave them some brief cover as they scrambled up it, but then they were fully in view of the Great Redoubt, Gowing recalling: 'We were only about 600 yards from the mouths of the guns; the thunderbolts of war, therefore, not far apart – and death loves a crowd.'[201]

As the British marched upward, the Russian gunners fired frantically at the approaching red line and a column of the Kazan Regiment prepared to counter-attack and force them back into the river. As the column advanced, the leading regiments of the Light Division halted and fired upon them. Used to close-range musket fire, the effect of Minié rifles shooting at a distance of a few hundred yards came as an unpleasant surprise to the Russians, and dozens of men fell in the leading ranks. In the face of disciplined and accurate fire, the Kazan Regiment fell back up the hillside and the British advance resumed. The Great Redoubt was wreathed in smoke as the gunners slammed round shot and then case shot down the slope, cutting wide gaps in the British line that closed up as they marched steadily upward.

> *With a ringing cheer we topped the Heights, and into the enemy's battery we jumped, spiked the guns, and bayoneted or shot down the gunners. Here we lost a great number of our men and, by overwhelming numbers, we (the 23rd, 33rd, 95th and Rifles) were mobbed out of the battery and a part of the way down the hill again.*[202]

Menshikov had committed four battalions of the Vladimir Regiment (almost 3,000 men) to drive the British out of the position and the 1st Division was too far away to give immediate support as the Duke of Cambridge, lacking clear orders, paused at the Alma: Raglan sent Airey to urge him onwards. Captain Jocelyn of the Royal Scots Fusiliers remembered how they endured an intense barrage of case shot, rocket fire and musketry as his regiment struggled up the slope, only 80 yards from the Russian entrenchments:

> *The fire for the next half-hour was awful. Several old Peninsular Officers – General Brown amongst others – said he never saw a heavier; and yet through it all I was most miraculously preserved. 10 of my brother officers were down and I lost one third of my Company. One of our colours had 24 Bullets through it, and the Staff of it shot away, which will give you a pretty good idea of what it was like.*[203]

Airey got the 1st Division moving but this was not enough for his commander-in-chief. Accompanied by his staff, Raglan crossed the river under heavy fire and took up position on an unoccupied knoll in clear view of Russian troops above them. Calthorpe described how two horses were killed as they forded the Alma and bullets began to hiss around them as they surveyed the Light Division being forced out of the Great Redoubt. At least two staff officers were hit. Remarking that the position was a good one for artillery, Raglan ordered up two guns of Turner's Battery who added their support to a renewed attack on the redoubt from there as the Light and 1st Divisions renewed the assault. Calthorpe added: 'In a minute more we were among the French skirmishers, who looked not a little astonished to see the English Commander-in-Chief so far in advance.'[204]

The French now requested urgent support from Raglan, but in fact the guns of Canrobert's 1st Division proved sufficient to hold Menshikov's counter-attack at bay. As their Allies began to reinforce their position on the right flank, the British felt able to commit the Guards Regiments in the 1st Division into an attack on the Great Redoubt whilst the 2nd and 3rd Divisions began to cross. The Coldstream, Grenadier and Scots Guards Regiments pressed on and forced their way into the Redoubt despite taking 171 casualties storming the fortification.[205] Meanwhile, the Scots Brigade of the 1st Division under Sir Colin Campbell crossed to the east of the Lesser Redoubt and assailed the uncommitted troops of the Russian Susdal Regiments drawn up in four battalions on the slopes to the right of the Russian position. Though Prince Gorchakov led two battalions of the 14th Division in a counter-attack to regain the Greater Redoubt, they were forced back by intense rifle fire and the Prince's horse was shot from under him.

Shocked at the determination and ferocity of the troops that had overrun his carefully prepared defence, Menshikov now ordered a general withdrawal as the British prepared a pursuit that might turn the Russian retreat into a rout. As Lord Raglan rode along the line the victorious troops cheered him heartily and cries of 'Huzza for Old England!' echoed along the heights. Calthorpe recalled feeling 'very choky about the throat, and very much inclined to cry, as one wrung the hand of a friend; and "God bless you, old fellow – so glad to see you all right!" and like expressions, were heard on every side.'[206] Around 8,000 men had fallen at the Alma: 5,709 of these casualties were Russian whilst the British lost 362 killed, 1,640 wounded and 19 missing. The French claimed to have suffered 1,600 casualties, though Raglan believed they had lost far fewer men.[207]

Raglan is often criticized for failing to pursue the retreating Russians and possibly gaining a decisive victory by destroying their army before it reached Sevastopol. Calthorpe recorded that he wished to do so but was dissuaded by French refusals to provide troops for a mixed force that could provide effective pursuit, despite having large numbers of uncommitted troops. St Arnaud complained that the infantry's packs had been left across the river and that the artillery on the heights had exhausted their ammunition. Already a sick man, he had been of little use to Raglan during the battle, concentrating most of his efforts on the French 1st Division alone and losing track of the course of the battle.

The Light Brigade, which had been unengaged, carried out a limited pursuit only to be recalled by Raglan. The Russians were withdrawing in some disorder but soon rallied and had at least 3,000 fresh cavalry who vastly outnumbered the 900 British cavalrymen, whose mounts were tired after three days' march. Nolan believed: 'The Russians after the battle said our attack had fared badly and our cavalry were *very* cautious.'[208] Yet with the steep nature of much of the ground, the Alma was always going to be an infantry affair and the Russian cavalry had also remained inactive. Realistically, the cavalry could only respond to a Russian flank attack before the heights were taken, which never came, or pursue the Russians after their position was carried. Nevertheless, Lord Cardigan's actions on receiving the order to abandon the chase seemed illogical and perhaps churlish:

> *from some misconception of orders Lord Cardigan would not allow any prisoners to be taken. An officer of the 8th Hussars, who was somewhat in advance with his troop, and who captured some 60 or 70 Russian soldiers, was ordered by Lord Cardigan to let them go again, quite as much to the astonishment of the Russians who had been taken, as to the Hussars who had captured them.*[209]

According to William Russell, special correspondent for *The Times*, Nolan later criticized Lord Raglan's failure to pursue with startling vehemence, saying: 'There were one thousand British Cavalry looking on at a beaten army retreating – guns, standards, colours and all . . . within a ten minutes' gallop of them – enough to drive one mad! It is too disgraceful, too infamous.'[210]

Nolan entered a damning passage in his journal, placing equal blame upon Lucan for not seizing the initiative and acting as the Russian positions began to crumble:

> *An enterprising leader would have crossed, gained the heights in the right rear of the Enemy & when the Infty had driven them from their Redoubts the Cavly should have prevented them from carrying off their guns . . . but no attempt was made to cross the River . . . The deeds of our horsemen in India of late years prove what they can do when led by men like Cureton, White, Smyth, Lockwood & Pearson & many others whose glorious feats of arms were all performed with but a handful of*

> *horsemen compared to what we had in the field of Alma, therefore the*
> *plea of want of numbers is inadmissible. At no time should Cavalry stand*
> *fast to count the opposing squadrons. Frederick the Great gave an order*
> *that any Cavly Officer meeting the Enemy and not charging should be*
> *cashiered! When a routed army was in full retreat what excuse can any*
> *one find for those horsemen who did not do their duty & whose chief*
> *replied to an order to advance that the Russians were very numerous!!*[211]

Louis was certainly forthright in his opinions but it must be borne in mind that these revelations were written in a private diary never intended for publication. Had he been able to write up these notes for a book on the campaign, he would certainly have toned down his criticism of individuals or possibly modified his views with the benefit of hindsight. Even so, his journal gives valuable insight into his views immediately after the Alma.

However, it was true that cavalry had achieved results disproportionate to their numbers in the past, especially against a disrupted or retreating enemy. At the Battle of Jena 1806, Marshal Murat's cavalry had done just that while chasing the defeated Prussian Army from the battlefield and beyond, inflicting great losses and capturing hundreds of demoralized soldiers. Though the Russian cavalry had not been committed and must have been relatively fresh, they had seen their army forced into retreat and, since many of them were irregular Cossacks, their capability for opposing a determined body of regulars was debatable. It was possible to argue the matter either way, but Raglan had decided that, lacking sufficient infantry support, he would take no chances. After all, the Allies lacked local intelligence in a foreign country, faced an indeterminate number of the enemy and were encountering difficulties securing forage and water. The cavalry were under strength and Raglan depended on their services so he was wise not to risk them. It is easy to imagine the criticism he would have faced if he had lost the only cavalry available to him at the outset of the campaign.

The Battle of the Alma may not have been a crushing victory but it marked a crucial point in the campaign. In strategic terms, the Russians had lost little by opposing the march since they still had Sevastopol. Though it was true that they had suffered 5,000 casualties and a blow to their morale, they possessed enormous manpower and to some extent could afford the sacrifice. In contrast, the Allies could not afford a defeat at this stage and even a temporary reverse or an engagement drawn out over several days would have created difficulties. They were on a hostile coastline, without sufficient shelter and reliant on supply by sea. A defeat or a crippling blow to the Allies' morale might have resulted in a laborious retreat back to Kalamita Bay and a difficult embarkation that could have ended in disaster. Instead, the Allies had received a boost to their spirits and could advance on their objective.

Although Raglan's leadership had not been inspired, he had kept his nerve and won a convincing victory against a strong defensive position. It had been an old-fashioned frontal assault but he, his command system and the army had prevailed, his brave but reckless 'forward reconnaissance' notwithstanding. In contrast, Menshikov's performance had been poor. Despite the advantage of large numbers of troops and a strong position, he had panicked, riding from one threat to another when he should have stayed in position and sent subordinates to deal with crises as they arose, the lack of a decent staff crippling his command structure. Gibbs believed that he had two opportunities to win the battle. When the French attempts on the heights were faltering and Canrobert briefly fell back before Kiriakov's counter-attack, the Russians could have followed up the attack in strength and pushed the French 1st Division back across the river. They could then have turned on Prince Napoleon's Division, which was already in some disorder. On the British side of the battlefield, a determined cavalry attack down the river valley while the British 1st Division was in the process of crossing could potentially have thrown the British attack into chaos.[212] Bold moves on Menshikov's part could have had dire repercussions for the Allies, but he failed to take advantage of the opportunities that he was offered.

Once more, Raglan disagreed with St Arnaud over their plan for marching on Sevastopol. Initially they had agreed to attack the city from the northern side, despite the vast expanse of the harbour that effectively split the city, the southern half being the larger. However, the French commander had changed his mind and wished to march around the city to attack the southern side's weaker defences. The French also considered the northern defences very strong, particularly the large star fort on the north side of the harbour. It was also likely that better landing sites and havens for the fleet could be found along that coastline. Raglan agreed to the French demands with reluctance; the slowness of the march on the city has been criticized. With the benefit of hindsight, a swift advance on Sevastopol may have caught the mauled Russian Army unprepared and denied the garrison the time they needed to improve their defences. Some officers, like Calthorpe, believed that the Russians might try to impede their march again on the Kacha or the Belbek. However, the shock of seeing their seemingly unassailable position on the Alma fall discouraged the Russians from making any serious attempt to delay them.

As the Allies advanced, Menshikov judged that the city had enough defenders and, unwilling to add more hungry mouths to a garrison likely to be besieged, marched the bulk of his forces into the hinterland. He also hoped for an opportunity to attack the Allied flank when they marched upon the city or to interfere with their operations as they prepared to lay siege to Sevastopol. The route of the flank march was difficult, running through hills, scrubland and woods. Considering Raglan's former caution, he was now taking a major risk since, while they were cut off from the fleet, the army was vulnerable. The cavalry were crucial to Raglan at such a time, under strict instructions to avoid engagements if possible and await support if they encountered the enemy. According to Russell, Louis overheard Raglan justifying this approach and commented scathingly: 'we ought to be kept in a bandbox. Did anyone ever hear of cavalry in a bandbox doing anything?'[213] However, even a good journalist like Russell was willing to find fault and send back lurid reports to Britain to entertain his readers. In his journal Nolan displayed a slightly different attitude. The cavalry may have been proceeding tentatively but the flank march was an act of daring:

> *This flank march is unmatched in the annals of war for its strategic importance, bold conception and brilliant execution . . . Our army drawn now to a narrow thread by the difficulties and impediments... could have been cut through at any time by a bold and erudite enemy. Our men were exhausted, our artillery horses actually drifting down and dying on the roadside... we had but one line of march, the road on our right lay under the guns of the enemy the country on our left was occupied in force, thus this movement hazardous at all times was 'neck or nothing' in our case, and a little dash and a little daring on the part of our foes might have brought our expedition to a . . . less glorious close than we now fervently anticipate.*[214]

In the rough country they encountered, the British cavalry in the advance lost their way and Lord Raglan and his staff unexpectedly came upon the last elements of Menshikov's rearguard crossing their path. Finding himself in the vanguard, Raglan was understandably curt towards Lord Lucan when the latter joined him in some haste. He could have been captured by the enemy and Lucan's justifiable protests, that it was the staff officers sent by Raglan to guide him who led them astray, were ignored. Some of the Heavy Brigade had now

Map 3: *The Flank March*

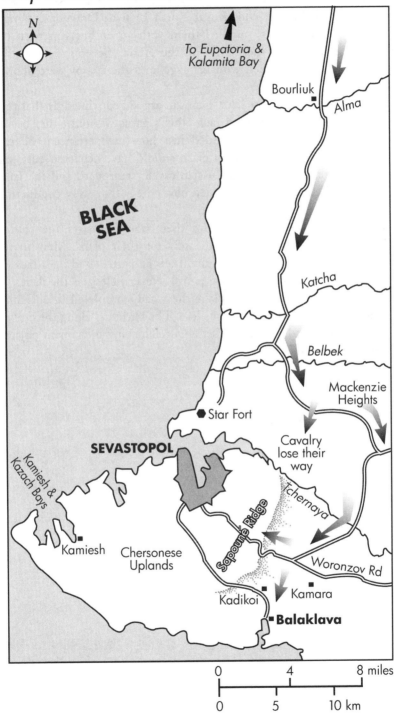

landed and when artillery fire and a determined advance put Russian infantry before them to flight, the 2nd (Royal North British) Dragoons, commonly known as the Scots Greys, pursued them with an enthusiasm born out of frustration after missing the Battle of the Alma. Several Russian supply wagons were taken, crammed with baggage, and the troops were allowed to plunder them.[215]

Writing twenty-three years later, Denison argued convincingly that the fact that two large armies had crossed each other's paths without either becoming aware of an enemy presence revealed just how inexperienced the cavalry leaders on both sides were. Such a clash should have occurred between the British cavalry vanguard and the Russian cavalry rearguard and the fact that neither met in the engagement revealed how poorly they were conducting the 'most important sphere of their duty'.[216]

The Allies spent a week caring for their wounded after the battle and completing the flank march.[217] Fortunately for their plans, Menshikov had remained blissfully unaware of their intentions and attributed the attack on his rearguard to the actions of a forward patrol. Nevertheless, as the Allies began to emerge on to the Balaklava plain they had completed a difficult and dangerous manoeuvre without serious loss. The harbours along the coast were now open to them and they could set about achieving their main objective – capturing Sevastopol.

Chapter 8

Balaklava

As the leading elements of his army entered the Tchernaya river valley, Raglan knew that it was imperative to secure practical landing points along the southern coast. The difficulties encountered by the Allies on the flank march convinced him that there was no possibility of maintaining reliable communications along that route, especially with a Russian army nearby. Crossing the Balaklava plain and the Woronzov Road the British entered the small village of Kadikoi. Most of the inhabitants had remained and showed no reluctance in giving them information about Balaklava, saying that the place was virtually undefended.

Balaklava has a small harbour so closely encircled by steep hills that from a distance it appears to be an inland lake, its entrance concealed. An old, crumbling Genoese fortress glowers over the small fishing village from the heights, established to protect this entrance. On 26 September Raglan and his staff rode with the vanguard as they approached Balaklava, where they were offered bread and salt by some of the inhabitants, symbolizing submission. They were therefore quite surprised when guns from the fort began to fire upon them. The Light Division were called upon to assault the fortress and riflemen began to clamber up the heights with Brandling's troop of horse artillery in support. A brief exchange of fire took place and the arrival of the navy at the harbour mouth provided further supporting fire that soon persuaded the garrison to surrender. Most sources agree that the fight for the fort was very brief and that only token resistance was offered. However, Nolan met one rifleman who claimed to have exchanged fire at close quarters during the struggle:

> *On going into Balaklava immediately after the action I met a fine young lad of the Rifles his face radiant with pleasure and excitement he said 'Look Sir, they have spoilt my hat' in fact a bullet had torn off the crown and he was evidently glad of the fact.*[218]

Angered at being fired upon after tokens of surrender had been received, Raglan's fury was mollified by the garrison's commander, who had been wounded in the action. This was Colonel Monto, a Greek officer in Russian service who commanded the town's militia. He would have surrendered immediately when confronted with an overwhelming force, he explained; but, as he had not been called upon to do so, honour compelled him to resist.[219]

The British rapidly set about occupying the town, and as HMS *Agamemnon* entered the harbour, soundings were taken to determine the depth of the waters. Despite its small size, the anchorage was deep enough for ships of the line, and soon it was choked with vessels of all kinds as stores were unloaded at the quayside. Admiral Lyons advised Raglan about the Royal Navy's requirements for resupply, saying that they must retain Balaklava in spite of a previous agreement with the French.[220] Their Allies were unhappy that Raglan had occupied Balaklava when it was they who were supposed to take up positions on the right of the proposed siege operations. St Arnaud had finally succumbed to sickness and relinquished command, only to die on 29 September. On the same day Nolan rode with Airey to Kadikoi to liaise with his successor, General Canrobert. Annoyed that the British had reneged on their agreement, Canrobert conceded that the pressing need to begin operations and the fact that the British were already in possession meant an exchange would take too long. Furthermore, after seeing the inlet he felt it was too far away from the city and too small to accommodate French needs.[221]

The French moved on to secure the bays of Kamiesh and Kazatch, which fell to them without serious difficulty. Both were larger and better suited for landing supplies than Balaklava. In addition, Kamiesh was closer to the new French positions. For the British, claiming Balaklava also entailed defending the Allied right, which was the point of the Allied position most vulnerable to Russian counter-attack. Even a partially successful attempt to cut off the British supply line could cause severe disruption to their siege operations. Hindered by lack of intelligence on the Crimea and hoping that the city would fall swiftly, Raglan's hasty decision to retain Balaklava would prove unwise. However, the swift and unexpected flank march appeared to have caught the Russians by surprise as an early patrol discovered:

> *They have just set fire to a large building outside the town (that the savans say is a depot of grain). This, together with the fact of the wells in the farmhouses not being destroyed, their buckets even being left, confirms the belief of how little they expected an attack from this side.*[222]

Now that their communications with the navy were re-established, the Allies set about besieging Sevastopol. Nolan was among those who helped mark out divisional campsites to the south of the city. The French took up positions to the west in the area known as the Chersonese uplands, with the British encampment placed upon their right. British troops were committed to defend Balaklava while a French corps of observation took up position on the Sapouné ridge to monitor the area where enemy attack was most likely to come from. Once again there was a firm belief in the army that an immediate assault on the city might bring swift success with the lack of fortifications. Sir George Cathcart believed that:

> *I am in the strongest and most perfect position I ever saw. Twenty thousand Russians could not disturb me in it with my division . . . pay me a visit, you can see everything in the way of defences, which is not much. They are working at two or three redoubts, but the place is only enclosed by a thing like a low park wall, not in good repair. I am sure I would walk into it, with scarcely the loss of a man . . .*[223]

Raglan agreed to an extent, but the French insisted on a methodical approach and he was bound to conform to their wishes. Storming the city with infantry was likely to entail great loss of life for the besiegers under any circumstances, but a preliminary bombardment would reduce Russian capability to resist. However, even some Russian officers later agreed that they would have been lucky to withstand a determined assault at this stage. The likelihood of such an attack succeeding was debatable, but some felt that another good opportunity had been squandered. The Allied armies began digging siege trenches and establishing batteries for their artillery while the Russian guns fired upon the engineers sapping trenches closer to their defences. It would take time to land the heavy guns and manhandle them up to the siege lines.

It was an unusual siege because the Allies lacked the men to completely encircle the city and, although the port was effectively blockaded from the sea, the Russians could still send men and supplies into Sevastopol from the north without serious difficulty. Naval reconnaissance had revealed that, in addition to the harbour being well protected by several modern fortresses, the Russians had sunk block ships to impede an amphibious attack. The Allies based their strategy on weakening the city defences enough to allow a land-based assault, since starving the Russians of food and supplies during a long siege was out of the question.

As soon as they arrived at Balaklava, the staff had been in a state of frenzied activity with so much to organize. Since Raglan relied increasingly on General Airey's counsel, Nolan was constantly on the move relaying orders over a wide area. The need to travel across country made Nolan's ability as a horseman invaluable and his fluent French made him a regular choice for liaison duties. Within a week the British were cursing their luck in having the steep climb from Balaklava to the siege lines and camps. Dragging heavy artillery and carts along roads that barely qualified as tracks was already proving a problem. Nolan had little time for rest but revelled in the work: 'It was dusk when I gained the plateau where the staff are in position, my horse was tired and I let him walk gently towards McKenzies . . . All the French bands were playing and many a well remembered melody carried my thoughts away to past and distant scenes.'[224]

Airey and his staff were initially based in Balaklava village, where the general took over a house as his office, but Louis and his fellow aides slept under canvas like the majority of the army. The villagers were well treated but Raglan ordered them to take what possessions they could carry and leave during the occupation as every building was needed and he had no wish for potential spies to remain. After ten days in the village, Raglan moved his headquarters to a farmhouse on the plateau, carefully chosen so that it was close to the siege lines but also allowing him to ride in a few minutes to the Sapouné escarpment and observe the approaches to Balaklava. The quartermaster general and the adjutant general joined him there with their respective staffs, pitching their tents around the building.[225]

Protecting Balaklava was vital, but it would take time to prepare a defence in depth, considering the demands the siege lines made on the army's manpower. Raglan initially placed Lord Lucan in command of the area. The final elements of the Heavy Brigade had arrived by early October and Lucan now had his entire division encamped on the Balaklava plain. However, sickness had thinned the ranks, and the stormy passage they had suffered crossing the Black Sea cost the Heavies 226 horses. While Lucan remained in camp with the men, for health reasons Cardigan was permitted to sleep aboard the *Dryad*, his private yacht in the harbour. This meant that he often failed to arrive at camp before 10.00 am and subordinates were obliged to carry out his duties. However, George Paget remarked that this was not always the case: 'Cardigan dines always on board his yacht, and sometimes returns here to sleep.'[226]

Raglan intended to throw up earthworks in two lines to strengthen the defence, but by 4 October little had been done and Louis was concerned: 'No

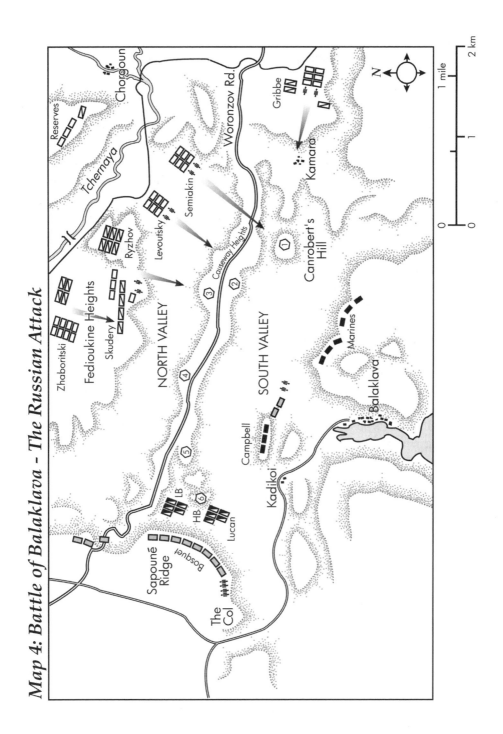

Map 4: Battle of Balaklava – The Russian Attack

plan of defence has yet been fixed upon in Balaklava and the valley through which our communications (pass) . . . To guard these against infiltration . . . (we must) occupy and fortify the ridge and heights forming a natural bastion across the Valley of Balaklava.'[227] The threat to their communications was serious; Nolan believed that thousands of British lives were at risk if their lifeline to the harbour was not secured. To approach, the Russians would have to cross the Balaklava plain. The Fedioukine Hills lay to the north overlooked by the Sapouné ridge where Bosquet's French Division (Corps of Observation) was placed since the ridge dominated the plain. In front of this lay the Balaklava plain, divided by a low ridge roughly 3 miles long, known as the Causeway Heights. This divided what the British called the North and South Valleys. The Woronzov Road lay along this ridge, running from Sevastopol to Baidar and eventually on towards Yalta. The British planned to raise six redoubts along it overlooking the North Valley. The land sloped down beyond the ridge into the South Valley that was edged with several hills before winding steeply downward towards the harbour.

While work on the siege lines was proceeding well, everyone was anxious to start the bombardment as soon as possible. A close watch was maintained on the enemy, and Nolan 'Rode out on the extreme right in a Reconnaissance with Genl. Airey and . . . de Lacy Evans . . . Our Reconnaissance drew a heavy fire from the White Tower. Battery after battery is rising . . . to confound us . . .'.[228] While the Allies were assembling an impressive array of siege batteries to pound the city's defences, every day the Russians were strengthening them and adding new works. Admiral Kornilov, in command of Sevastopol, believed himself to be in a strong position and was determined to resist, particularly since the city could be resupplied and a Russian field army lay in the interior ready to harass the besiegers and potentially relieve him. His chief engineer, Lieutenant Colonel Franz Todleben, was also confident that the defences could be drastically improved if allowed sufficient time. At first the garrison comprised 18,500 sailors and 4,000 marines and reservists, but by 9 October, when Menshikov reinforced them with regular army troops, it had been increased to approximately 25,000 men. The southern defences were also being bolstered by the addition of naval guns disembarked from the remaining ships in the harbour.

The British plan to protect their supply line and Balaklava was now taking shape. The cavalry were encamped in the South Valley behind the Causeway Heights with the duty of maintaining reconnaissance and responding to enemy movement. Campbell had been given 1,200 Marines in addition to the 93rd

Highlanders and Turkish battalions to guard the heights around Balaklava as the second line of defence. Nolan recorded that seventeen guns had been landed to be placed in the redoubts by 7 October and that the earthworks along the Causeway were under construction:

At last to my great satisfaction it has been decided to occupy and strengthen the chain of heights from which Balaklava is first seen on crossing from the bridge of Tchernaya. For this purpose two battalions of Turks have been lent to us by the French. These are now posted on the heights which are to have 5 enceinte redoubts and hold each 250 men. The works are under the direction of Mr Bergman (name unclear) of the Turkish Service and will be thrown up by the Turks themselves who are excellent workmen.[229]

These small fortifications were placed in a chain about a mile long. No. 1 Redoubt, the strongest and best built, was mounted on a large eminence known as Canrobert's Hill. Garrisoned by the Turks, it contained three 12lb iron cannons. Redoubts No. 2 and No. 3 held two guns each while No. 4 Redoubt held three guns. Redoubts No. 5 and No. 6 were in the process of construction. Further redoubts were also planned to protect the gorge known as the Col where the supply road climbed up to the Sapouné Heights, since the French guns could not cover it from their positions along the ridge. However, the Causeway redoubts could only hope to delay a large enemy force even with the infantry in support camped on the hills above Balaklava where a second line of earthworks was also planned. Raglan's dilemma was that large numbers of troops were needed to conduct the siege operations and the plan to protect the supply base was forced to rely on support arriving in time from the Chersonese plateau in the event of a major attack.

The Russian field army were beginning to send patrols with increasing frequency to observe Allied activity. The outlying British picquets were constantly giving reports on enemy activity; on several occasions the entire division was called to arms when an imminent attack was anticipated.[230] Some officers wrote that they were overreacting to these potential threats and Paget remarked: 'If the Russians are clever they will take care that we have no more repose, for they can easily see that we all turn out on the appearance of a few of them.'[231] However, the Russians soon began to send larger cavalry patrols, sometimes supported by horse artillery and losses were incurred among the picquets and patrols across the river. Knowing that the Russians possessed large numbers of cavalry and were far more familiar with the ground, Raglan ordered Lucan to keep his men on the southern bank of the Tchernaya and to act defensively. On 7 October a small patrol of the 4th Dragoon Guards under Cornet Fisher-Rowe unexpectedly encountered a strong Russian force on the southern bank. They were immediately attacked and, with only ten men, Fisher-Rowe beat a hasty retreat, but not before several men had been speared by Russian lancers who pursued them some distance.

Lord Lucan called out most of the cavalry division in response and observed a large force of Russian cavalry in the North Valley. Believing that they were likely to withdraw, he contented himself with observation alone. Although their seeming inactivity appeared to invite an attack he remembered the trap the cavalry had nearly been lured into on the Bulganek and had no wish to risk losing men just to discourage a patrol. When Captain Maude's troop of horse artillery came up, Lucan allowed him to open fire upon the Russians after pondering his options for a while. This inflicted losses and persuaded them to retire in some haste. When Nolan rode up to assess the situation for Airey, he was among those in favour of an immediate counter-attack:

> *The Russians could be seen with the Telescope on the farther side of the River. I asked Ld. Lucan had he pushed forward any force to watch their movements, 'No but look at the disposition of my Troops it is not good.' His troops looked very well but they were a long way from the Enemy.*[232]

Nolan wanted to go forward to see what the Russians were up to, and Lucan permitted him to take a squadron of the 17th Lancers to do so. Reconnoitring as far as the river, he observed significant numbers of Russian troops retreating towards the Mackenzie Heights, estimating that there were eight infantry battalions and five regiments of cavalry. He believed that the Russian withdrawal should have been aggressively followed up; but Lucan, true to his instructions, was not going to be rushed into any hasty decisions and refused to mount a pursuit. Disappointed by this passive attitude, Nolan was equally unimpressed when he learned how the enemy had been driven off before his arrival:

> *thus the Enemy went off leaving on the field such arms & accoutrements as they had thrown away in their haste as a Trophy to the Victors, who calmly sat on their horses & looked at them from above! thus contributing a strong case in favour of the Russian assertion that our*

Captain Louis Edward Nolan of the 15th Hussars. *(Illustrated London News)*

The Military Pioneer School at Tulln in Austria, where Louis studied as a military cadet. *(Courtesy of Tulln Tourist Information Office)*

A parody on the British Army's purchase system, which blighted Nolan's early career. *(Punch)*

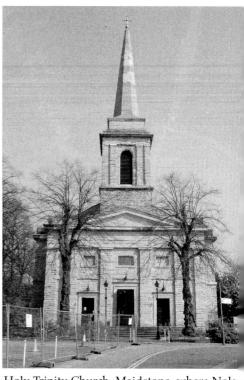

Holy Trinity Church, Maidstone, where Nola worshipped. A commemorative plaque was laid here in his memory.

The former officers' mess for Maidstone Barracks, where Louis was quartered, the only military building of its kind left in existence.

olan's recommended military seat or riding posture. *(The Training of Cavalry Remount Horses)*

:cruiting for the cavalry in London. Nolan considered short, light men the ideal recruits. *(Illustrated ndon News)*

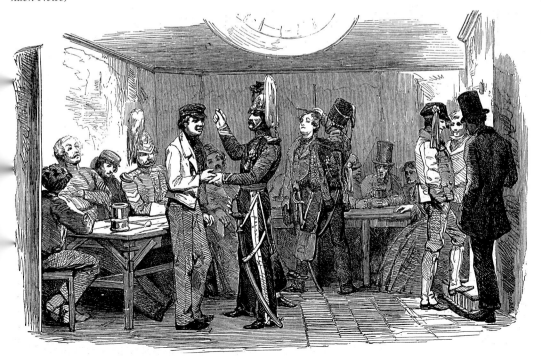

Demonstrating the act of reining back. *(The Training of Cavalry Remount Horses)*

Demonstrating the pirouette, a manoeuvre Nolan favoured for the mêlée. *(The Training of Cavalry Remount Horses)*

The slope before the two redoubts at the Alma taken from just beyond the river. The Great Redoubt was situated approximately where the Russian memorial can be seen.

Allied guns bombarding Sevastopol. *(London Journal)*

The small harbour of Balaklava, which became the British supply base for the siege of Sevastopol.

A view of the Causeway Heights across the South Valley from where the 93rd Highlanders stood. The prominent hill is the site of No. 1 Redoubt.

Looking into the South Valley and towards Balaklava from the Causeway at No. 4 Redoubt's site. The 93rd Highlanders were positioned just before the cluster of buildings on the right.

view from the Sapouné escarpment near Raglan's position. It shows how shallow the Causeway pears from this perspective, running diagonally from right to left. During the charge, the Light igade rode parallel with the Causeway towards the white building on the left.

ken from the site of Redoubt No. 4 where Nolan is supposedly buried, showing the area where the ght Brigade deployed for the charge, overlooked by the escarpment.

Midway down the North Valley just before the likely position of the Don Cossack Battery. A spur of the Fedioukine Hills can be seen on the left.

A view of the North Valley from the eastern end of the Causeway. The Don Cossack Battery was positioned just beyond the row of trees in the centre.

e moment when the first line of the Light Brigade charged into the Russian battery. *(Illustrated don News)*

Lord Raglan, commander-in-chief of the Allied forces in the Crimea. *(Illustrated London News)*

Lord Lucan, commander of the cavalry division, who said 'They have sacrificed the Light Brigade they shall not the Heavy, if I can help it.' *(Illustrated London News)*

General Bosquet, who reputedly said 'C'est magnifique, mais ce n'est pas la guerre!' while watching the Charge of the Light Brigade. *(Illustrated London News)*

General Prince Alexander Menshikov, commander-in-chief of the Russian Army. *(Illustrated London News)*

...e North Valley beyond the guns where elements of the Light Brigade pursued the Russian cavalry.

...e charge of the French Chasseurs d'Afrique against Russian infantry and artillery on the Fedioukine ...lls. *(Illustrated London News)*

A Russian statue depicting the mortally wounded Admiral Kornilov exhorting his men to defend Sevastopol to the last.

Following the battle, the British were reduced to using poor-quality tracks to supply the siege lines after yielding the Woronzov Road.
(*Illustrated London News*)

THE ROAD TO SEBASTOPOL.—COMMISSARIAT WAGGONS, CONVEYANG OF FASCINES, ETC.

The British memorial to those who fell at the Battle of Balaklava.

...elics displayed at the Balaclava ...estival in 1875 at Alexandra Palace ...London. *(Illustrated London News)*

| 1. Trophy in Central Hall. | 3. Pioneer's Sword. | 5. Pipe. | 7. Bugle (Inkerman). | 9. Leather Gauntlet. | 11. Head of Ronald, Lord Cardigan's horse. |
| 2. Russian Helmet. | 4. Knapsack (Balaclava). | 6. Drum. | 8. Helmet. | 10. Horse-pistol (Balaclava). | 12. Epaulet (Alma).   13. Powder-horn (Redan). |

RELICS AT THE BALACLAVA FESTIVAL.

A wounded soldier at the Military Hospital in Haslar. The human cost of war should never be forgotten.
(*Illustrated London News*)

'The witness that ought to be examined.' A cutting satire on the inquiry held into the Crimean War.
(*Punch*)

Cavalry are very cautious, a quality quite unknown to the British Dragn. of former days who's rash & headstrong courage was his only fault.[233]

He was not the only officer to think so. Several accounts reveal that the army, especially the infantry, believed that the cavalry were purposefully holding back from action. It was clear that the Russians were sending increasingly strong forces over the river to observe their positions and many agreed this suggested that a major attack was imminent. Had this reconnaissance in force been driven off with heavy loss, demonstrating the strength of the British position, it might have discouraged them. Brighton believes that Lucan's nickname of 'Lord Look-on' originated from this incident more than from the action on the Bulganek and that the infantry began to refer to cavalrymen in general as 'Look-ons'.[234] Even Paget, as a cavalry officer, commented 'We hear the cavalry are supposed to have made rather a muck of it the other morning. At daybreak a reconnaissance came round upon Balaclava, which it is said they lost an opportunity of cutting off. Mind, this is only hearsay, and we were out of it fortunately.'[235]

There was still discord in the cavalry: Lucan constantly asserted himself in a draconian manner while his brother-in-law complained incessantly about his interference with the Light Brigade. Even the level-headed Raglan was frustrated by their continuing enmity, and Paget believed that the decision to place the camps of the Light and Heavy Brigades apart was partially motivated by a desire to separate the feuding pair. On 14 October he placed Major General Sir Colin Campbell in overall command of Balaklava's defence. Campbell was an officer of great experience. Aged 62 he had served in the Peninsular War, the First China War and the Second Sikh War. He was one of the best officers in Raglan's command and a dependable man to put in the role. Lucan retained independent command of the cavalry – this was perceived as a slight by many and a comment on his recent performance. Whether Lord Raglan had intended to convey this impression or not, Lucan felt humiliated and it affected his standing within the Army of the East.

While Fanny Duberly had accompanied the army to Balaklava, the cold and lack of privacy under canvas, and her husband's sharing a tent with three men, meant that she took quarters on board one of the ships in the harbour. Nevertheless, she rode up to the Light Cavalry camp every day. On Monday 16 October she wrote:

> *Captain Nolan came in, and we had a long and interesting conversation. After discussing my afternoon's amusement, I determined on accepting his horse and saddle, with a tiger-skin over the holsters; while he borrowed a pony, and we rode together to see Henry at the camp.*[236]

Idle tongues suggested that Nolan had become Fanny's lover, but there is no evidence to suggest this in any of her letters home: there were several unsubstantiated rumours about Duberly's 'affairs' with other officers, which were probably little more than malicious gossip. After Nolan's demise, she seemed less affected by his death than one would expect from a close relationship.[237] Louis told her that the bombardment would begin the next day, and Fanny recorded tremendous gunfire beginning on 17 October that carried on far into the night as she watched the flashes of the guns from the deck that evening.

The navy fired on the sea forts and batteries protecting the harbour, which proved to be immensely strong. The return fire of the Constantine, Alexander and Quarantine forts in particular caused more damage to the Allied ships than they inflicted on the coastal defences. On land considerable damage was wrought upon Sevastopol's defences, particularly on the Redan, and Admiral Kornilov was killed while inspecting the Malakov redoubt. Nevertheless, Russian artillery fire proved highly effective and numerous guns were dismounted on both sides. Over the following weeks it became apparent that the siege of Sevastopol was unlikely to come to a swift conclusion. Though the French and British efforts were inflicting considerable destruction, every night Russian work parties came out to repair the damage and the larger redoubts proved very difficult for the Allied gunners to reduce. Vast amounts of ammunition had to be carried up to the lines to maintain the cannonade and this battle of attrition seemed likely to go on for some time. Campbell confided in Paget that 'people must be disappointed who expected such a place as that to fall in a few hours'.[238]

Yet Nolan was far from despondent. Though in his opinion the cavalry arm could be performing better under different leadership, it looked as if the campaign would continue for some months and much could change in that time. Conflict was the ideal time for a soldier and he was gaining valuable experience in a European war that would further his career. One officer wrote: 'The day before his death . . . I met him, and he said, "Well, Bob, is not this fun? I think it is the most glorious life a man could lead."'[239] Nevertheless, he was well aware of the hazardous nature of the campaign and the risk to life and limb, through sickness as much as enemy action. During the flank march he had renewed his acquaintance with Captain Morris and the pair had taken the gloomy but sensible precaution of exchanging letters to send to each other's next of kin in the event of the other's death. Morris wrote a poignant letter to his wife while Nolan wrote to his mother.[240]

Russell spoke to several men who thought the Allies were in a precarious state when he rode into the Light Brigade camp on 24 October. Louis was amongst them and was vocal in his condemnation:

> *I was told 'that the Ruskies were very strong all over the place,' that reports had been sent to headquarters that an attack was imminent, and that Sir Colin Campbell was uneasy about Balaclava. As I was leaving Nolan overtook me . . . The evening was chilly. He remarked that I ought to have something warmer than my thin frock, and insisted on my taking his cloak – 'Mind you send it back to me tomorrow; I shall not want it tonight.' Nor did he next night or ever after! I bought the cloak at the sale of his effects, and I have it to this day. All the way back he 'let out' at the Cavalry Generals, and did not spare those in high places. 'We are in a very bad way I can tell you.'*[241]

The gossip in the camp was well founded: the Russians were not going to wait while the Allies strengthened their positions and built up their resources. Prince Menshikov's probes on the Allied positions around Balaklava had revealed that their earthwork defences were incomplete and manned by second-grade Turkish troops.[242] The relatively passive British defence also implied that they were reluctant to risk losing men. Furthermore, Menshikov needed to give the Tsar some kind of victory, having played down the scale of the defeat on the Alma. Morale in his army had improved after the reverse but the men needed further inspiration as they watched the Allied guns pound their city. Though he was reluctant to take the offensive, the Allies appeared to be offering him an opportunity which he would be foolish to ignore. If he advanced swiftly enough with a large force, support from the main Allied army might take too long to arrive before he captured their base or cut their supply line. Even with the French bays still in Allied hands, such a blow would severely disrupt British operations and possibly even persuade the Allies to lift the siege entirely.

The cavalry were now being called out on a regular basis to respond to enemy incursions. On 19 October the Russians carried out another probe onto the plain: three large infantry columns approached the Causeway Heights and were fired on at long range by the redoubts. Raglan was concerned enough to order up 1,000 infantrymen under General Goldie from the Chersonese plateau to add to the defence, but Campbell sent them back insisting that they were not required.[243] The significance of this was twofold. The infantry took time to assemble and set off at 3.00 am to arrive at Kadikoi at around 7.10 am on 20 October, having marched around 10 miles to get there. Secondly, Campbell's rather abrupt refusal of their services made them feel unappreciated: both these factors would be relevant to the action five days later.

Prince Menshikov had now formed his plan of attack, intending to seize both lines of defence on the plain to cut the British off from Balaklava. Although capturing the harbour was a secondary objective, possession of the hills and ridges above it would probably render it untenable for the Royal Navy once Russian artillery was in place since, being overcrowded with ships, concentrated gunfire would wreak havoc. A presence had already been established at the village of Tchorgoun when Colonel Rakovitch led a mixed force down from the Mackenzie Heights. By 23 October this had been placed under the command of General Liprandi and was made up of 17 infantry battalions, 30 squadrons of cavalry and 64 guns. A separate force under General Zhaboritski had 8 battalions of infantry, 4 squadrons of cavalry and 14 guns and would act in close cooperation with Liprandi's force. Altogether the Russians were committing a formidable force of around 25,000 men and 78 guns to the assault.[244]

The Russians moved into position on the night of 24 October. General Liprandi stood by the Tractir Bridge as the troops marched across shouting that he 'hoped they would fight as well as they had done on the Danube!'[245] and was answered with resounding cheers. The Russian cavalry were eager for action after a long period of relative inactivity, and General Ryzhov concentrated them on the Mackenzie Heights that night in preparation to follow up the infantry attack on the Causeway. Once the earthworks were taken, he intended to seek out the Allied cavalry and engage them.

The Russian attack began at around 7.13 am on 25 October. Paget was in command of the Light Brigade in Cardigan's absence and, after overseeing morning roll call, rode with Lucan to the Kamara ridge towards Canrobert's Hill to check the piquets. They observed the flag signalling 'enemy advancing' run up by the Turks in No. 1 Redoubt and almost immediately a shot crashed out as the redoubt began to engage the advancing Russians. Lucan 'lost no time in ordering the Cavalry Division under arms; an affair of only a few moments, as the cavalry are always ready to turn out an hour before daylight.'[246] Riding to confer with Campbell, the two commanders saw large numbers of Russian troops entering the north-eastern side of the North Valley and crossing the Fedioukine Hills towards the Causeway. Obviously a major attack was beginning. Lucan deployed the Heavy Brigade in a show of strength to the right of No. 3 Redoubt along with Maude's Horse Artillery troop, who swiftly unlimbered their guns and added their fire to the redoubts as three Russian columns approached across the North Valley.

General Gribbe with a combined force of infantry and cavalry advanced along the Baidar valley taking Kamara in order to cover the left flank of the Russian attack. Rapidly deploying his ten guns, this force began to fire on Canrobert's Hill, the first Russian objective. General Semiakin led a column against No. 1 Redoubt comprising five battalions of infantry preceded by riflemen with ten guns. The Turks had not had time to cut down the scrub and thorn bushes before the slopes of Canrobert's Hill and Semiakin's skirmishers used these to good effect as they advanced to cover the assault.[247] Two other attack columns advanced on Semiakin's right. General Levoutsky's column of three battalions and ten guns approached No. 2 Redoubt whilst Colonel Scudery with four Odessa battalions, a company of riflemen, a field battery and three sotnias of Cossacks aimed for No. 3 Redoubt. The main body under General Ryzhov advanced to the edge of the North Valley ready to give support to any of these attacks should it prove necessary.[248] A large force under Zhaboritski remained on the Fedioukine Hills.

No. 1 Redoubt was the main focus of the first assault and it soon came under heavy fire. Opposed by at least 11,000 infantry and 38 guns the defenders could only bring the five guns of the first two redoubts against Semiakin's column with six of Lucan's field pieces in support. It was an uneven struggle and the defenders' guns soon fell silent as they withdrew to the far side of their fort to await the inevitable assault, where they enjoyed better shelter from the sustained cannonade. Maude's Troop were also heavily outgunned and forced to retire when ammunition ran low and Maude was badly wounded when a shell struck his horse.

Liprandi later wrote how No. 1 Redoubt was stormed by Colonel Kridener's Azovsky Regiment in two lines in company column. As they crossed the ditch and climbed over the low parapet, they were aided by the fire of two other battalions forming a third line in support.[249] With a hoarse roar of 'Uraah!' they rushed into the fort where the Turks stood fast to meet them with the bayonet. A savage fight ensued, which the Turks, facing overwhelming numbers, were doomed to lose. The Russians recorded 170 Turks killed out of the 500–600 strong garrison; the survivors rapidly fled down the southern slopes. No. 2 and No. 3 Redoubts resisted the Russian advance briefly but were subjected to very heavy fire. Seeing large numbers of Russians approaching and having witnessed the fate of No. 1 Redoubt, they abandoned their works and fled towards Kadikoi. In fairness, the second (inner) defence line was out of range and unable to support them with cannon fire and they could see no relief forces approaching. Luckily the British sappers in the redoubts managed to spike their guns before retreating.

Lucan attempted to cover the retreating Turks, but the Heavy Brigade was now receiving musketry fire in addition to cannon fire and he felt compelled to withdraw. The Heavy Brigade then took up position towards the end of the valley facing east where they could assail any attack crossing the South Valley in the flank as it advanced. Major Forrest of the 4th Dragoon Guards remembered:

> *several round shot fell into (the) ranks, breaking the legs of two Horses and one large ball struck a man named Middleton right in the face . . . killing him instantly . . . they opened such a fire upon us that we could do nothing but retire which we did about half a mile behind our encampment. Our tents had in the meantime been struck but because of the confusion they could not be packed up and we had the pleasure of galloping over our little property.*[250]

The southern slope was covered with fugitives, some of whom were ridden down by Cossacks as the Russian horse followed up their infantry's success. Calthorpe, now observing from the Sapouné ridge with Raglan and the staff, remembered hearing the harsh yells of these irregulars as they killed fleeing Turks with their lances.[251] The Russians swiftly occupied the first three redoubts and sent men to disable No. 4 Redoubt and tip its guns over into its ditch. Raglan had arrived on the escarpment by 8.00 am but well before 8.30 am all the redoubts on the Causeway had fallen. Having witnessed the final stages of the reverse, Raglan was still uncertain whether this was a prelude to a move on Balaklava or a distraction in support of a large sally against the siege works from the city. ADCs were sent to order the 3rd Division under arms in anticipation of a move from Sevastopol and to order the 1st and 4th Divisions to march to the Balaklava plain. In addition, Canrobert ordered two infantry brigades and several squadrons of the Chasseurs d'Afrique to reinforce the defences.

As the Russians began to secure the heights an artillery exchange took place. Although Maude's battery had withdrawn, guns manned by the Marines and Lieutenant Wolfe's battery began to target the area around the redoubts, forcing some Russian units to fall back over the Causeway or take shelter in the forts. Russian gunfire was also effective and Campbell ordered the 93rd Regiment, drawn up on a low hill before Kadikoi, to withdraw to the reverse slope when round shot began to inflict losses.[252] In his First Order to Lucan that day, Raglan told him to move the cavalry further back out of range. Lucan was annoyed since he held good ground that was perfect for mounting a counter-attack should the Russians move into the South Valley. He was also tired of taking the blame for what many took to be excessive caution when he was in fact preserving the cavalry according to his commander's orders.

Now the Russians wished to probe the British positions and follow up on their success. Liprandi later reported to Menshikov that a strong cavalry force under Ryzhov comprising two hussar regiments, three sotni of the 53rd Don Cossacks, one sotnia of Ural Cossacks and horse artillery was sent forward into the North Valley.[253] Ryzhov detached four squadrons who rode over the Causeway into the South Valley heading towards Kadikoi. The 93rd now advanced to line the crest of the hill and prepared to receive them. Campbell was with them and rather than form a defensive square to repel them, he directed their colonel to keep the men in a line two ranks deep. He also had two Turkish battalions along with fugitives rallied from the retreat, whom he posted on both sides of the 93rd, along with around forty men on detached duties and one hundred invalids on their way from the trenches into Balaklava. In all he had around 1,000 infantrymen. Observing from the ridge, Russell described this combined unit as a 'thin red streak'[254] that later became immortalized as 'the thin red line'. The Russians maintained their course straight for the hill and, when they advanced within range, the infantry opened fire. Several saddles were emptied and a number of riders were observed clinging to their mounts in a way that suggested they had been hit. The 93rd's colonel recalled:

> *The Cavalry could not bear the fire, and swept off to their left, trying to get round our right flank, and cut in on the Turks. But C. wheeled up the Grenadier Company to its right, and peppered them again, and sent them back with a flea in their ears.*[255]

Though some of the Turks had fled after firing the first volley, the Russian cavalry then turned and withdrew in some disorder over the Causeway, pursued by cannon fire from Barker's Battery stationed near Campbell's position. The line had fired at least three volleys, but at medium range it is likely that only a few casualties had been inflicted. Although a great moment in British military history, it is debatable how much the Russians wished to gain from the attack. Denison believed that they had no intention of charging Campbell's line and were probably making a demonstration to get the Allies to reveal their positions.[256] Campbell's reluctance to form the infantry into squares also implies that he guessed the Russians had no intention of charging him, especially as they were unsupported, and that this was merely a reconnaissance. As the Russians retired he commented to his ADC: 'Shadwell! That man understands his business.'[257]

Observing the action from the ridge and seeing large numbers of Turks in retreat, Raglan was concerned enough to order Lucan to provide close support to Campbell. Raglan's Second Order to him that day instructed him to send eight squadrons of heavy dragoons to reinforce Campbell's infantry. Scarlett led his squadrons in two columns through the South Valley parallel with the Causeway. As they rode towards Campbell, Lieutenant Elliot drew his commander's attention to a line of lances appearing along the skyline of the ridge. The main body of the Russian cavalry were attacking!

The Russians were now making a far more serious move with almost 2,000 cavalry who rode over the ridge just before No. 5 Redoubt in a gigantic column, with 'Ryzhov, like Murat, riding out in front and not deigning even to draw his sabre'.[258] Undeterred by their sudden appearance, Scarlett immediately ordered 'left wheel into line' and prepared to charge. With their backs to the enemy bearing down upon them, the officers dressed the lines but the nature of the ground hampered them. Though Scarlett wished to attack in two extended lines the tangled remains of the Light Brigade's camp impeded them on the right and a fenced vineyard on their left meant that the two squadrons of the Scots Greys and the 2nd Inniskillings had to take ground to the right and advance through the guide ropes and partially struck tents. There was no time to do anything else.

Perhaps surprised at the presence of a large body of cavalry immediately below him, Ryzhov slowed and halted his column. Had he charged headlong into them, the Russians' momentum would almost certainly have swept all before them but Ryzhov hesitated and redeployed, having Cossacks fan out in 'wings' on both flanks, hoping to use his superior numbers to envelop the enemy. This gave Scarlett five valuable minutes to dress his lines and seize the initiative. Lucan now rode up with his staff, commanding Scarlett to immediately charge the Russians, although he was already on the verge of doing so. The 5th Dragoon Guards were advancing some way behind him, slowed by the remains of the encampment, and the 1st Squadron of the Inniskillings were on his right flank.

The 4th Dragoon Guards also came up on the left to act in support but Scarlett's initial charge began with the Scots Greys and the 2nd Inniskillings, only 300 men charging uphill, over broken ground, towards a vastly superior enemy force. With the Russians only about 100 yards away, they had hoped to charge from a standing start but this proved impossible. Therefore the trumpeters sounded the trot, gallop and charge in rapid succession. The watchers on the ridge could see the action distinctly and held their breath as the riders galloped up the ridge. Although a few of the Russian hussars wore blue pelisses, the majority of the Russians were clad in grey coats topped with black shakoes. Against this the red-coated British stood out starkly against the hillside, wearing either black bearskins or brass helmets. Riding as fast as they were able, Scarlett's tiny group of staff officers, followed by the leading squadrons, penetrated the grey mass to be swallowed up as it closed in around them.

With the Russians only moving at a walk, the Heavies had the advantage of momentum as they struck the enemy line. Some of the leading Russian horsemen opened fire with carbines and pistols just before the first clash and several riders fell, among them Lieutenant Colonel Henry Griffith of the Scots Greys. Then, as the two lines met, swords rose and fell in a savage mêlée. The edges of the heavy cavalry swords and the light Russian sabres had suffered in the wet weather and many found them ineffective for a slashing blow:

> *My own attention was occupied by the hussar who cut at my head, but the brass pot stood well, and my head is only slightly bruised. I cut again at him, but do not believe that I hurt him more than he hurt me. I received a blow on the shoulder at the same time, which was given by some other man, but the edge must have been very badly delivered for it has only cut my coat and slightly bruised my shoulder.*[259]

However, Lieutenant Elliot had a different problem as he rode into the Russian ranks. Delivering a fine point with his sword, he impaled a Russian officer but had difficulty withdrawing his weapon after his horse's momentum drove his sword right up to the hilt in his opponent's body. Dressed in the distinctive cocked hat of the staff, several Russians set about him thinking he was a senior officer and Elliot suffered no less than fourteen sabre cuts to his head and upper body. Scarlett was also struck numerous times, taking five wounds, although his helmet deflected many blows.

The two wings began to close in around the British, but the 1st Inniskillings now slammed into the Russians' left wing catching them in their flank. As the Russians reeled from this fresh onslaught, the 4th Dragoons mounted another charge against the Cossacks on the Russian right, driving into the swirling mass. Ryzhov was unhorsed when his mount was shot from under him and was only saved from capture by an NCO from the Ingermanlandsky Regiment as the riders hacked and stabbed at one another in the mêlée. He later wrote: 'I have served for forty-two years, having taken part in ten campaigns, among them Kulm, Leipzig and Paris, but never before have I seen such an action where both sides slashed away at each other for so long . . .'[260]

The final charge by the 4th Dragoons drove deep into the Russian right flank and decided the matter. The Royals, who had been left with the Light Brigade, advanced under the personal initiative of Lieutenant Colonel Yorke and followed up on the 4th Dragoons' charge but only had the chance to exchange a few blows before the Russians broke and galloped back over the Woronzov Road in considerable disorder, hurried on their way by cannon fire. Tired, dazed and spattered with blood, the troopers of the Heavy Brigade began to wave their swords and cheer as the enemy fled. They had suffered seventy-eight men killed or wounded but the Russians lost considerably more. Having watched the unequal struggle with bated breath, the watchers on the ridge broke into loud 'huzzas' as the Russians withdrew. Raglan sent a dispatch to Scarlett bearing the simple remark, 'Well done!'[261]

Nolan had witnessed an extremely successful cavalry attack and must have been impressed. Earlier he had written, 'The most difficult position a cavalry officer can be placed in is in command of cavalry against cavalry, for the slightest fault committed may be punished on the spot, and a reverse lead to the most disastrous consequences.'[262] Considering the rapid nature of most cavalry encounters this was certainly true. Scarlett had won a considerable tactical victory against superior numbers and over very difficult ground. Likewise he had shown no hesitation whatsoever in attacking the enemy, being completely undaunted by their numbers and acting with commendable aggression. Admittedly, Nolan might have commented that manoeuvring within reach of the enemy was asking for trouble,[263] but Scarlett had little choice, being caught marching in column and in no position to charge. In contrast, Ryzhov had far less excuse for pausing and redeploying when an immediate advance might have disrupted and shattered the British cavalry dressing their ranks below him. He had also proved Louis's point about the folly of adopting large, unwieldy formations. Even though they heavily outnumbered the British, the rapid succession of charges by smaller units against them prevailed over the huge Russian column with many riders unable to engage the enemy in the press and chaos that ensued. However, Louis must have been irritated that this stunning feat of horsemanship had been performed by heavy rather than light cavalry. Cardigan's inaction in the immediate aftermath of the charge must have dismayed him even more.

The Light Brigade were drawn up only 500 yards from the action and were allowed ample opportunity to charge the Russians' exposed flank as they began to waver or to mount a pursuit. However, Cardigan refused to charge despite the fact that some officers urged him to do so. Captain Morris was among them and later claimed to have requested permission to advance with the 17th Lancers alone, which Cardigan later denied. Nevertheless, several witnesses saw him speaking earnestly with his commander and one recalled:

> *We heard nothing of the short conversation except Cardigan's hoarse sharp closing words – 'No, no, sir!' – whereupon Captain Morris fell back, uttering the words as he wheeled his horse in front of the right squadron – 'My God, my God, what a chance we are losing!' – at the same time slapping his sword sharply against his leg, as if in anger.*[264]

Cardigan maintained that he was under strict orders to act only in defence, but Lucan later refuted this, saying that he had permitted him to charge any enemy force that came within reach. Cardigan's inaction went against everything Nolan believed about cavalry being an offensive arm, whose effective use depended on a commander using his own initiative. In essence he argued that the 'tactics of cavalry are not capable of being reduced to rule . . . With the cavalry officer almost everything depends on the clearness of his *coup d'oeil*, and the felicity with which he seizes the happy moment of action . . . .'.[265] Cardigan later insisted that he desperately wanted to attack but felt compelled to remain in position, saying at the time, 'Damn those Heavies! They have had the laugh of us this day!'[266]

No pursuit was mounted into the North Valley by either brigade. The Russians had not suffered serious losses, but in their state of disorder the fresher battalions of the Heavy Brigade or the uncommitted Light Brigade could have pursued them and created havoc. However, although they had been driven back, it is possible that the Russians broke off the engagement with the partial intention of luring the British cavalry within the range of their guns and the decision not to pursue was probably sound. Although the watching staff officers on the ridge were euphoric at the success of the Heavy Brigade, it was believed that the light cavalry had missed an opportunity to hasten the Russians on their way at least. Nolan must have viewed these events with mixed feelings: the heavy cavalry that he considered almost obsolete had conducted a brilliant charge while the light cavalry stood by as a broken enemy fled beyond their reach.

Chapter 9

The Fateful Message

After the repulse of their cavalry the Russians seemed reluctant to advance any further and clung to their territorial gains awaiting developments. Raglan believed that the time had come to mount a counter-attack on the Causeway as the first three redoubts seemed to be lightly held, yet Canrobert believed that Russian inaction may have been an attempt 'to entice us down from our excellent positions . . .'.[267] The infantry were slow in marching down to the plain and, although the 1st Division under the Duke of Cambridge were well on their way, marching along the Woronzov Road as ordered, the 4th Division under Cathcart took time to get under arms. Cathcart was reluctant to mobilize his command, suspecting another false alarm or a minor affair of outposts, and his men were weary having spent most of the night in the siege trenches. Instead of taking the more direct route he marched slowly towards Balaklava via the Col. Raglan sent several messengers to speed his progress and finally dispatched Airey himself in the hope of spurring the infantry into greater efforts. He told Cathcart unequivocally, 'Lord Raglan wishes you to advance immediately and capture the redoubts.'[268] He was instructed to move along the Causeway as the 1st Division moved into the South Valley to protect his flank. He left Captain Ewart with Cathcart to show him the ground.

Raglan was frustrated that the infantry were taking so long. Every minute of delay increased the possibility of the Russians reinforcing the Causeway or even mounting another attack. Balaklava was still under threat and Raglan was concerned about his supply line. Despatching another aide, Raglan instructed Lord Lucan to act: 'Cavalry to advance and take advantage of any opportunity to recover the heights. They will be supported by the infantry which have been ordered (to) advance on two fronts.'[269] This was Raglan's Third Order to the cavalry that day. Lucan ordered the cavalry to mount and redeployed the Heavy Brigade on the slope of the Causeway whilst placing the Light Brigade across the end of the North Valley. The way he chose to interpret this instruction was to await the promised infantry support before going on to the offensive.

About thirty to forty minutes or more had elapsed as Raglan and his staff waited impatiently. Not only did the Russians show no sign of renewing their attack, the redeployment of their cavalry and artillery seemed to suggest that

Map 5: The Charge of the Heavy Brigade

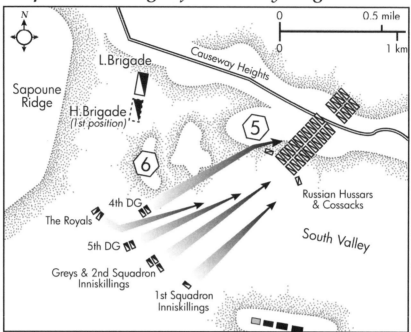

Map 6: The Charge of the Light Brigade

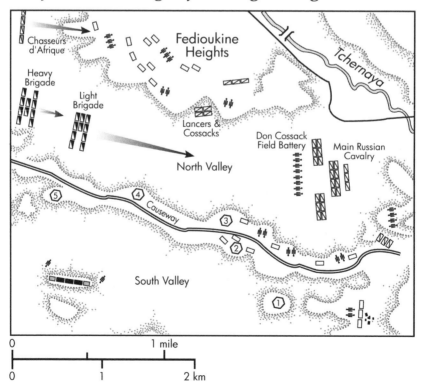

they contemplated withdrawal. It was the ideal time for a show of force, but Lucan remained inactive. Watching the Causeway through telescopes and field-glasses, staff officers spotted Russian artillery teams with lasso equipment approaching the redoubts. The number of guns captured in an action was often quoted to claim victory in battle, and the enemy appeared to be removing the cannons. Concern at this development probably spurred Raglan into action. Dictating what became known as the Fourth Order to Airey, he beckoned to an aide to carry his dispatch. Although Captain Calthorpe was next in line for duty, Raglan wanted the message relayed as swiftly as possible, which is probably why he insisted that Nolan should carry it. Airey handed him the following note, hastily scribbled in pencil:

> *Lord Raglan wishes the cavalry to advance rapidly to the front, and try to prevent the enemy carrying away the guns. Troop of horse-artillery may accompany. French cavalry is on your left. Immediate. (Signed) R. Airey.*[270]

Both Airey and Raglan spoke with Nolan to clarify their intentions. This was commonly known as the 'word of mouth' whereby an aide would provide further information if requested by the recipient. They then sent Louis on his way but as he rode off, Raglan shouted after him, 'Tell Lord Lucan the cavalry is to attack immediately.'[271] Instead of picking his way carefully down the steep 700-foot slope of the ridge, he took a very direct course, riding almost straight down the escarpment. His confident horsemanship astonished some onlookers.

Despite Raglan's impatience, the Russians had barely moved since Lucan received the Third Order. The Fedioukine Heights were still held in considerable strength by General Zhaboritski with at least eight battalions of infantry, four squadrons of cavalry and fourteen guns. Liprandi had deployed infantry in the first three redoubts and the Odessa Regiment were drawn up in the region of No. 3 Redoubt. However, in the centre the Russians had pulled back through the North Valley and Ryzhov had deployed his cavalry roughly half a mile from the aqueduct behind an artillery battery. This was the No. 3 Don Cossack Battery under the command of Colonel Prince Obolensky. Though the standard number of guns for horse artillery was eight, some observers believed that a battery and a half was present with at least twelve guns drawn up in line to enfilade the valley.[272] Liprandi also had six squadrons of Jeropkine's lancers that he divided and placed on both sides of the valley, one at the foot of the Fedioukine Heights and the other in a ravine to the side of the Causeway. Kinglake believed that the Russians intended to conduct a gradual withdrawal as the British infantry came up and had no intention of holding the Causeway. From his position Liprandi could clearly see the approaching infantry divisions marching down from the Chersonese, but he made little attempt to consolidate his position.[273] The Russian commander certainly seemed to have abandoned any further designs on Balaklava but, having pushed in the first line of Allied defences, he had inflicted some losses and certainly disrupted the enemy's siege operations.

As Nolan cantered across the plain towards his destination, many men in the ranks turned to watch as the staff officer rode through the interval between the regiments. Although tired and hungry after missing their morning's rations, many were eager to fight, particularly after watching their rivals defeat a Russian attack while they remained idle. Private Wightman saw him ride up to his commanding officer:

> *'Where is Lord Lucan?' 'There,' replied Morris, pointing – 'there, on the right front!' Then he added, 'What is it to be, Nolan? – are we going to charge?' Nolan was off already in Lord Lucan's direction, but as he galloped away he shouted to Morris over his shoulder, 'You will see! You will see!'*[274]

Nolan rode up to Lord Lucan and handed him the message. According to many witnesses, the pair debated a while and Nolan pointed towards the enemy. Exactly what was said during this brief conversation would become the subject of heated debate and play a crucial part in the myths that arose about Louis Nolan.

Lucan then rode over to confer with Lord Cardigan and ordered him to advance. The Light Brigade was formed up in two lines; Lucan altered their disposition slightly, ordering the 11th Hussars to fall back behind the first line in support, reducing the frontage of the brigade to two regiments – the 17th Lancers and the 13th Light Dragoons. The 4th Light Dragoons and the 8th Hussars formed the second line. Lucan said that he would personally lead the Heavy Brigade in support. Cardigan later wrote that he:

> *came in front of the Brigade, ordered the 11th Hussars to fall back in support and told me to attack the Russians in the Valley, about 3/4 of a mile distant with the 13th Lt. Dragoons & 17th Lancers. I answered 'Certainly but allow me to point out to you that the hills on each side are*

covered with Artillery & Riflemen.' The Lt. General replied 'I cannot help it, you must attack, Lord Raglan desires the Lt. Brigade immediately to attack the enemy.'[275]

Lucan's recollection differed: he claimed he instructed Cardigan to advance down the valley and, if no opportunity to take his objective presented itself, he was to retire.[276] Their mutual antipathy made this conversation typically short. As he rode to the head of his brigade, Cardigan supposedly muttered, 'Well, here goes the last of the Brudenells!'[277] Before advancing, he spoke to Paget insisting, 'You will take command of the second line, and I expect your best support, *mind, your best support.*'[278] Indignant at his commander's unnecessary emphasis, Paget assured him that he would have it.

Instead of returning to Raglan, Louis asked to join the brigade for the action and permission to do so was granted. One trooper recalled:

I distinctly remember that Nolan returned to the brigade, and having a mere momentary talk with Cardigan, at the close of which he drew his sword with a flourish, as if greatly excited. The blood came into his face – I seem to see him now; and then he fell back a little way into Cardigan's left rear, somewhat in front of and to the right of Captain Morris . . .[279]

Cardigan now ordered the brigade to draw swords and then gave the order to advance at a walk, with the first squadron of the 17th directing, heading straight down the valley. The Odessa Regiment on the Causeway, observing their advance, fell back towards No. 2 Redoubt. Here they began to form squares, anticipating attack. The brigade had begun to increase their pace to a trot and had covered about 200 yards when Captain Nolan spurred his horse forward and towards the right in the direction of the Causeway. Startled, Captain Morris shouted at him: 'That won't do Nolan! We've a long way to go, and must be steady.'[280] Cardigan was incensed to see him gallop ahead, it being a breach of discipline to ride before a brigadier without good reason. What on earth was he doing? Turning in his saddle, Nolan waved his sword aloft and shouted. At that moment the Russian guns on the Fedioukine spoke for the first time and a shell exploded between Nolan and Cardigan. Louis was struck full in the chest by a shell splinter and though his arm remained raised, his sword fell from his grasp:

but all the other limbs so curled in on the contorted trunk as by a spasm,

*that we wondered how for the moment the huddled form kept the saddle.
It was the sudden convulsive twitch of the bridle hand inward on the chest
that caused the charger to wheel rearward so abruptly. The weird shriek
and the awful face as rider and horse disappeared haunt me now to this
day, the first horror of that ride of horrors.*[281]

Nolan's horse carried him back through the interval between the first two
regiments, the stricken rider emitting an unearthly death cry. The horse carried
him almost as far as the point where the brigade had started before Nolan fell
from his saddle and lay dead on the valley floor.

Rhyzov later wrote that around ninety minutes had elapsed since his clash
with the Heavy Brigade. He had ridden forward to speak with Colonel
Obolensky at the battery when the gunners observed the dust cloud that
heralded the Light Brigade's approach. As soon as they were in range they
opened fire with shot and shell, changing to case shot as their target drew
closer.[282] Initially the Light Brigade were fired upon by the guns on the
Fedioukine Heights but as they rode further into the valley they came under
rifle and musketry fire from skirmishers and infantry around the Fedioukine
and on the Causeway: 'As we neared the battery, a square of infantry . . . gave
us a volley in flank. The very air hissed as the shower of bullets passed through
us; many men were now killed or wounded.'[283]

Paget's second line began to encounter more and more difficulty as the
volume of fire increased. He had chosen the 4th Light Dragoons as the
directing regiment and initially feared following the first line too closely. The
opposite problem now arose with the line falling too far back within the first
300–400 yards of the advance and the 8th Hussars beginning to veer to the
right. Paget kept shouting, '8th Hussars, close in on your left. Colonel Shewell,
you are losing your interval.'[284] As casualties mounted they found their way
impeded by riderless horses and walking wounded. Increasingly they had to
ride around men and horses lying dead or injured on the valley floor. Although
the officers did their best to keep formation, the 8th gradually drew away in the
dust and smoke and Paget eventually lost sight of them.

Cardigan rode steadily onwards, sitting straight-backed and holding his
sword at the slope, he looked neither left nor right as he led the brigade
forward. A few times he shouted hoarsely at the men to be steady as huge holes
were torn in the line and the sergeants tried to get the men to close the ranks.
He also shouted at some officers to fall back and not to try to force the pace as
they began to ride faster, drawing nearly level with him. The guns of the

battery in front now opened fire, rarely having had such a large and clear target. Dozens of men were falling:

> *I rode near the right of the line. A corporal . . . was struck by a shot or shell full in the face, completely smashing it, his blood and brains bespattering us who rode near. His horse still went on with us. By this time, the ranks being continually broken it caused some confusion. Oaths and imprecations might be heard between the report of the guns and the bursting of the shells, as the men crowded and jostled each other in their endeavour to close to the centre.*[285]

As the round shot struck, it bounded along the valley floor, often hitting several targets, taking off limbs or killing men and horses outright. Shell bursts showered the advancing squadrons with metal fragments maiming or killing as horses were brought crashing to the ground. Occasionally one cannon shot alone would bring down four horses and those nearby were hard pressed to avoid riding into them in their ruin as they tried to close up the gaps in their formation. As they neared the Don Cossack Battery, the guns in the redoubts added their fire to the fusillade.

Following in their wake, Lord Lucan led the Heavy Brigade onward and came under artillery fire from the Fedioukine Hills. Appalled, the watchers on the Sapouné Ridge looked on as the cavalry rode headlong into the middle of the Russian Army. Shot at from three sides, they rode into a maelstrom of dust and smoke and were soon lost to view. Lucan rode on with the Heavies as round shot fired from the Causeway began to plough up the ground in front of them and plunge into their ranks. Looking ahead, he saw the Light Brigade disappearing into the swirling dust cloud ahead. Men and horses were falling and Lucan sustained a slight wound as he ordered his trumpeter to sound a halt. He was taking fire from both flanks and decided that to press onward was futile. He stopped the Heavy Brigade level with and roughly midway between the third and fourth redoubts, remarking to Lord Paulet, 'They have sacrificed the Light Brigade; they shall not the Heavy, if I can help it.'[286] Ordering the brigade about, Lucan led them back along the valley, still being fired upon by the Russian guns. General Scarlett fell back with great reluctance and only on his commander's direct order. Lucan led the Heavy Brigade back along the valley, intending to cover the Light Brigade's withdrawal if he could.

General Morris, in command of the French cavalry division, had squadrons of the Chasseurs d'Afrique drawn up about half a mile from the British cavalry's initial position. Although Lucan had not requested their help, he ordered an advance on the Fedioukine in an effort to support the attack. Major Abdelal now led four squadrons against the Russian batteries. Advancing steadily, the Chasseurs were fired upon by Russian skirmishers but these soon fled to the safety of their infantry who were forming square against them. Distracted from the British advance, the Russian gunners were thrown into uproar as the French cavalry bore down upon their right flank. Chaos ensued as they stopped firing and tried to limber up their guns and retreat.

Riding up the shallow slope, the French tore into the batteries and a fierce fight around the guns ensued. The Russian artillerymen managed to carry off some of the guns but others were abandoned as the Chasseurs rode around them, their sabres rising and falling as they struck down at the gunners. From the relative safety of their squares, the nearby Russian infantry fired stoically at the cavalrymen but failed to drive them off. Zhaboritski ordered a counter-attack and the Vladimir Regiment advanced along the heights against the French. The cavalry was dispersed, fighting around the batteries and beginning to come under sustained rifle and musket fire, so the recall was sounded. They withdrew in good order, having suffered ten killed and twenty-eight wounded, but they had effectively silenced the batteries on the Fedioukine.[287]

Despite the intense fire of the cannonade, the Light Brigade kept going. As the cavalry bore down upon them, the gunners swabbed out their barrels and rammed charges down as fast as they could, changing to case shot as the enemy approached, which brought down dozens of riders. They were now at a gallop and around 50 yards from the battery, swords and lances were levelled and they increased to charging speed. Ryzhov had ridden back to his command and ordered his cavalry forward to protect the Don Battery as the British were clearly not going to be stopped by gunfire alone. Though the battery was wreathed in its own smoke, the artillery realized that the cavalry must be nearly upon them and they struggled to hitch their guns to their limbers and withdraw. They were too late as the first line hurtled into them.

A savage fight now took place as the riders set upon the gunners and drivers trying to withdraw. Having endured a devastating cannonade, the first line stabbed and hacked down at the gunners who had wrought such destruction upon them. The excitement and terror of their incredible ride now welled up into a fearsome battle fury as they took revenge on their persecutors. Some stopped to exchange blows with or cut down fleeing artillerymen, whilst others rode straight through the battery, delivering cuts at the gunners as they went

Map 7: The Guns and Beyond

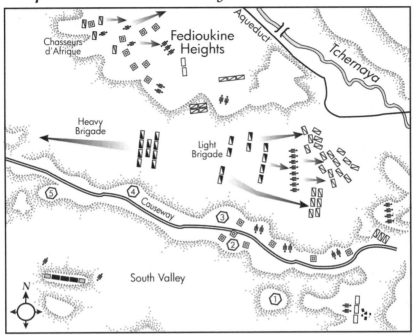

Map 8: The Retreat

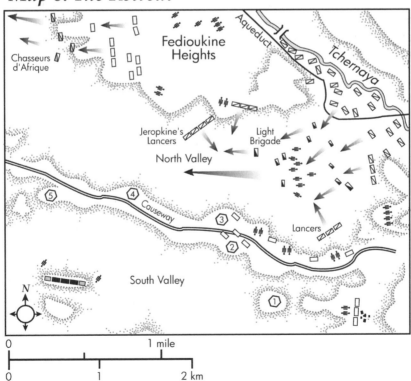

past. Cardigan himself rode through the guns with his sword still held at the slope and some yards further on, reined up at the sight of the Russian cavalry deployed to his front. Incredibly, he had survived the charge unscathed. In the Russian ranks Prince Radzivill recognized the earl, having met him years before in England, and sent forward some Cossacks to capture him. Evading a few thrusts from their lances, Cardigan wheeled about and rode back the way he had come, receiving only a slight injury.[288]

Numbers of cavalrymen began to emerge from the fight and dash onwards past the guns towards the approaching Russians. One officer recalled that the Cossacks at the front of their advance were already 'frightened by the disciplined order of the mass of cavalry bearing down on them, did not hold, but, wheeling to their left, began to fire on their own troops in their efforts to clear a route of escape'.[289] Colonel Douglas of the 11th Hussars led his regiment behind the guns rather than engaging the gun teams, unaware of how badly outnumbered he was by the enemy cavalry.[290] The sight of this formed body of men advancing determinedly upon them added to the Russians' alarm. The regular troopers of the Ingermandlandsky and Kievsky regiments were disordered by the unnerved Cossacks who rode through and into them and a general rout ensued as the struggling men broke and fled. Ryzhov looked on aghast as some officers tried to rally their men, only to be cut down by the enemy.

The 4th Light Dragoons in the second line now thundered into the battery. Around the guns troopers cut at the traces of the gun teams to prevent them dragging cannons away and some dismounted and attempted to spike some of the guns.[291] Private Grigg of the 4th Light Dragoons rode at a mounted driver:

> *He cut me across the eyes with his whip, which almost blinded me, but as my horse flew past I made a cut and caught him in the mouth, so that his teeth all rattled together as he fell. I can hear the horrible sound now. Then I made for another driver, cut him across the back of the neck, and gave him a second cut as he fell . . .* [292]

Carrying on past the battery Grigg joined in as groups of riders, their blood up, pursued the Russian cavalry in a running fight down the valley. As Kubitovich observed: 'most of the cavalry continued the headlong chase after the hussars, slashing at them without mercy . . . the English chased them almost as far as the transport lines.'[293]

Lieutenant Kozukhov of the 12th Artillery Brigade was stationed with his light battery covering a gorge near the Tractir Bridge. He recorded how they looked on disgustedly as their cavalry broke and fled, but he believed that it was the hussar regiments and not the Cossacks who began the stampede to the rear. The Russian cavalry milled around trying to reform, having been driven there by an enemy that Kozukhov estimated they outnumbered by five to one. The British were clearly unsupported and he expected them to throw down their weapons and surrender but:

> *It is difficult, if not impossible to do justice to the feat of these mad cavalry, for having lost a quarter of their number and being apparently impervious to new dangers and further losses, they quickly reformed their squadrons to return over the same ground littered with their dead and dying. With such desperate courage these valiant lunatics set off again . . .*[294]

Many of those who had pursued the Russians this far failed to regain their lines, being either killed or captured, but the enemy cavalry took some time to reform, convinced that they were opposed by superior numbers rather than 'a handful of red-coated desperadoes',[295] as Kozukhov scornfully remarked.

Back at the guns, Paget did his best to ensure that his troopers managed to put as many guns out of action as possible. Yet, soon realizing that no support was coming, he tried to rally as many men as he could for the inevitable retreat. Many officers and NCOs were doing the same:

> *we heard the familiar voice of Corporal Morley, of our regiment, a great, rough, bellowing Nottingham man. He had lost his lance hat, and his long hair was flying out in the wind as he roared, 'Coom 'ere! Coom 'ere! Fall in, lads, fall in!' . . . with shouts and oaths he had collected some twenty troopers of various regiments.*[296]

Paget managed to assemble around sixty or seventy men, largely from the 4th Light Dragoons and 11th Hussars. Many men and horses were injured and their mounts were flagging if not blown. Nevertheless, Paget began to retire, trying to maintain as much order as possible. They were still being fired upon by infantry and artillery, though the guns on the Fedioukine had fallen silent. Groups of Cossacks were becoming bolder, riding out to capture the fine English horses and finish off wounded or isolated men. Private Firkins was set upon as he rode back from the battery:

> *I had only got a few yards when I saw two Russian Lancers coming*

> *towards me with clenched teeth and staring like savages. I prepared to*
> *meet them with as much coolness and determination as I could command,*
> *the first one made a thrust at me with his Lance, it is a heavy weapon and*
> *easily struck down, which I did with my sword, thrusting it at the same*
> *time through the fellows neck . . . the shock nearly brought me from my*
> *saddle . . .*[297]

Losing his sword in the encounter and being nearly exhausted, Firkins was
saved from his other assailant by the timely intervention of one of the 17th,
who speared his lance directly into the man's back. Shortly afterwards, his
horse was struck and killed by a shell and, like so many others, he struggled
back on foot.

The 8th Hussars under Colonel Shewell had missed the guns completely,
arriving on the Causeway side of the battery a few hundred yards behind it.
Bringing his regiment to a halt, Shewell observed the swirling mêlée still taking
place in and around the battery and that the majority of the Russian cavalry
were in retreat. He could see no formed bodies of British cavalry but there were
Russian formations to his front, standing inactive. Resuming his advance, small
groups of riders from other regiments rode to form on the 8th as they emerged
from the battery or returned from the pursuit. The colonel was contemplating
attacking the Russian cavalry to his front when he was informed that enemy
cavalry had ridden down from the Causeway to block their withdrawal.
Effectively surrounded, Shewell wheeled his men about and began to retire.
Finding themselves caught between two enemy lines, the 8th attacked the
lancers before them and cut their way through. Lieutenant Seager later wrote
that many in the Light Brigade appreciated the fact that their regiment was
able to provide some form of cover in this manner for the survivors making
their way back from the guns.[298]

The withdrawal of Paget's command was being hard-pressed by Russian
cavalry, although he recalled that they advanced in a disorderly fashion, seemed
unwilling to engage and they appeared 'not to know what next to do'.[299]
Nevertheless, he felt increasingly threatened by their numbers and 'I shouted
at the top of my voice, "Halt, front; if you don't front, my boys, we are
done!"'[300] This discouraged their pursuers who halted once again but then they
realized that enemy lancers were approaching from behind in an effort to head
them off. Paget gave the order 'threes about' to face this threat and with an air
of desperation ordered an attack. The tired horses surged forward in a slow,
ragged advance and he was amazed when the fresh enemy troops, who were

formed up and prepared for a charge, stopped. Although they heavily outnumbered his group, the lancers were hesitant and, though a few half-hearted blows were exchanged, they managed to push and jostle their way through: 'Well, we got by them without, I believe, the loss of a single man. How, I know not! It is a mystery to me! Had that force been composed of English *ladies*, I don't think one of us could have escaped.'[301] In contrast, Loy Smith with a small group of about twenty men encountered considerable opposition; his group were pursued by hussars with several men overtaken and killed before being caught between them and the waiting lancers, resulting in a sharp skirmish. Similarly, he recorded that the lancers seemed reluctant to attack when a charge would have carried the tired British riders before them, but his group was dispersed and he returned to the Allied lines alone.[302]

Russian accounts differ considerably over the manner of the retreat. Kubitovich with the Eropkin Uhlans had been posted near the Causeway and they were ordered by Liprandi to cut off the enemy retreat. Riding down from the Causeway they were fired upon by their own infantry, who mistook them for the enemy. He recorded that the parties he tried to intercept rode in remarkably good order, considering the trial they had just gone through and that both sides charged, resulting in a fiercely fought mêlée: 'The English fought with amazing bravery, even the dismounted and wounded fighting on until they dropped.'[303] During the mêlée, Russian guns opened fire on them from the Causeway, and possibly the reoccupied Don Battery, knocking down friend and foe alike. He believed that very few in his part of the field escaped them and that his unit chased them as far as No. 4 Redoubt (although No. 3 is more likely) before retiring. Kubitovich commented that his opponents were riding in formation; so it is likely that he encountered elements of the 8th or the 11th Hussars in this fight. Ryzhov, aware that his cavalry had not performed well during the battle, exaggerated their success claiming, 'From this moment the battle might have been compared to the coursing of hares. Even the enemy reserve, seeing how matters stood, turned back, not being able to save their fellows.'[304] However, Kozhukhov refutes this, stating that the only 'hare coursing' he saw that day occurred during the pursuit of the Cossacks and hussar regiments from the battery. Furthermore, in his opinion, the enemy were pursued from the field with little enthusiasm.[305]

With such conflicting accounts, the truth of the matter may never be known, but the North Valley presented a sad spectacle uncontested by either side. The valley floor was a harrowing scene, with men and horses lying scattered along the route of the charge. Men struggled back to the Allied lines either mounted or on foot, still being fired upon by the troops on the heights. Wounded horses lay kicking and struggling on the plain or lay deathly still. The valley was strewn with the dead, and those wounded who were able limped or crawled back, desperate to avoid groups of looting Cossacks picking their way through the carnage. Mitchell returned on foot, and though riderless horses, maddened by gunfire, galloped about the plain, he was unable to catch one. As he staggered back he came across a solitary figure who, hearing him approach, called:

> *'Is that an Englishman?' I answered, 'Yes', and on going to him found he had been wounded by a piece of shell just between the eyes, which had blinded him. He had bled very much, and was still bleeding. I had a handkerchief. . . which I bound round his wound, and taking him by the arm, led him along.*[306]

The entire incident lasted only twenty minutes. For roughly half of that time the guns of the Fedioukine Hills had been out of action; had they not been so, losses would have been much higher.

Captain Morris was one of the men stumbling back across the plain. Covered in blood, he had been hit many times during the charge and wounded during hand-to-hand fighting with the Russians. Briefly taken prisoner, his captors left him for dead when he lost consciousness and, though he caught a riderless horse, his second mount was shot from under him. Coming across Nolan's body he knew he must be approaching safety as he had fallen at the beginning of the charge. However, he had reached the limit of his endurance and, seeing the shattered form of his friend, fell unconscious beside him.

Captain Ewart was still riding with Cathcart's infantry division, now emerging on to the plain. Hearing from a retreating group of troopers that a fellow staff officer lay grievously wounded out in the valley, he obtained permission to investigate. Riding down onto the valley floor, he was stunned by the scene of devastation that greeted him but managed to find Nolan and Morris. In scarlet forage cap and gold-braided uniform, Nolan's body was easy to spot. Seeing that Turkish troops had reoccupied Redoubt No. 4, Ewart persuaded some of them to help him carry them off the field, until Russian gunfire forced them to retire. Eventually a group of officers and men managed to rescue Morris and recover Nolan's body, despite being fired upon and harassed by scavenging Cossacks. Captain Brandling saw the body and noted the severe burns on Nolan's uniform, revealing how close he must have been to the exploding shell. Louis's chest was almost completely torn open, exposing the heart.[307]

Brandling saw to it that Nolan was buried in the ditch of one of the redoubts. There is some dispute over whether this was Redoubt No. 4 or No. 5 but, considering the difficulty in carrying a dead body, it is likely to have been the nearer No. 4 Redoubt. The party of limber gunners who dug the shallow grave also came under intermittent enemy fire, which implies that it was the nearer redoubt. One year afterwards, officers visiting the scene heard the following account of the aide's burial from a medical orderly:

> *'It was in this ditch,' said this gentleman, reining sharply up, 'we buried poor Nolan. I knew him', he said: 'he was a good fellow, but an ugly man, and made a still uglier corpse'; he lay on his back, with a deep wound in his left breast. Dr _____ had just had his fingers in it, and was wiping them in his handkerchief. Some spoke of carrying the corpse back to our lines. 'No,' said Lord Look-on, 'he met his deserts – a dog's death, – and, like a dog, let him be buried in a ditch.' 'I thought it a hard and cruel speech,' said our informant, 'but if the poor fellow erred, he suffered for it, and there ought to have been nothing of the sort uttered at such a time – tread lightly on the ashes of the dead.'*[308]

This account is unsupported by other sources, though it does reveal the extent of the controversy that had arisen by 1855 over the Charge of the Light Brigade. Whether Lucan was present at the burial in the aftermath of the charge is questionable, as is his callous epitaph on the deceased, the habit of the day being to keep one's feelings firmly in check especially within the hearing of subordinates and those of a lower class. Nonetheless, a talented and promising officer now lay in a shallow unmarked grave. Most of the bodies lying in the valley below suffered a similar fate, some remaining exposed on the valley floor for months. An anonymous mass grave awaited them but, unlike many who fell in the Crimean Peninsula, neither they nor Captain Nolan would be forgotten.

Lord Raglan was dismayed. How could his instructions have been so completely misunderstood or even deliberately disobeyed? Riding with a knot of staff officers down to the plain he confronted Lord Cardigan. White with rage he demanded: 'What do you mean, sir, by attacking a battery in front, contrary to all the usages of warfare, and the customs of the service?'[309] Seemingly indifferent, Cardigan decried all responsibility and referred him to Lord Lucan as his superior officer. When Lucan eventually reported to his commander, Raglan greeted him with the cold accusation: 'You have lost the Light Brigade!'[310] Lucan strongly denied this charge; but the furore about who had sent the Light Brigade into the North Valley was only just beginning.

British infantry were now in position and Cathcart sent light infantry along the Causeway. Redoubts 5 and 4 were reoccupied and some limited skirmishing took place with the Russian infantry. One infantry officer recalled how the French and Russian batteries continued to exchange fire for some time. The first three redoubts were still held in force by the Russians: 'We expected to have to storm them that night, but little did we know the extent of the reverse which had befallen our cavalry, and which made our chiefs tired of fighting for the moment. After dark we quietly withdrew in skirmishing order, leaving the plain in possession of the enemy.'[311]

The high command agreed to give up the first three redoubts, Canrobert arguing that they could ill afford the troops to garrison them adequately and still have sufficient manpower for the siege works. They had always been a weak defence and, even if strengthened, the second defensive line was too far away to give them proper support. However, by this act the Allies lost control of the Woronzov Road. According to Fortescue, the loss of the only metalled road between Balaklava and Sevastopol was the key point that the battle should have been remembered for.[312] When the winter set in and the already poor Crimean tracks became quagmires of mud and sludge, the loss of the Woronzov was keenly felt. The acts of the 'thin red line' and the cavalry charges were heroic but strategically irrelevant. The remnants of the Light Brigade were sent to camp beyond the Sapouné Ridge while the Heavy Brigade remained as part of Balaklava's defence and two more infantry regiments from the Highland Brigade were brought down to support Campbell.

The Russians had not taken many prisoners – less than fifty men fell into their hands, most of whom were wounded. Wightman was one and recalled how General Liprandi came to visit them, enquiring with a spirit of wonderment, 'what did they give you to drink? Did they prime you with spirits to come down and attack us in such a manner?'[313] One of the men responded that had they done so they would have taken half of Russia by now. The general smiled indulgently and assured them that he was sympathetic to their plight and would ensure that they were well treated in captivity. Yet the Russians were baffled by this ferocious and seemingly suicidal attack on their positions and many surmised that the Light Brigade must have been either mad or fired with alcohol. Kozhukhov disagreed:

> *As for drunkenness, there was some talk of it at the time but no one*
> *seriously believed it. I, at any rate, saw most of the enemy wounded, and*

> *I saw none drunk. It is indeed difficult to imagine that drunken cavalry could have achieved what those English horse actually did.*[314]

The Russians were pleased with the Battle of Balaklava. Liprandi's report to Menshikov played down the reverses his cavalry had suffered and claimed that the Light Brigade had charged with over 2,000 men, though it should be remembered that his estimate may have been based on the numbers of a comparable Russian force. In fact the Light Brigade was greatly under strength at the time: estimates of the number who actually took part in the charge vary between 658 and 690.[315] Liprandi also claimed to have taken eight guns in the redoubts though the Allies admitted to only seven. Writing to the Tsar, Prince Menshikov raised this figure to eleven guns. Russian casualties sustained in the battle were estimated at 300, although they were probably far higher, and the capture of the guns and the Causeway allowed them to claim a limited victory. After the demoralizing reverse at the Alma and the slow, squalid butchery of the siege, their spirits had been raised by this success. However, many had formed the opinion that the British cavalry were dangerously unpredictable and possibly composed of reckless fanatics.[316]

The men of the Light Brigade spent a dismal night contemplating their losses. Many horses were so badly wounded that they had to be shot and at least six wounded died in the night. Seager lamented that 'Many a poor fellow was laid low.'[317] Even though the 8th Hussars had been in the second line and veering off course spared them some of the cannon fire in front, they had still suffered twenty-eight killed and nineteen wounded. Other regiments had fared even worse, with the 17th in the first line losing 36 men of all ranks killed and 38 wounded. Mrs Duberley rode with her husband to the Light Brigade camp enquiring after their friends and was shocked at how many had been lost or injured:

> *Many had a sad tale to tell. All had been struck with the exception of Colonel Shewell, either themselves or their horses. Poor Lord Fitzgibbon was dead. Of Captain Lockwood no tidings had been heard... Mr Clutterbuck was wounded in the foot; Mr Seager in the hand. Captain Tomkinson's horse had been shot under him; Major De Salis's horse wounded. Mr Mussenden showed me a grapeshot which had 'killed my poor mare.' Mr Clowes was a prisoner. Poor Captain Goad of the 13th is dead. Ah, what a catalogue.*[318]

The exact numbers of those lost have caused some debate over the years, but the official casualty report recorded a total of 110 killed outright, 130 wounded and 58 assumed missing or captured. The Light Brigade had suffered 40 per cent losses. This was horrific but, contrary to some of the myths that arose about the action, the brigade was not destroyed. Less than 200 *mounted* men reported to roll call at the end of that day. The horses were in fact more difficult to replace than trained cavalrymen. The cost and difficulty in buying and shipping horses out to the Crimea made them a valuable commodity; in total 381 horses had been killed outright during the charge or put down shortly afterwards.[319]

Many men died of their wounds over the next few months. Shipped out to the hospitals in Turkey, some endured and survived the squalid conditions but many succumbed to their injuries. Nurse Sarah Anne Terrot recorded some of the human cost of the charge, speaking to many survivors. Nearly all were young, she recalled, and most had been wounded by cannon fire. She wrote down the experiences that some of these men related:

> *Ward in front of me was blown to pieces. Turner on my left had his right arm blown off, and afterwards died, and Young on my right also had his right arm blown off. Just then my right arm was shattered to pieces. I gathered it together as well as I could, and laid it across my knees.*[320]

The amputees were particularly difficult to save, and those who did recover faced an uncertain future back home since there was little provision for the disabled in Victorian society. As historian Moyse-Bartlett pointed out, 'It was a poet, not a soldier, who glorified the Charge of the Light Brigade.'[321]

Chapter 10

Recriminations

In the immediate aftermath of the Battle of Balaklava, a whispering campaign began in the Army of the East about the disaster. Some felt that Nolan bore responsibility, often citing his supposedly reckless temperament as reason enough for suspicion. Others blamed Raglan or Lucan. Lord Lucan was outraged that Raglan held him accountable and bitterly objected when accused of losing the brigade. According to Lucan, Raglan retorted 'you were a lieutenant general and should, therefore, have exercised your discretion and, not approving the charge, should not have caused it to be made.'[322] This infuriated him, since in his view he had been obeying Raglan's specific order. However, Raglan never confirmed making this statement: if divisional commanders had a degree of latitude when given a *direct* order, it would have serious implications regarding the chain of command.

Lucan felt he had done his best under difficult circumstances and was now being victimized after acting on his commander's express instructions. Visiting his chief, Paget observed: 'Lucan is much cut up; and with tears in his eyes this morning he said how infamous it was to lay the blame on him.'[323] Guessing Lucan's mind, two days later Raglan asked Airey to try to placate him. He found Lucan brooding over the matter in his tent and tried to console him, saying, 'These sort of things happen in war; it is nothing to Chillianwallah.' Lucan said, 'I know nothing of Chillianwallah; but I tell you . . . that this is the most serious affair; and . . . I do not intend to bear the smallest particle of responsibility.'[324] The recollection of a notorious cavalry failure during the Second Sikh War did little to calm the embittered Earl, but Airey's insistence that Raglan would write a fair-minded report partly reassured him.

Raglan did his best to minimize the scale of the loss in his dispatches home. Kindly to a fault, and perhaps knowing that he was not entirely blameless himself, he tried to be subtle and made a great deal of the success of the Heavy Brigade's action in his dispatches. Nevertheless, his report and letters made it clear that he held Lucan responsible: one line read, 'From some misconception of the instruction to advance, the Lieutenant General considered that he was bound to attack at all hazards.'[325] It was also very difficult to be totally positive about infantry's role in the battle. Although he mentioned the 4th Division's counter-attack against the Causeway, it was difficult to conceal the fact that Cathcart took a long time to get his division into position and, had the infantry arrived on time, the cavalry attack might have had a very different outcome.

After witnessing the action from the ridge, Russell rode down to speak with survivors of the charge. His hurried notes written in camp that night and the dispatch he sent to his newspaper were the first public reports of the incident. Despite his liking for Nolan, many gave him the impression that Nolan had issued a confusing message in great haste and he agreed:

> *A braver soldier than Captain Nolan the army did not possess. A matchless horseman and a first-rate swordsman, God forbid that I should cast a shade on the brightness of his honour, but I am bound to state what I am told occurred. When Lord Lucan received the order . . . he asked . . . 'Where are we to advance to?' Captain Nolan pointed with his finger to the line of the Russians, and said, 'There are the enemy, and there are the guns,' or words to that effect . . .*[326]

However, he qualified his remarks by saying that Nolan's interpretation of the order and Lucan's were very different, and 'The result of the confusion caused by Lord Raglan's lack of precision can hardly have been what he intended.'[327] Russell may have believed that Louis was in error but clearly felt that others were also accountable.

After the Battle of Balaklava, the weather began to deteriorate. Although the Crimea has an almost Mediterranean climate, the winter of 1854/1855 was the harshest the region had suffered in decades. Following the Battle of Inkerman 5 November 1854 when the Russians marched out of Sevastopol attempting to break the siege, the Light Brigade was moved up to monitor the area. They were now six miles from Balaklava and due to the shortage of baggage animals and the muddy road being nearly impassable to carts, both cavalry brigades had to use their chargers for menial supply work. When the snow began in earnest, the men suffered under canvas but the horses had no shelter whatsoever and occasionally stood up to their knees in mud, exposed to freezing winds, sleet and snow. Occasionally reduced to a handful of barley a day, they began to gnaw at each other's saddle straps, blankets and tails. Overworked, underfed and subjected to appalling conditions, large numbers died from exposure and want.[328] The Russian guns had taken a heavy toll on the Light Brigade but it was the Crimean winter that finished them off. Nearly all the horses died and, since remounts were not arriving fast enough, the Light Brigade became ineffective. It would be months before the situation was resolved.

Another possibility was that Raglan may have unintentionally misled Nolan. Calthorpe believed that Nolan had misunderstood Raglan's instructions,[329] but there is no previous record of Nolan failing in this regard – in fact rather the opposite, considering what is known about his staff work. Calthorpe was also Raglan's nephew and after the battle may have been more concerned with his uncle's reputation than that of his dead friend. However, there is no record of exactly what Raglan and Airey said to Nolan by way of clarification, and Raglan's last shouted instruction added the fatal word 'attack', which was not included in the written order and may have conflicted with Nolan's previous instructions. Frustratingly, without an exact record of Raglan's final conversation with Louis, the truth of this matter will never be known.

Partly convinced by Airey's entreaties, Lucan had calmed down but was incensed once more when he read Raglan's letter in the newspapers. Confronting Raglan and Airey, he insisted that his own side of the story should be made known to Horse Guards. Though his commander earnestly advised him to reconsider, he submitted a letter for the Duke of Newcastle, following the proper army channels for such a complaint. Suspecting that this might not be sent, he dispatched a copy to his solicitor to release to the press. Knowing that this could only inflame the situation, his solicitor did no such thing. In fact, Raglan was as good as his word and sent Lucan's missive but included a covering letter of his own.

He refused to withdraw any of his remarks and repeated that Lucan was in error to think he was obliged to attack and certainly in the manner in which he did. Furthermore, 'he is wholly silent with respect to a previous order which had been sent him.'[330] This was the Third Order, which emphasized the need to recover the heights and that the infantry were to support the cavalry, not the other way around. It left far less reason for confusion when read in conjunction with the Fourth Order: 'This order (meaning the Third Order) did not seem to me to have been attended to, and therefore it was, that the instruction by Captain Nolan was forwarded to him. Lord Lucan must have read the first order with very little attention, for he now states that the Cavalry was formed to support the Infantry.'[331] He had failed to use the horse artillery or act in conjunction with the French cavalry that Raglan had mentioned in the Fourth Order and was also 'so little informed of the position of the Enemy, that he asked Captain Nolan, "where and what he was to attack", as neither Enemy nor Guns were in sight.'[332] This was a serious point as, although Lucan would make a great deal of his inability to see important areas of the field, it was a vital part of a cavalry commander's business to seek out such information; Lucan should not have needed to ask Nolan to provide clarification.

Lucan's letter was too much for Viscount Hardinge at Horse Guards, as the one thing the army could not tolerate was disloyalty within the command structure. Lucan's culpability was irrelevant since Raglan could hardly rely upon him in the field if he was trying to undermine him; such recriminations were best left until after the campaign. Lucan was asked to resign his command and return home. Though many in the Army of the East considered Lucan a bully and a tyrant, Paget at least was sorry to see him go under such circumstances: 'I have always felt very keenly that he was a hardly used man . . . No cavalry man was ever heard to say anything against Lord Lucan; all had respect for his military character, and all sympathised with him on his recall.'[333] Not everyone agreed: Lieutenant Walker Heneage of the 8th Hussars was one of those who contradicted this, admitting, 'I always hated him, and so did the whole Cavalry Division, but for heaven's sake let a man have fair play.'[334] Major Forrest went even further:

> *Captain Nolan may have been, and I believe was, somewhat to blame about that Light Brigade tragedy, but I think my Lord Lucan the most to blame. If a lieutenant general will not take any responsibility upon himself, a lance corporal might fill his place, he should have waited until the infantry on their way up had arrived, or sent to inquire whether that was not Lord Raglan's intention.*[335]

Considering his place in the military hierarchy, Lucan had the rank to overrule Nolan and seek direct confirmation from Raglan if he had sufficient cause. And so, having personally put the order into effect, he clearly bore some responsibility for it, given his position of authority. Nevertheless, in spite of his unpopularity both at home and in the Army of the East, many felt that Lucan was being used as a scapegoat.

Shocked and angry at his abrupt recall, Lucan sailed for England determined to clear his name. Unlike the hero's reception that Cardigan had received, his welcome was decidedly muted. On 3 March 1855, the day after his arrival, he sent his son to request a court martial from Horse Guards so that he could state his case before the army. This was refused, as was his renewed insistence when on 5 March he learned of the contents of Raglan's covering letter.[336] There had already been criticism of his actions in the press and Anthony Bacon, an officer who bore him ill will, even published a pamphlet that damned him as an antiquated and inefficient officer. The pamphlet also questioned his personal courage, suggesting that he should have led the charge in person.

Though friends and relations urged restraint, Lucan felt unable to let the matter lie, and challenged his detractors. He wrote a pamphlet of his own, entitled 'A Vindication of the Earl of Lucan from Lord Raglan's Reflections'. He also sent several letters to *The Times* proclaiming his innocence and refuting allegations made against him. When his letter to Newcastle was finally published verbatim in *The Times* it revealed that Raglan's written instructions were rather ambiguous and not the kind of dispatch required by an officer under pressure on the battlefield. The Duke of Wellington would probably have been appalled at the way in which it had been phrased, having always made great efforts to ensure his orders were clear and concise. Yet Lucan also revealed that the manner in which they were delivered was suspect:

> *After carefully reading this order I hesitated, and urged the uselessness of such an attack and the dangers attending it. The aide-de-camp, in a most authoritative tone, stated that they were Lord Raglan's orders that the cavalry should attack immediately. I asked him, 'Where, and what to do?' as neither enemy nor guns were within sight. He replied, in a most disrespectful but significant manner, pointing to the further end of the valley, 'There, my Lord, is your enemy; there are your guns.'*[337]

According to Lucan, Nolan had pointed straight down the North Valley, clearly indicating the Don Cossack Battery as their objective. His tone of delivery had been imperious to the point of insubordination. This is the key account of what passed between Lucan and Nolan, and only Lucan and John Blunt (Lucan's interpreter and Turkish expert) heard the entire conversation. Blunt confirmed that Nolan spoke in a vehement manner towards Lucan and was surprised that Lucan did not place him under arrest.[338] Whether Raglan's written instructions were unclear or not was now a separate issue. Lucan had requested clarification from an aide-de-camp who gave instructions that were not actually in the written order. Furthermore, Nolan allegedly insisted that the order was urgent and had to be carried out straight away. Although Lucan realized that such an attack would be fired upon from both flanks as well as in front and was likely to suffer heavy losses, he felt obliged to obey a direct order: 'Having decided, against my conviction, to make the movement, I did all in my power to render it as little perilous as possible.'[339]

Raglan later claimed that some animosity existed between Lucan and Nolan, commenting: 'I have heard that there was some bad feeling between Captain Nolan and Lord Lucan, and that the former entertained it on account of the latter having spoken disparagingly of the horses he had purchased in Syria.'[340] Lucan later denied this, but acknowledged that he had publicly expressed strong views about Nolan's Syrian horses. Following Nolan's death Lucan became aware that Nolan had made disparaging remarks about his leadership, but insisted that he hardly knew him and that any resentment that existed was entirely one-sided.[341] However, Lucan stated, 'I altogether deny that I was influenced by anything said or done by that aide-de-camp . . . To impute to me that I allowed my feelings or temper to influence my conduct is not doing me justice.'[342] From this it appears that Lucan, though objecting to the manner in which the message was delivered, placed the blame squarely upon Lord Raglan.

In January, Mr H Berkeley MP, representing Bristol, requested that papers relating to the charge be laid before the House and asked whether there would be an inquiry 'on the subject of the melancholy disaster which occurred at the battle of Balaklava'.[343] This was postponed on the grounds that the government possessed insufficient information to make a decision at that time. Lucan raised the issue three times in the House of Lords, defending his own position. His utter refusal to let the matter rest testified to his sincerity in his cause. Had he believed himself to be even partly at fault it is likely that he would have quietly accepted the situation, as the army wished. He believed that a court martial would have exonerated him and stated his case at great length. In his opinion the Fourth Order was 'a fresh order, quite independent of any previous order, and having no connection with No. 3 or any other order'.[344] Furthermore, he believed that Cathcart had no instructions to act in conjunction with his command and that 'It is generally admitted that, had I disobeyed this order, I should have been held responsible for the loss of the guns, which it was erroneously believed were being removed.'[345]

A number of members rose in reply to Lucan's speeches, including both Viscount Hardinge and the Duke of Newcastle. They pointed out that there was no legal precedent for Lucan to request a court martial and that his allegations undermined a superior officer in time of war: 'any military man acting under a Commander in Chief placed himself in an improper position by volunteering a controversy of that description.'[346] Although his use of the House of Lords to express his grievances was considered highly irregular, Lucan gained a largely sympathetic hearing. Some members, regardless of whether they held him accountable or not, thought that he had been denied a fair chance to defend or explain his actions.

Contrary to popular opinion, Lucan was a competent solider who led from the front, shared in the privations of his men to some extent and was diligent regarding his duties almost to the point of obsession. His inability to get along with Lord Raglan and unfortunate association with his volatile brother-in-law have led many to think too harshly of him, though it is notable that some officers like Campbell, who placed more value in competence than affability, thought highly of him. Yet he was also a bitter man and resentful for having taken the blame for Raglan's persistent caution regarding the cavalry. Although his commander's desire to preserve his mounted arm was a sound strategy, Lucan's reputation suffered because of it and, smarting under such criticism, he may have acted in haste when finally ordered to attack. While he may have been victimized by the establishment to conceal greater failings in the system, of the three individuals concerned he bears the greatest share of responsibility for the Charge of the Light Brigade.

Others rallied to Nolan's defence and his supposed culpability was hotly debated within the army. One former comrade of Nolan wrote to *The Times*:

> *Sir, - I am sure you will not allow the serious imputation of giving a false order to tarnish the memory of a most devoted and chivalrous officer. I have known Captain Nolan from our earliest years, and I know that his ideas of discipline and passive obedience to superiors... were carried to perhaps an extreme point... he was by no means rash or inclined to act on the inspiration of a momentary enthusiasm . . .*[347]

The writer went on to say that he could not believe Nolan responsible for the accusations made against him and made an impassioned plea for the public to suspend their judgement until the full facts were known.

So opinion was deeply divided. Seizing upon such a scandalous tale, the newspapers discussed the issue of accountability at great length. While Lucan's comments were widely reported, they did not go unquestioned, and the loss of life provoked harsh condemnation of whoever did bear responsibility: 'Never was more wilful murder committed than in ordering an advance against such fearful odds and certain destruction.' The *Morning Chronicle* continued that while many considered Nolan at fault, 'what baffles the understanding is, in what respect Captain Nolan, whose position was merely that of an aide-de-camp, should thus have proved the unwitting instrument of the light brigade's destruction.'[348] It went on to emphasize that a senior officer like Lucan must have had the benefit of a written order and should have possessed sufficient self-command to act on his own initiative regardless of what an aide had said.

The *Daily News* was even more forthright. At first it remarked sarcastically that no one was willing to take responsibility for the order and that blame was being levelled at a dead man, 'who, if living, would be tried by court-martial. But as this officer fell in the attack, of course he cannot be tried, and there is no means of unravelling the mystery'.[349] As more information came in, they published a report by their special correspondent who had interviewed members of the Light Brigade in the Crimea. Wild tales and rumours abounded, some even claiming that Nolan ignored Lucan and gave the order to Cardigan. Others claimed that Louis had referred to 'our guns' rather than 'the guns' in his explanation of the order. Yet the majority roundly damned him and their correspondent considered many of their elaborate tales entirely discreditable:

> *I cannot help remembering that Captain Nolan was one of our most distinguished cavalry officers – a man who . . . had acquired a thorough knowledge of his arm, and who, more than any one else, was able to make a fair estimate of its capabilities. He was not a mere routine soldier . . . he had also been a deep thinker on his profession, and he was the author of one of the best books on cavalry service. To lead cavalry, unsupported by foot, through a cross-fire of two batteries, in order to cut down the support and the gunners of the third, is so adventurous and unmilitary a proceeding that Captain Nolan is the last man whom I can believe to have been capable of so much thoughtlessness and folly.*[350]

Many in the press agreed that Nolan was only a messenger and, having no personal authority over Lucan, did not have the influence that some sought to imply. If Lucan had disagreed so strongly with the aide's explanation, they asked, surely he was at liberty to enquire further over such a serious matter?

Nevertheless, the establishment was unwilling to pursue the matter and events in the Crimea soon overshadowed the debate. Reports about the way the war was being fought and the terrible conditions attending it provoked scandal in Great Britain. Many of these originated from Russell's dispatches, who wrote disturbing accounts for *The Times* alleging gross mismanagement. On 18 June 1855, a major Allied infantry assault took place against Sevastopol. Despite the incredible pounding the city had received from the Allied guns over the preceding months, the Russians managed to repulse the attack, inflicting severe losses. Ailing from cholera and weakened by the burdens of command, Lord Raglan died ten days later.

Although Sevastopol was eventually stormed again and the Allies destroyed the dry docks and other naval facilities, the Russians clung tenaciously to the northern side of the city, which was well protected by the dividing harbour and the strong fortifications there. The victory was therefore only partial, and the war in the Crimea became a stalemate. Ultimately it was the far less famous actions in the Baltic that in 1856 persuaded the Tsar to seek a negotiated peace. While the Allies had achieved their war aims and could justifiably claim a victory, they paid a heavy price: thousands of lives had been lost and the war had cost a vast amount of money. Many foreign observers judged that the British Army had given a poor performance in the Crimea; the damage to the army's reputation was one of the reasons that Indian troops felt confident enough to rebel in the Indian Mutiny of 1857, which came close to provoking a national uprising and wresting control of the Indian subcontinent from the British. Russia's reputation suffered even more. The performance of its high command had been inferior even to that of the Allies and the war proved that its armed forces were incapable of matching a modern army despite their numbers. Only Turkey had any cause to celebrate the Allied victory, with the temporary reduction of Russian power in the Black Sea region and the frustration of her imperial ambitions. In the final analysis, few of the European powers concerned were satisfied with the outcome of the war.

Public concern about the war led to the 'Commission of Inquiry into the Supplies of the British Army in the Crimea', held under Colonel Alexander Tulloch and Sir John McNeill. With the severe winter conditions, malnutrition, rampant disease and lack of supplies that the soldiers had to endure, even the horrors of the North Valley paled in comparison. The commission's findings provoked a storm of controversy with both Airey's and Filder's conduct called into question.[351] Allegations of incompetence were also levelled against Lucan and Cardigan amongst others, with elements in the press openly calling for their dismissal. Losses sustained in battle were one thing, but the avoidable deaths and unnecessary suffering of both men and horses in the Cavalry Division that winter were quite another. Both angrily defended their actions and were eventually exonerated by a Board of General Officers convened at Chelsea to look into the commission's findings. In fact nobody was really held accountable for anything, with supply problems largely blamed on the initial lack of resources before the war. Nicknamed 'The

Whitewashing Board', its judgement was questioned in many quarters, since the commissariat in particular had not been fit for purpose. However, the British Army learned many lessons from this war and, while its reputation had suffered, many reforms were agreed and quietly put into practice over the following years.

Meanwhile the Charge of the Light Brigade became one of the most celebrated incidents of the war. It may have been a terrible mistake, but newspaper articles and Alfred Lord Tennyson's famous poem in particular, emphasized the heroism displayed in the charge above all else. Though it had achieved very little in military terms, the courage displayed by all concerned was undoubted and the image of a magnificent and glorious tragedy ensured its fame. In a war notable for appalling conditions attended with great loss of life, many saw it as one of the few high points in an increasingly grim conflict. The controversy over the errors that caused the action lent it even more appeal to a public tired of reading about supply problems and human suffering. The debate over Nolan's responsibility continued and his image became one of a tragic anti-hero whose true intentions were obscure. In the immediate aftermath of the charge, the Light Brigade mourned the loss of comrades and many were despondent over the futility of a costly action that to them had achieved nothing. Glorified accounts of the charge in the newspapers sent to the Crimea puzzled them and, on their return to Britain, many were astounded at the extent of the public reaction to their feat. The men who had charged into the North Valley came to symbolize the very epitome of courage to the Victorian public and even those who had taken part came to view the incident in a different light.

Alexander Kinglake spoke with or wrote to many participants whilst writing his monumental work on the Crimean War. He was particularly intrigued by the Charge of the Light Brigade and the circumstances that brought it about, engaging in lengthy correspondence with many of those involved and with Lord Cardigan in particular. His presence during the early part of the campaign and unrivalled access to eyewitnesses ensures that his eight volume work is still considered one of the definitive accounts of the war up to the death of Lord Raglan, and his views had a considerable effect on contemporary opinion.

The view that Kinglake formed of Nolan was that of a committed soldier who suffered from an intense belief in the effectiveness of cavalry, 'an enthusiast unchilled and unshaken. His faith was that miracles of war could be wrought by squadrons of horse . . . if only it could be properly constituted and properly led'.[352] Gaining access to Nolan's journal, he deemed it the work of a highly impatient individual that revealed the writer's belief that Lucan was responsible for the allegedly poor performance of the cavalry during the early campaign.[353] Although Kinglake viewed Nolan as a near fanatic, his opinions over his part in the lead-up to the charge were surprisingly charitable.

Kinglake considered the Third and Fourth Orders to be fairly comprehensible, especially since the Fourth contained the directive to 'prevent the Enemy carrying away the guns'. Out of all those present, Lucan should have been aware of which guns Raglan intended him to advance upon because he had witnessed their capture and positioned his cavalry with a view to attack the heights following the Third Order. The fact that the first three redoubts were out of the line of sight from his position did not detract from this as, having defended it for the last few weeks, he must have been very familiar with it. The historian also considered Nolan to be fully aware of the strategic layout of the battlefield, at least from Raglan's position, and that any misunderstanding was unlikely to have been on Lucan's part.

As far as the altercation with Lucan was concerned, he allowed that Nolan may have been guilty of using too harsh a tone when speaking to a divisional commander but that this was definitely out of character: 'Nolan was a man who had gathered in Continental service the habit of such extreme and such rigid deference to any general officer, that his comrades imagined him to be the very last man who in that point would ever prove wanting.'[354] His excitement at the prospect of action and possible impatience with a man he viewed as incompetent may have led him to lose his temper. One important point is that the Fourth Order was essentially a reiteration of the Third Order, which Lucan had failed to put into effect. When he hesitated to obey what was almost a clarification of a previous order, the suggestion that Nolan may have given a heated response seems credible.

Yet it was Kinglake's view on Nolan's final act that was most important. His conversations with Lord Cardigan on the subject were revealing. On first seeing Nolan ride out in front of him, Cardigan had assumed that 'Capt. Nolan came in front of the Brigade with a view as it appeared of hurrying it on.'[355] At the time he had been extremely angry, his first words after the charge being a complaint about Nolan's conduct:

> *I rode slowly up the hill, and met General Scarlett. I said to him, 'What do you think, General, of the aide-de-camp, after such an order being brought to us which has destroyed the Light Brigade, riding to the rear*

and screaming like a woman?' Sir J. Scarlett replied, 'Do not say any more, for I have ridden over his body.'[356]

After some reflection Cardigan changed his view and agreed that in all likelihood, seeing the brigade was heading in the wrong direction, Nolan had ridden out to warn him. The course he took towards the Causeway seemed to reinforce this view and he probably died in the act of shouting that this was the direction they should be taking. He had been killed in the very act of trying to correct the mistake which he saw unfolding before him, and in Kinglake's view, 'I have no reason for supposing that Nolan had the least idea of the mistake which was about to be perpetrated until he saw the brigade begin to advance *without having first changed front*. After that . . . he did not lose a moment in his efforts to rescue the brigade from the error into which he saw it falling.'[357]

Considering the origin of the Fourth Order, many said from the outset that Lord Raglan must accept at least part of the blame for setting the Light Brigade on their fatal course. Although the order is actually signed by Airey, he cannot be held accountable as it was his duty to write down Raglan's instructions verbatim. The meaning of the Fourth Order has been debated endlessly ever since the day it was written. Significantly, it requests that Lucan should advance yet fails to mention the word 'attack'. Its key phrase is 'try to prevent the enemy carrying away the guns'. Although this seems clear enough, there were three artillery concentrations in the vicinity and it may have been clearer had Raglan substituted the words 'our guns' instead. However, the assumption that Lucan would compare this with the Third Order was not an unreasonable one, and Lucan should therefore have known which guns Raglan meant. In fairness, from his position Lucan could not see the guns referred to nor any guns on the move, but it is difficult to accept how he found this confusing unless he was led astray by what Nolan may have said. Nevertheless, the guns of the Don Cossack Battery, while directly to his front in conformity with the Fourth Order, were certainly not being removed at this time, which begs the question as to why he believed that these were the target. Although the Fourth Order may seem unclear to modern eyes, it is notable that not all Lucan's contemporaries (for example Kinglake and Calthorpe) considered it so.

To the author's mind what Raglan actually intended was a threatening advance against the redoubts rather than a fully fledged attack. Although he does not mention the intended route in the Fourth Order, Raglan probably left this to Lucan's discretion, and it was logical that the cavalry would advance through the South Valley, directly along the Causeway or by both routes. He hoped that the Russians were wavering: a display of aggression may have speeded them on their way. Events proved that this was not the case but, even taking this into account, the presence of cavalry in the area would certainly have discouraged the enemy from trying to take away the guns. Although horse artillery was capable of moving at some speed, the guns in the redoubts were cumbersome, being of heavy calibre and not intended for rapid movement. A team of artillerymen dragging them would be unlikely to outrun cavalry.

In addition, cavalry could take guns but not hold them. Raglan would have been aware that infantry were needed to hold and defend the guns but evidently wished the cavalry to initiate the affair before they could be moved. They could have done this without actually charging the redoubts. Limited attacks, aimed more at harassment than being pressed home, would have prevented the guns being carried off and induced the infantry to form squares or seek shelter in the redoubts. If this could be carried out successfully it would certainly prepare the ground for an infantry assault that could regain the heights.

The forest on the Sapouné escarpment today makes it extremely difficult to stand at or see from Raglan's exact position, but slightly further along the ridge it is evident that the Causeway looks almost flat from this altitude and distance. It is quite possible that Raglan *assumed* that Lucan would be able to see the Russian-occupied redoubts from his viewpoint below. In 1855 an officer of the militia and two companions wished to see the site of the famous charge and were quite surprised at the nondescript appearance of the location: 'Well, look yonder,' said one, 'at that rising ground; it was there the Russians were posted.' 'I thought it had been on a hill or mountainside,' said another. 'Just what you see; little better than an inclined plain of easy ascent.'[358] However, from Lucan's position, the Causeway is certainly high enough to obscure the first three redoubts from direct view.

If Raglan had taken it for granted that Lucan could see along the Causeway from his position, it was a regrettable oversight, but considering that Lucan had been guarding the area for weeks, and given the contents of the Third Order, it was natural for Raglan to assume that he knew exactly which guns were meant. Furthermore, it is very surprising that Lucan had not made an adequate reconnaissance. The target may have been out of his line of sight but his failure to send out scouts to keep himself informed was a serious omission for a cavalry commander. It is notable that this requirement was also overlooked by both Scarlett and Ryzhov earlier that day, unless one regards Ryzhov's first cavalry advance as a reconnaissance in force.

In the final analysis, Kinglake conceded that Nolan may have been sufficiently angered at Lucan's response and querying of Raglan's order to have spoken out of turn. If this was true, it was serious enough, since Lucan's resulting indignation may have clouded his judgement. However, Kinglake considered it highly improbable that Nolan misunderstood Raglan's instructions, mistook the Don Cossack Battery for the true objective or deliberately indicated the wrong target. Acknowledging that accusations continued to be made against him, he commented on the remarks of an unnamed Guards officer who suggested that Nolan's demise made him a convenient scapegoat. He was not the only one to think so: Lieutenant Seager believed that 'Lord Raglan is very angry, he says he did not order us to go through such a fire, but the man who carried the message from him to Lord Lucan – Captain Nolan – is killed, so I suppose the blame will be laid to his account.'[359] Written the day after the charge, this prophetic remark proved all too true.

Chapter 11

Nolan's Legacy

The Charge of the Light Brigade may not have seen the last of the Brudenells but it was the end of Nolan's line. Although his mother survived him, Louis was the last male member of the family and only she was left to mourn him. However, many friends expressed their heartfelt sorrow at Louis's untimely death and obituaries appeared in several newspapers and periodicals. The *Gentleman's Magazine* printed a summary of his life and achievements, remarking on his varied service, his writing and the remount mission to Syria. As far as the furore about the Light Brigade was concerned it commented: 'The error, however, was not his, for the order was a written one,' and concluded, 'Captain Nolan has left a widowed mother, who had already lost two sons in the service, to mourn the early fall of the last, who was her only pride and hope.'[360]

The *Illustrated London News* printed a lengthy obituary and included a portrait derived from a painting of Louis made in India, which became the most famous image of him. The obituary recorded his service and mentioned his mastery of several Indian dialects in addition to his other languages, along with a brief reference to his sporting achievements in India. The writer recorded that they held his second book in high regard and that it had brought him to the attention of Horse Guards. Regarding the charge, they believed that 'the rash movement in question was so opposed to his own published theory on the subject, that he could never have willingly countenanced, much less directed it, even under an excess of zeal.'[361] In support of this, they included a quotation from his work outlining his warning that charges should never be made against masses of troops unless previously weakened by fire.

Many newspapers carried some kind of brief record of Nolan's life, but the *Annual Register for 1854* printed half a page on his career, and expressed the view that 'Nolan was too good a soldier to have recommended a charge like that of our Light Brigade at Balaclava. His book is full of warnings against such rash enterprises'.[362] However, it did comment that the surprising success of the charge, when the brigade should have been cut to pieces, seemed to support Nolan's claims that cavalry could achieve great things.[363]

In the military, a number of Nolan's friends and acquaintances paid to have a marble plaque erected to his memory on the wall of Holy Trinity Church in Maidstone, close to where the cavalry depot officers usually sat. General Berkeley and General Airey both contributed to this fund, along with Colonel Key and many of Nolan's fellow officers in the 15th Hussars. It stated that 'his brother officers and other friends have erected this tablet as a slight tribute of their esteem and affectionate regard for the memory of one of the most gallant, intelligent and energetic officers in Her Majesty's Service.'[364] He was also honoured by the Army and Navy Club in London along with ten other members who had fallen in the charge.[365] These were hardly the acts of men who believed Nolan guilty of offence.

Louis bequeathed most of his possessions to Colonel Key. His will had been witnessed by John Thompson of the 10th Hussars and Lieutenant Chapman RN and Lieutenant Stope RA aboard the steamship *Trent* as they sailed back from Syria. Though it appeared to disinherit his mother, the will contained the codicil: 'Should my estate take place previous to that of my mother I make it my last request to my mother that she should make her will in conformity with this one.'[366] Louis probably believed that Eliza would predecease him, but in fact she outlived him by many years. However, a document of this kind can only tell a historian so much. It is possible that he had made some kind of informal agreement with Key that he would look after his mother in the event of his death; the reason for Nolan not making his mother a beneficiary remains obscure.

Louis bequeathed the houses in London, his interests in the Adelphi Estate in Tobago and the property in Canada to Key along with any miscellaneous goods and sums of money. He also left him 'the Copyright of a book called "Cavalry its History and Tactics" published by Bosworth'.[367] The copyright for *The Training of Cavalry Remount Horses* he left to Lennox Berkeley, a fellow staff officer in India and one of his companions and supporters during his horse-racing days at Madras.

Since Louis had been Eliza's only real means of support, she applied for a pension as an army widow, worth £50 per annum. The large number of casualties in the Crimea had led to a royal warrant being issued in 1855, granting gratuities to officers who had fallen there. Eliza eventually received the value of Louis's staff commission, which came to £3,306 18 shillings and sixpence. When she died on 17 July 1870 she had reached the grand age of 92, living out the final years of her life in Bruges. She still owned the Bloomsbury houses and land in Scotland, leaving property to the value of around £4,000 in her will. She did not make it in conformity with Louis's wishes but left Colonel

Key a likeness of her son and his Balaklava medal, which he had received posthumously.[368]

The years failed to diminish the fame of the charge and the acclamation of its spectacular heroism grew. Veterans met at an annual dinner held by the Balaclava Commemoration Society, and in 1875 the *London Illustrated News* showed these stalwarts on its front cover, raising a toast to their fallen comrades at a banquet held at Alexandra Palace. The Balaclava Festival was held in conjunction with that event, including an exhibition in the Central Hall. The prominent exhibit was an obelisk: 'The Principal object in this trophy was the colossal figure of Honour standing on a pedestal, at the base of which were relics of the engagement'.[369] Bedecked with standards, the names of several officers were inscribed upon the plinth, including those of Winter, Charteris, Goad, Lockwood, Oldham and Webb. Central among these in a much larger type size was the name Nolan.[370] Although the recollections of some of the veterans were printed, little was said about Nolan, though it is unlikely that his name would have been given such prominence without their approval.

Nolan's true legacy, or at least the most enduring memory that he left behind him, had nothing to do with the valuable work he had carried out or the influence he had on his profession. The events during his last few moments and their consequences overshadowed everything he had achieved in an eventful life, and the argument over whether he bore the blame for the Charge of the Light Brigade started immediately after the event and continues unabated 150 years later. During this time new evidence has emerged periodically and the fame of the incident encouraged participants to write memoirs, many of which expressed opinions on who had caused the action. Writers, journalists and historians have all contributed to the debate, and many theories have emerged over the years.

It seems that Raglan was certainly guilty of making assumptions. His orders were poorly phrased and certainly not the kind of simple messages required by men acting under the stress. His famous good manners prevented him from delivering the terse, stern commands that Wellington would have uttered in his place. But in many ways, the Fourth Order was a clarification of the Third – and in any case his aide was there to confirm his intentions. Although Raglan's words to Nolan are unknown, as an experienced aide it is likely that Nolan knew exactly what Raglan intended, having been present with the staff for most of the morning, watching the battle from a grandstand position. As their full conversation remains a mystery, whether Nolan had been confused by Raglan's remarks or not remains a matter for speculation. Ultimately, Raglan had failed to issue precise instructions but his intentions should have been clear to those concerned in carrying out the order. He certainly contributed to the error indirectly but was not the only one at fault.

The argument that Nolan had misrepresented the order to Lucan or had misunderstood his own instructions largely relies on rumours about Nolan being an impatient, irascible man, prone to fits of temper. What is known of Nolan's life prior to the charge seems totally at odds with this image of his personality. Firstly, Nolan was an experienced, highly professional horseman. Horses simply do not react well to excitable, angry or impatient riders, and if they sense that something is wrong they can be provoked to aggression. It is important to remember that Nolan's exhortation to use kind and gentle methods above all else in handling horses was at the core of his theories on horsemanship. The fact that he was an exceptionally gifted horseman tends to imply that he was anything but a headstrong and impulsive man.

Louis may have assumed that Lucan knew which guns he meant and may not have meant his gesture to be taken literally. He knew that Lucan must have been well acquainted with the territory and believed that, as a repeated instruction, following on from the Third Order containing the key words 'recover the heights', Lucan must have realized it could only mean the guns in the redoubts. However, it is always dangerous to make assumptions: the only guns Lucan could actually see from his position were the Don Cossack Battery directly down the valley. On this basis it has even been surmised that Lucan may have thought the guns had already been removed and that Nolan was pointing in the direction in which they were being taken.

That the altercation became heated between them is easy to imagine. Lucan was very conscious of the fact that he had lost face within the Army of the East over the preceding weeks and hardly wished to damage his reputation even further. Aware of Raglan's orders to act defensively and preserve the slowly dwindling cavalry division, he was understandably reluctant to take risks; but at the same time was determined to fulfil his duties. He was a man weighed down by the responsibilities of command and, as one of the strictest disciplinarians in the army, highly unlikely to tolerate insubordination from a junior officer under any circumstances.

From Nolan's point of view here was a man whom he believed elevated beyond his abilities by his social standing and wealth. Although the previous charge by the Heavy Brigade had been well executed he must have been mortified by Cardigan's inaction when a well-timed charge might have turned a success into a devastating tactical victory. After all, Lucan had had time to ride to the Light Brigade and order them to attack if he had been aware of the opportunity. Lucan's calm demeanour when another chance was slipping away may have enraged Nolan, flushed from a hard ride, into speaking hastily and disrespectfully. He must have known the contents of the Third Order and, read in conjunction with each other, their intent seems plain enough. It is easy to picture him flinging out an arm to indicate without really looking. Standing at the approximate position of the Light Brigade today where Lucan received the Fourth Order, it does appear to be a matter of a mere twenty degrees angle of difference when one points at the Causeway Redoubts or the likely position of the Don Cossack Battery. This is just as Kinglake claimed[371] and if it was a matter of judging the error on Lucan's interpretation of Nolan's gesture alone, the decision to charge the wrong guns is not as foolish as it first appears.

Allegations have also arisen that during their brief conversation before the charge, Nolan accused both Cardigan and his brigade of cowardice after the brigadier confided in him that he was reluctant to carry out his orders. As far as eyewitnesses are concerned, both Loy Smith and Wightman, despite being too far away to hear what was said, record a conversation taking place. However, several secondary accounts record Cardigan, enraged by Nolan's taunts, roaring, 'By God! . . . If I come through this alive, I'll have you court-martialled for speaking to me in that manner!'[372] This account seems highly improbable. There is no hint of Nolan being openly insubordinate or disrespectful to authority up to 25 October. It is true that he may have voiced his concerns about his superiors in private but this had not manifested itself in an open contempt for authority until, allegedly, his conversation with Lucan. Most of his contemporaries believed quite the opposite, writing that he showed considerable deference to his senior officers. Even allowing for his supposed anger at the Light Brigade's earlier inaction, his altercation with Lucan and dislike for Cardigan, this seems out of character. For a career-driven man, he would also have been aware that such a wild accusation could only harm his prospects.

This account also fails to fit with Cardigan's reputation. In Victorian times any officer admitting to feeling afraid would be looked down upon, and, as one of the vainest officers in the army, Cardigan is unlikely to have confessed to this even if it were so, and certainly not to a subordinate he hardly knew. The fact that Cardigan's allegedly loud and furious response apparently passed without being remarked upon by other witnesses – and Cardigan's failure to mention such an outrageous allegation himself – are enough to raise serious doubt over Nolan making such comments. The allegation is probably the result of malicious gossip; it is far more likely that, during his brief talk with Cardigan, Nolan merely requested permission to join the brigade for the action.

Recently the idea that Nolan deliberately set the Light Brigade on its course has gained credence. Adkin is one supporter of this theory: he believes that a combination of anger and frustration with Lucan, along with a burning desire to prove his own theories, drove him to intentionally set the Light Brigade against the wrong target.[373] The foundation for this is a belief that Nolan's contempt for Lucan and his excitement on the verge of going into action had got the better of him. Yet there is very little hard evidence to support this theory. Several contemporaries, including Russell, Calthorpe and Paget, believed that he was indeed to blame for the disaster, but through misadventure rather than malicious intent.

One factor against Nolan was his unpopularity in some quarters, partly deriving from natural resentment at staff privileges. His supposedly opinionated manner alienated some, and the fact that he both knew his subject and had written successful books on it aroused jealousy, as Paget's remarks reveal: 'There is, or rather was, an officer named Captain Nolan, who writes books, and was a great man in his own estimation, and who had already been talking very loud against the cavalry, his own branch of the service, and especially Lucan.'[374] He went on to refer to him as a man known for his bravery but also for being headstrong and potentially reckless. Bemoaning the fact that Calthorpe should have been sent in his stead, he referred to him as 'the madman who was the chief cause of the whole'.[375] However, he blamed Lucan to an extent, saying that he should have dealt with Nolan in a more professional manner, and considered him negligent in not sending out scouts. The pair's unfortunate history had exacerbated the affair, he conceded, as did the antagonism between Lucan and Cardigan.[376] Since Paget had undoubtedly proved himself a hero during the charge, his views were respected.

The idea that Nolan thought there was something to gain by launching an attack against such overwhelming odds seems discreditable and is partly based on judging the stunning performance of the light cavalry after the event. With the benefit of hindsight, the Light Brigade did extremely well even to reach the guns, let alone what they accomplished afterwards. Most military men would have predicted the near annihilation of the brigade; in fact they sustained 'only' 40 per cent losses. An attempt to threaten, or even to take the Causeway Redoubts, was a hazardous undertaking; to have accomplished it successfully would have promised sufficient glory, assuming this was Nolan's aim. It has been suggested that the broken and sloping ground of the Causeway would have severely hampered the cavalry's ability to manoeuvre making even Raglan's actual intention a dangerous order.[377] However, a look at the Causeway Heights today, along with Fenton's photograph of the scene, confirms that they were accessible by cavalry, if imperfect ground for horses. The earth redoubts were also relatively poor structures, which earlier in the day the Russians had been able to take with relative ease – though admittedly with a force of combined arms – as they had galloped over this low ridge during their earlier manoeuvres; and there was always the possibility of advancing directly along the road or along the South Valley during an attack.

This charge against seemingly insurmountable odds stood more chance of making the cavalry looking ridiculous than demonstrating their worth as the superlative military force. At the very least such a foolhardy attack would result in heavy losses and the brigade was likely to be repelled by cannon fire long before they reached the enemy. After the fact, it is difficult to imagine a better demonstration of how vulnerable cavalry were to modern small arms and artillery than the charge. Had Nolan intended to set the brigade on such a hazardous course, it would have revealed in him a remarkably callous mind, given the near certainty of heavy casualties. Although there is no evidence that he entertained deeply held religious beliefs, he does not appear to have been an immoral man, and the idea that his sense of ambition extended to sacrificing hundreds of lives to prove a point is suspect. Even if this had been the case, the chances of getting away with such a reckless act were negligible and were certain to result in court martial and disgrace – an unlikely risk for an ambitious, career-minded officer to take.

Another reason for this theory gaining some credence is the view of his comrade Sergeant Henderson, who recalled:

> *I well remember how often I have heard him express his conviction that cavalry could accomplish almost anything, where it had a fair scope to act. ...putting a case hypothetically of cavalry charging artillery in a plain, Captain Nolan drew with a piece of chalk on the wall of the Quartermaster's store in Maidstone barracks a rough sketch which as nearly as possible represented the relative positions of the Russian artillery and the British light cavalry at the battle of Balaklava; the only thing he was not quite right in was the result. He assumed in such a case the certain capture of the guns. His glorious death at Balaklava prevented his being undeceived in this world.*[378]

Considering that Henderson was a close associate of Louis's and in no way unfriendly towards him, this account is probably reliable. Nevertheless, Nolan was expounding a theory here and, although it is tempting to draw an instant parallel with what happened years afterwards, it does not prove that he wished to put his hypothetical case into practice. Many an expert has expanded on what is theoretically possible but would hesitate to put such a theory to the test when lives were at stake. Henderson also mentions the qualifying remark 'where it had a fair scope to act'. This is relevant since the situation at Balaklava contrasts with what Louis put forward as good conditions for a cavalry attack, namely that a formed body of troops should be softened up by the fire of infantry or artillery and, in the case of artillery, advancing cavalry should advance in small, dispersed groups, preferably when the guns were being limbered up or were in the process of being deployed.

Furthermore, many officers and private soldiers had gained an entirely different impression of Nolan's conduct both in barracks and in the field. For example, General De Lacy Evans mentioned Nolan during his testimony to the Crimean Commission. Airey had been ill at the time, Colonel Gordon acting in his stead. De Lacy Evans distrusted Gordon and on 23 October was placed in an awkward position when commanded to take his 2nd Division down towards the Tchernaya to capture a Russian supply convoy of around 1,000 wagons. De Lacy Evans was unable to locate the convoy and indeed doubted its existence. Furthermore, the enemy were present in strength and he believed that well-positioned Russian batteries on the heights would be able to bring the fire of twenty guns against him if he advanced. After some debate with the aide who delivered the order he requested clarification and sent him back to Gordon to confirm Raglan's instructions. The aide returned with 'the slight qualification that I should exercise my discretion in the matter, and that I should do nothing against my own judgement'.[379] Evans then insisted on knowing the exact location of the convoy before moving:

> *I told Captain Nolan to go with another staff officer, examine the position, and return and tell me whether he did not think the British troops would be completely compromised by any such movement . . . Many attacks, which I cannot answer, have been made upon Captain Nolan for his conduct in another affair, but I must say that his reply to me on that occasion showed anything but imprudence and want of sense. He assured me, as I had myself anticipated, that if I moved the troops into the valley they would have been utterly compromised; and that fact*

induces me to hope that some of the statements made to his disadvantage regarding the affair at Balaklava are not altogether well founded.[380]

This statement was met with the cry of 'Hear, hear' from those listening in the gallery. De Lacy Evans's example bears a remarkable similarity to the position which Lucan faced only two days later over almost the same ground. It is very interesting to see how an infantry commander reacted to a situation directly comparable to what occurred only two days afterwards. The cavalry's main strength – their mobility – was both a blessing and a curse in this regard. Often required to make swift decisions, their speed theoretically allowed them to correct an error with similar rapidity. Although a much more versatile arm by this period, the infantry moved comparatively slowly: De Lacy Evans knew that once he was committed, it would take considerable time to withdraw and that he may even need assistance in extricating himself if faced with significant opposition. Had an infantry division advanced down the North Valley on 25 October they would have taken far longer to retreat than the Light Brigade.

De Lacy Evans's refusal to be hurried and his repeated requests for clarification are of even greater interest in comparison to later events. Far from reproaching him, Raglan advised him to act on his own discretion and, even after receiving two orders, he still insisted on further reconnaissance. When this confirmed that his suspicions were correct, he sent a response to Raglan stating that he was unable to comply without repercussions. Nolan's role in the affair is a remarkable coincidence and his collected demeanour and considered advice are very revealing. From an officer of great experience and considerable repute, the opinions of De Lacy Evans carry some weight.

One of the most intriguing angles on the Nolan myth is that he died in the very act of trying to avert the tragic mistake. This is a tempting hypothesis, since it fits with many interpretations of the facts. Dwelling over his altercation with Lucan he may have suddenly realized that his words had been misinterpreted, especially if he perceived that the Light Brigade were heading in the wrong direction. The theory can also be supported by the idea that, had he ordered the move intentionally, the enormity of what he had done suddenly dawned upon him and he hurried to put things right. Either way, considering that riding ahead was at the very least highly irregular for a man of his experience and knowledge, it is tempting to suppose that warning the brigade was his intention. However, there are some who dispute this.

Marching down with the 1st Division before the charge, Captain Higginson of the Grenadier Guards met Louis returning from an errand: 'the impression he gave me during the short conversation we held together, [was] that under the stress of some great excitement he had lost self-command'.[381] However, Nolan was pausing during an important mission and was doubtless eager to get back to the staff, possibly speaking in great haste. However, Calthorpe, in spite of their friendship, also believed that the excitement of going into action had got the better of him and that he 'galloped some way in front of the brigade, waving his sword and encouraging the men by voice and gesture'.[382] This led to the theory that, rather than trying to warn the brigade, Nolan was in a state of great excitement and, in common with other officers later in the charge, was trying to force the pace. Nonetheless, Calthorpe was too far away to see Nolan's final act and must have been reliant on hearsay or second-hand testimony. Considering that Nolan had been under fire on many occasions at the Bulganek, the Alma, Balaklava and while reconnoitring Sevastopol and during the defence of Balaklava, the idea that going into combat would have led him to lose control seems implausible. His repeated stress on the necessity of maintaining formation and discipline during cavalry manoeuvres also implies that he would not have broken formation without a very good reason.

Kinglake believed that Nolan died trying to warn the brigade, but Kelsey pointed out that Kinglake referred to only two sources for his theory. The officer who drew the diagram illustrating Nolan's final movements chose to remain anonymous, so his testimony is open to question. Also, Kinglake summarized Cardigan's change of heart over the incident, rather than quoting his views directly, and the Earl's death before publication meant that this remained unchallenged. Furthermore, Cardigan said nothing about Nolan riding diagonally across the front of the brigade, merely recording that he rode ahead. With some justice he stated that the romanticized view of Nolan dying in a desperate attempt to avert disaster should not be based on only two sources.[383]

Recently the journal for the Crimean War Research Society carried a fascinating series of articles debating this subject. Major Colin Robins mentioned that Kinglake wrote twelve years after the event and, biased in favour of Raglan, could be considered partisan.[384] In response, Douglas Austin pointed out that Woods mentioned similar theories in his *Campaign in the Crimea*, published in 1855, and in his *History of the War Against Russia*, published in 1857, E H Nolan (no relation) also thought that Louis had tried to alter the course of the charge. Furthermore, there were several primary sources such as Private Mitchell of the 13th Light Dragoons who saw Nolan struck before him, which clearly indicated that he had moved to the right from his initial position riding in front of the 17th Lancers.[385]

Several participants in the charge believed that Nolan's movement was involuntary and possibly caused by the fact that he had been hit. Lieutenant Maxse (Cardigan's ADC) and Private George Badger both claimed that Nolan's horse almost collided with them when it swerved and rode to the rear, which reveals how close they must have been and, because of their own positions, suggests that Nolan had remained to the front and centre of the brigade. Indeed, after reading Kinglake's theories, Maxse wrote that Nolan had been quite definite about their objective and that he had 'no recollection of Nolan having attempted to create a divergence either by deed or gesture'.[386] Such accounts had previously been used by John Harris, who also disbelieved the idea that Nolan was trying to warn the brigade.[387] Austin countered this with the testimony of Captain Soame Jenyns of the 13th Light Dragoons who saw Nolan killed right in front of his regiment; he suggested that Jenyns may even have been Kinglake's anonymous source. In addition Austin referred to another six sources in support of the theory that Nolan did indeed ride diagonally across the brigade, just as Kinglake had claimed.[388]

Corporal Nunnerley of the 17th Lancers strongly implied that Nolan died in the very act of trying to redirect the brigade:

After giving a kind of yell which sounded very much like 'Threes right,'
and throwing his sword hand above his head, his horse wheeled to the
right and he fell to the rear. As though obeying his death-like order, part
of the Squadron wheeled 'Threes right.' I immediately gave the order
'Front forward' and so brought them into line again.[389]

Corporal Morley, also of the 17th, supported this view, although Adkin believes that he may have formed his opinion after talking with Nunnerley and that both were writing some years after the event. Furthermore, he argues that they had misheard what was merely Nolan's death cry.[390] While it is possible that the noise and confusion of the firing were partly to blame and that the pair were stating what they *wanted* to believe, the similarity between the sound of the command and a scream of agony seems tenuous at best. Nevertheless, two veterans who rode in the charge both claimed to have heard Nolan trying to influence the direction of the brigade and it is difficult to wholly discredit such close eyewitness testimony.

However, Adkin makes the much more serious point that Nolan could not have realized they were heading in the wrong direction since the brigade had only advanced 200 metres.[391] This is partly supported by the fact that the Odessa Regiment on the Causeway had formed square, believing that the British cavalry were about to turn and attack their position. Although there is some substance to this, firstly Nolan was an acknowledged expert and may have guessed from the manner and direction of the advance that Cardigan intended to carry on straight down the valley rather than turn. Furthermore, had Cardigan intended to attack the Causeway he probably would have repositioned the Light Brigade to advance against it directly rather than moving into the valley before turning. This however does not alter the fact that had Nolan realized his words had been ambiguous, may have ridden ahead just to confirm that the order was being carried out correctly. Whether he rode straight forward or across the brigade, he could still have been trying to warn Cardigan that he was heading the wrong way, and by waving his sword and shouting he was certainly trying to attract attention, whatever his motives may have been. The incident is confused by conflicting evidence, but the likeliest supposition is that Nolan died trying to deliver a warning.

So was Nolan to blame for the tragedy that struck the Light Brigade? The case has certainly not been proven. In this writer's opinion, of the three leading suspects he deserves the smallest portion of the responsibility. The Charge of the Light Brigade was brought about by a combination of errors that started with Raglan and ended with Lucan. Raglan's ambiguously worded orders undoubtedly confused the matter, making him at least partially accountable. Nonetheless, as his written orders did not instruct Lucan to attack the Don Cossack Battery and, in the absence of conclusive evidence regarding his verbal instructions, he can only be held indirectly responsible.

In his role as Raglan's messenger, Nolan's actions can be interpreted in a number of different ways, but it is impossible to hold him solely accountable. There is only circumstantial evidence available to support the theory that he deliberately ordered the charge and it certainly appears highly implausible. It is largely reliant on quotations, often taken out of context, from his book on cavalry, Henderson's recollection of him expounding on a *theory* and assumptions over his state of mind. It is possible that he misunderstood the order but considering his previous good service on the staff this seems unlikely and, due to his death, this can never be firmly established.

If Nolan misled Lucan, it was almost certainly unintentional; whether he lost his temper during their brief conversation is open to debate. Perhaps the worst that can be said of him is that his sense of urgency, exacerbated by Raglan's final shouted command, led him to deliver a hasty and confusing message. It is possible that he failed to explain Raglan's orders adequately, but, according to the accounts available, he was not asked to go into great detail. By Lucan's own admission their conversation was brief and, since it appeared to have left Lucan dissatisfied, he should have sternly demanded an explanation in full, especially if Nolan had been impertinent. The idea that a Lieutenant General should indignantly ride off to put orders into effect, of which he had an imperfect understanding, because a junior officer had spoken harshly to him seems absurd. Lucan's reputation as a disciplinarian suggests that he would have reprimanded Nolan at the very least if his conduct had been improper and it is far more likely that he misinterpreted Nolan's words and gesture, emphasizing Nolan's supposed impertinence in mitigation for his own actions.

There is some evidence to support the theory that Nolan tried to divert the course of the Light Brigade on to its true objective, but not enough to make it a certainty. Although the opponents of this theory argue that it is adopted since it fits neatly with the circumstances, this can be countered by the fact that, had Nolan merely been the first man hit and his ride to the front was the act of his panicked horse, it must have been a remarkable coincidence. Circumstantial evidence seems to support the fact that he did try; the evidence of several eyewitnesses such as Morley, Nunnerley and Cardigan suggests that this is the most likely version of events.

The case against Lord Lucan, as the third suspect for responsibility over the charge, is far stronger. For him the idea of disobeying an order from a senior officer was anathema, and so, though bitterly disagreeing with the course of action he thought was being proposed, he still insisted on carrying it out. Yet he was in a position of considerable authority; blind obedience was not required of him. The testimony of De Lacy Evans recalling his own actions under remarkably similar circumstances reveals that Lucan had a number of options open to him, which he failed to use. His superior's instructions were ambiguous and it is possible that Nolan misled him, but he should have requested confirmation rather than adopt a course that he considered foolhardy. Looking at the written orders alone, he should have surmised Raglan's intent from the Third and Fourth Orders and acted accordingly, regardless of what Nolan told him.

The full truth of the matter will probably never be known, however. This is one of the reasons that this burning question of who was to blame still haunts people today almost as much as it did in the 1850s. The fact that the most famous cavalry charge in history occurred because of a mistake has always added an air of mystery to the question of accountability, and Nolan's alleged attempt to avert the disaster lends it dramatic appeal. To some he was a martyr whose convenient death was cynically used to cover up the mistakes of others. Some still believe that he threw his life and career away in a baffling and selfish gesture, though it is difficult to see what he hoped to achieve if this had been the case.

Nolan died young, at the age of 36. Looking over his eventful life, it is deeply unfortunate that his last few minutes came to dominate people's memory of him above all else. He had won a deserved reputation as a talented officer, rider and sportsman, gaining some popular renown. His writings on cavalry were justly celebrated and added to military thought, as did his methods of horsemanship and some of the suggestions and innovations he left behind him. His zeal had impressed many officers in India and in Maidstone and, had it not been for his untimely death, he would probably have added to his achievements. A book by Nolan on the cavalry's performance during the Crimean War would have been well worth reading.

During his career he had evidently worked extremely hard, and much that was said of him after 25 October 1854 was misleading or untrue. Though perhaps never fully accepted by the establishment, he was hardly the fanatic that some believed him to be and definitely not a wild, impetuous man prone to acts of recklessness. Admittedly his writing contained some controversial theories, but this was a very tame form of radicalism, merely asking for improvements to be made in an existing system. Earnest belief hardly equates with recklessness and lack of judgement, as some of his detractors would have us believe. Many supported his values and arguments, and his success in both the Austrian and the British armies speaks well of him. His acceptance onto the Austrian delegation to visit the young Queen Victoria was a firm endorsement, as were his two staff appointments. Furthermore, the trust conveyed in him with the mission to Syria would hardly have been bestowed upon an unreliable officer; on the contrary, it reveals that the establishment thought highly of him.

It is noticeable that most of those who considered him impetuous seemed to know him only slightly or were reliant on the views of others. The number of fellow officers and associates who thought him a level-headed and professional individual is far greater. This is shown in the fact that his brother officers made considerable efforts to commemorate his life and by a number of sympathetic obituaries and articles in the newspapers that spoke out on his behalf when he was no longer capable of defending himself.

Louis Nolan died a heroic death at Balaklava and was laid to rest in an unmarked grave in common with many of his fellow soldiers who fought in the

Crimea. Though he deserves to be remembered far more for his achievements during a full life, the controversy surrounding his final moments brought him not only notoriety but also a kind of immortality. There can be few men whose names have endured for so long because of the events of only a few minutes. Though his motives and the truth about the cause of the charge will always remain an enigma, perhaps he met a fate similar to that he would have wished for, as it is difficult to dispute the facts that he led a soldier's life and died a valiant death.

Notes

Chapter 1: A Family Tradition

1 Hubert Moyse-Bartlett, *Nolan of Balaclava* (London, Leo Cooper, 1975), p. 12.
2 Gwyn Harries-Jenkins, *The Army in Victorian Society* (London, Routledge & Kegan Paul, 1977), pp. 69–70. Considering that full pay was very low, half pay was a meagre amount of money intended as a kind of pension when an officer retired from active service. Promotion to general rank and above could not be purchased.
3 Philip J Haythornthwaite, *The Napoleonic Source Book* (London, Guild Publishing, 1990), p. 196. This practice was born out of long tradition: Charles I frequently granted such commissions to gentlemen who raised a large body of men to fight for the Crown during the Civil War. There is also evidence that the practice extends back to medieval times, before the existence of a full-time army establishment. See Harries-Jenkins, *The Army in Victorian Society*, p. 62.
4 Harries-Jenkins, *The Army in Victorian Society*, pp. 65–6.
5 Moyse-Bartlett, *Nolan of Balaclava*, p. 17.
6 Ibid., p. 23.
7 Ibid., p. 32.
8 Ibid., p. 41.
9 Robin Okey, *The Habsburg Monarchy c. 1765-1918* (London, Macmillan, 2001), p. 94.
10 Constantin de Grunwald, *Metternich* (London, Falcon Press, 1953), p. 276.

Chapter 2: Imperial Service

11 Moyse-Bartlett, *Nolan of Balaclava*, pp. 45–6.
12 Ibid., pp. 47–8. The regimental prefix of K.k. stood for *Kaiserlich-königlich*, which translates as Royal-Imperial. It was later changed to K.u.K. when the Habsburgs adopted the status of 'dual monarchy' over Austria-Hungary in the 1890s.
13 Ibid., p. 51. At this time staff officers, then under the command of the quartermaster general, were some of the few officers in the British Army likely to receive formal training at anything beyond regimental level.

14 Isabella Ackerl, 'Austria's Military Academy Founded by Maria Theresa', *Virtual Vienna Net*, http://www.virtualvienna.net/community, pp. 1–4. Most cadets were accepted between the ages of ten and twelve with the average course lasting around eight years. *Ex-propriis – Gemeine* were volunteers who wished to enlist not as private soldiers but with a view to becoming officers.

15 KT 4345, Grundbuch – Ludwig Eduard von Nolan.

16 F Loraine Petre, *Napoleon and the Archduke Charles* (London, Greenhill Books, 1991), p. 31.

17 Darko Pavlovic, *The Austrian Army 1836-66*, vol. 2: *Cavalry* (Oxford, Osprey, 1999), p. 3. Due to its multi-ethnic nature, the Imperial Army was divided into two branches, 'German' and 'Hungarian'. Kurassiers wore the distinctive breastplate (or cuirass) for protection in close combat and in common with Cheveauxlegers and Dragoons wore helmets and carried heavy swords. Cheveauxlegers were very similar to dragoons and the nearest thing that the German branch of the army had to light cavalry. They were classed in this fashion partly because of fears that the army might split along nationalist lines – which it came close to doing in the revolution of 1848. Cheveauxlegers wore the white uniforms that the Austrians were famous for, whereas Hussars had blue or green uniforms, much adorned with worsted cording and braiding, topped with a shako (a cylindrical felt hat) or a fur 'busby' rather than a helmet. They carried the lighter, slightly curved sabre rather than the straight swords of the heavy cavalryman. Light cavalrymen never wore even the limited armour that some heavy cavalry regiments affected in the form of breastplates that were fast becoming an anachronism on the modern battlefield.

18 Peter Newark, *Sabre & Lance* (Dorset, Blandford Press, 1987), p. 62.

19 A J P Taylor, *Europe: Grandeur and Decline* (London, Penguin Books, 1967), p. 127.

20 Alan Sked, *The Survival of the Habsburg Empire* (London, Longman, 1979), p. 2.

21 Ibid., pp. 7–8.

22 Ibid., p. 7.

23 Peter Evan Turnball, *Austria*, vol. 2 (London, 1840), pp. 292–93. Empress Maria Theresa decided that commissions would no longer be sold except for the two most junior ranks (2,000 florins for the infantry and 3,000 florins for the cavalry) of the cavalry and infantry. However, sums often changed hands unofficially in spite of this.

24 Gunther E Rothenberg, 'The Austrian Army in the Age of Metternich', *Journal of Modern History*, 40/2 (June 1968), pp. 155–65.

25 Sked, *Survival of the Habsburg Empire*, p. 9.

26 Ibid., p. 10.

27 Nowadays words like 'horsemastership' or 'horsemastery' are often used to define the equestrian arts of horse-breeding, raising, healthcare, maintaining fitness and breaking (training) of horses. Basically they are used to describe the host of tasks involved in the care and maintenance of horses as a form of animal husbandry. The word 'horsemanship' is sometimes taken to describe the ability to actually ride a horse alone. However, in spite of their common usage, these words do not appear in the current *Oxford English Dictionary*, so the author has decided to omit them in this study, using the term 'horsemanship' as an all-embracing term in preference.

28 Sked, *The Survival of the Habsburg Empire*, pp. 26–7.

29 Rothenberg, 'The Austrian Army in the Age of Metternich', pp. 155–65.

30 Sked, *The Survival of the Habsburg Empire*, p. 12.

31 Mark Boyd, *Reminiscences of Fifty Years* (London, Longmans, Green & Co, 1871), pp. 198–99. The Grand Duke was the emperor's brother and serving as the viceroy for the Austro-Italian states at this time. Another description of him that corresponds with Boyd's is contained in Germain Bapst's memoirs: 'He was a handsome fellow with large rather protruding blue eyes, a slightly receding chin, curly hair and a very neat fair moustache.' See Germain Bapst, *Le Marechal Canrobert: Souvenirs d'un Siècle*, vol. 2 (Paris, Librairie Plon, 1902), p. 319.

32 Sked, *The Survival of the Habsburg Empire*, pp. 14–15.

33 KT 593, Conduitteliste for Unterlietenant Ludwig Nollan 1835–1838.

34 Ibid.

35 Ibid.

36 Ibid.

37 Ibid.

38 Moyse-Bartlett, *Nolan of Balaclava*, pp. 62–4.

39 KT 593, Conduitteliste for Unterlietenant Ludwig Nollan 1835-1838.

40 Cecil Woodham-Smith, *Queen Victoria* (London, Hamish Hamilton, 1972), p. 150.

41 *The Times*, 10 July 1838, p. 5. This review included soldiers from the Royal Horse Artillery, Household Cavalry Brigade (Life Guards and Royal Horse Guards Blue), the First and Second Battalions of the Rifle Brigade,

Brigade of Foot Guards, detachments of the 10th Hussars and 12th Lancers (light cavalry) and several field batteries of artillery.

42 Sidney Lee, *Queen Victoria* (London, Smith, Elder & Co., 1904), pp. 87–8.

43 Ibid., p. 50.

44 *The Times*, 20 June 1838, p. 5.

45 Moyse-Bartlett, *Nolan of Balaclava*, pp. 56–7.

46 Stanley Weintraub, *Victoria: Biography of a Queen* (London, Unwin Hyman, 1987), p. 114.

47 Moyse-Bartlett, *Nolan of Balaclava*, p. 58.

48 Ibid., p. 60. It is remarkable that Babington had failed to stress Louis's abilities as a cavalry officer before this time. Perhaps he had despaired of getting one of his sons into the more prestigious branch of the service after so much effort and disappointment on behalf of his brothers.

49 KT5406, Oberst Ezvik to General Command of Hungary 1840.

Chapter 3: Home and Abroad

50 J M Russell, *The History of Maidstone* (London, Simpkin, Marshall & Co., 1881), p. 368.

51 The Marquess of Anglesey, *A History of the British Cavalry 1816 to 1919*, vol. 1: *1816–50* (London, Leo Cooper, 1973), p. 104.

52 Robert Henderson, *The Soldier of Three Queens*, vol. 2 (London, Saunders, Otley and Co., 1866), p. 190.

53 James Douet, *British Barracks 1600-1914* (London, The Stationery Office and English Heritage, 1998), p. 82.

54 Anglesey, *History of the British Cavalry*, pp. 101–02.

55 *The Queens Regulations and Orders for the Army, 1844* (London, 1855), p. 378.

56 Henderson, *Soldier of Three Queens*, p. 191. He continued that a soldier's prospects at Maidstone were better if he was well disciplined, dependable and caused no trouble rather than through any knowledge or skill displayed. Upon his application to join the army at the depot, the commandant guessed he was a former soldier and, when he confirmed this, was told that his experiences in Portugal and Spain would do him no good at Maidstone (Henderson, *Soldier of Three Queens*, p. 189).

57 Ibid., pp. 193–5.

58 Anglesey, *History of the British Cavalry*, pp. 96–7.

59 Ibid., p. 100.

60 Bernard Pool (ed.), *The Croker Papers* (London, B T Batsford, 1967), p. 237.

61 Moyse-Bartlett, *Nolan of Balaclava*, p. 91.
62 Anglesey, *History of the British Cavalry*, p. 96.
63 Moyse-Bartlett, *Nolan of Balaclava*, p. 101, citing Henry Franks, *Leaves from a Soldier's Notebook* (Thirst, 1904), p. 17.
64 KT 593, Conduitteliste for Unterlietenant Ludwig Nollan 1835-1838.
65 Charles Allen, *Plain Tales from the Raj* (London, Abacus, 2000), p. 129.
66 Moyse-Bartlett, *Nolan of Balaclava*, p. 107.
67 Ibid., p. 111. By 'entire' horses, Aitchison was referring to the regiment's use of stallions rather than geldings (horses that had been castrated to make them more manageable).
68 Anglesey, *History of the British Cavalry*, p. 110.
69 Moyse-Bartlett, *Nolan of Balaclava*, pp. 122–4.

Chapter 4: The Cavalry Fanatic

70 L E Nolan, *Cavalry: Its History and Tactics* (London, Thomas Bosworth, 1853), p. 277.
71 Philip Guedalla, *The Duke* (London, Hodder & Stoughton, 1933), p. 475.
72 Moyse-Bartlett, *Nolan of Balaclava*, p. 128.
73 L E Nolan, *The Training of Cavalry Remount Horses* (London, Parker, Furnival & Parker, 1852), p. 1.
74 Ibid., p. 38.
75 Ibid., pp. 13–14.
76 Ibid., p. 14.
77 Ibid., p. 14.
78 Ibid., p. 4.
79 Ibid., p. 40.
80 Nolan, *Cavalry: Its History and Tactics*, pp. 158–9.
81 Nolan, *Training of Cavalry Remount Horses*, p. 19.
82 Ibid., p. 41.
83 Nolan, *Cavalry: Its History and Tactics*, p. 61.
84 Ibid., p. 61.
85 Ibid., p. 78. Following some experience with firearms, the author believes this to be a slight exaggeration as three foot of earth will stop many bullets even today. However, it does prove a good point and there are numerous examples in military museums of breastplates fully penetrated by musket balls, let alone a conical Minié bullet, that appear to have penetrated both the rider's body and the plate on the other side. Nolan had discussed this with Captain Minié, who also claimed that his new rifle, adopted by the

British Army in the 1850s, was capable of hitting the mark seven times out of ten at 1,800 yards – a great improvement on previous models.

86 Ibid., p. 95.

87 Ian Fletcher, *Galloping at Everything* (Kent, Spellmount, 1999), p. 14. The ostensible reason for Wellington's decision was the lack of forage available in southern France, but it is significant that he felt he could do without the heavies while retaining his light cavalry who would therefore perform all the cavalry duties demanded by an army beginning an invasion of the most powerful state in Europe.

88 Nolan, *Cavalry: Its History and Tactics*, p. 124.

89 Vindex, 'The British Cavalry', *The United Service Journal and Naval and Military Magazine*, pt. 3 (1831), pp. 473–6.

90 Nolan, *Cavalry: Its History and Tactics*, p. 105.

91 Ibid., p. 107.

92 *The Times*, Thursday, 8 February 1855, p. 9. The writer had only just returned from the Crimea, after Nolan's death, and signed himself 'Experientia Docet'. He remarked that a previous correspondent's view on the matter seemed 'to have an eye more to the appearance of the British officers "at Her Majesty's Drawing Rooms" than to their service in the field.'

93 Nolan, *Cavalry: Its History and Tactics*, p. 115. While many uniforms of the day were the epitome of military fashion, plumes, gold braid and other decorations served little purpose other than making the wearer highly conspicuous. Although some items were removed on active service, such as the plumes from the Life Guards' helmets in the Crimea, recent innovations in firearm range and accuracy made increased visibility a dubious benefit in the field.

94 Nolan, *Cavalry: Its History and Tactics*, p. 97.

95 David Buttery, 'Hunting as Training for War', *Soldiers of the Queen*, 115 (December 2003), pp. 3–10. Field Marshal Sir Evelyn Wood and Major-General J G Elliot were among those writers who believed that fox hunting and pig-sticking were ideal training grounds for cavalrymen. Many officers practised these blood sports to the point of obsession in the nineteenth and early twentieth centuries.

96 Moyse-Bartlett, *Nolan of Balaclava*, p. 150.

97 Nolan, *Cavalry: Its History and Tactics*, p. 167.

98 Ibid., p. 153.

99 Ibid., p. 181.

100 Ibid., p. 216.

101 Ibid., p. 242.

102 Ibid., pp. 302–03.

103 Vindex, 'The British Cavalry', pp. 473–6.

104 Nolan, *Cavalry: Its History and Tactics*, p. 249.

105 Ibid., p. 272.

106 Ibid., p. 319.

107 Ibid., p. 317.

108 Ibid., p. 320. Nolan remarked that Johnson was 'a very intelligent, clever man' and acknowledged that he owed him a great debt for his work on the project.

109 *Illustrated London News*, 7 January 1854, p. 17.

110 *The Times*, Friday, 24 March 1854, p. 12.

111 Ibid., p. 12. However, the reviewer did qualify this remark with the observation that some wounds would be serious enough to stop a horse, for example when the skull was completely shattered.

112 *The Times*, Tuesday, 28 March 1854, p. 9. This letter was signed 'A Light Dragoon'.

113 Ibid., p. 9. However, the writer evidently agreed with some of Nolan's and the reviewer's points, ending his letter with the suggestion that hunting gear was more durable and applicable to the needs of the service and that cavalry uniforms should be adapted to emulate it.

114 Moyse-Bartlett, *Nolan of Balaclava*, pp. 149–50.

115 E G French, *Good-Bye to Boot and Saddle* (London, Hutchinson & Co., 1951), p. 156.

116 Ibid., p. 156.

117 Edward Hamley, *The War in the Crimea* (London, Seeley and Co., 1891), p. 115.

118 Moyse-Bartlett, *Nolan of Balaclava*, p. 151.

119 George T Denison, *A History of Cavalry – from the Earliest Times with Lessons for the Future* (London, Macmillan, 1877), p. 516. Denison mentions how much success officers enjoyed with their revolvers at Balaklava. This was supported by Robert Grant, formally a private in the 4th Light Dragoons, who recalled that during the charge: 'Our officers had revolvers, and they did great execution with them . . . In fact, the officers did a great deal more service than the men, because of the revolvers. Many of the Cossacks got shot foolishly like, for after one discharge they thought it was all over, but the revolver had several barrels (cylinders).' See

supplement to the *Illustrated London News*, 30 October 1875, p. 439.

Chapter 5: The Crimean War

120 TNA: FO 65/424/13, Letters from Sir George Hamilton Seymour to Lord John Russell.

121 *The Annual Register for 1853* (London, F & J Rivington, 1854), p. 180.

122 A W Kinglake, *The Invasion of the Crimea*, vol. 1 (Edinburgh and London, William Blackwood & Sons, 1874), pp. 79–80.

123 *The Annual Register for 1853*, pp. 380–1.

124 Norman Rich, *Why the Crimean War?* (Hanover, University Press of New England, 1985), p. 111.

125 Kinglake, *Invasion of the Crimea*, vol. 1, pp. 380–1. The Turks declared war on Russia on 5 October 1853.

126 *The Times*, 14 March 1854, p. 8.

127 Philip Guedalla, *Palmerston* (London, G P Putnam's Sons, 1927), p. 183. Palmerston had been in the Home Office and the War Office and eventually became Prime Minister in 1855.

128 Albert Seaton, *The Crimean War: A Russian Chronicle* (London, BT Batsford, 1977), pp. 21–2.

129 A J Barker, *The Vainglorious War 1854-56* (London, Weidenfeld & Nicolson, 1970), p. 15.

130 J N Barker, *Endurance and Endeavour: Russian History 1812-1992* (Oxford, Oxford University Press, 1993), p. 32.

131 Seaton, *The Crimean War*, p. 24.

132 Ibid., pp. 27–8.

133 Ibid., p. 33.

134 Robert H G Thomas and Richard Scollins, *The Russian Army of the Crimean War 1854-56* (Osprey, 1991), pp. 8–9.

135 J W Fortescue, *A History of the British Army*, vol. 13: *1852-1870* (London, Macmillan, 1930), p. 37.

136 Thompson, Captain John, 'The Turks in Kalafat', *Blackwoods Edinburgh Magazine*, 75 (January–June 1859), pt. 2, 449–61. John Wycliffe Thompson initially purchased a commission in the 3rd Dragoon Guards in 1844 and later transferred into the 10th Hussars as a lieutenant. He served in the Crimea and was wounded at the Battle of the Alma.

137 Barker, *The Vainglorious War*, p. 19.

138 Fortescue, *History of the British Army*, p. 36.

139 Trevor Royle, *Crimea: The Great Crimean War 1854-1856* (London,

Abacus, 2003), p. 107.

140 Fortescue, *History of the British Army*, p. 30.

141 Ibid., p. 36.

142 Philip Warner, *The Crimean War: A Reappraisal* (Chatham, Wordsworth, 2001), p. 22.

143 Christopher Hibbert, *The Destruction of Lord Raglan* (Chatham, Wordsworth, 1999), p. 42.

144 Woodham-Smith, *The Reason Why*, pp. 34–5.

145 Saul David, *The Homicidal Earl* (London, Abacus, 1999), pp. 112–13. During the 1830s and 1840s Cardigan shocked Victorian society with a succession of public scandals. The most notorious of these incidents was the house arrest of Captain Reynolds for failing to decant his wine in the mess, the so-called Black Bottle Affair, and the court martial of Captain Wathen, which eventually led to Cardigan's own dismissal from command of the 15th Hussars. In addition, he had fought a near fatal duel with Captain Tucket, one of his former officers, ending with a trial before his peers in the House of Lords, and suffered a deserved reputation as a martinet. Commanding several cavalry regiments during a stormy career, his behaviour embarrassed the army and led many to question the purchase system that had enabled him to rise so swiftly up the chain of command.

146 Hibbert, *The Destruction of Lord Raglan*, p. 137. Lord Lucan turned down Colonel Beatson who requested a place on his staff despite his considerable experience, having served in both Spain and India.

Chapter 6: Horse-Dealing with the Bedouin

147 Hansard's Parliamentary Debates (series 3), vol. 130, 31 January to 27 February 1854 (London, Cornelius Buck, 1854), p. 1134.

148 Ibid., p. 1134.

149 TNA: MM.182 RUSI, Raglan Papers. Letter from Newcastle to Raglan, 11 March 1854.

150 *The Times*, Friday, 27 April 1855, p. 10.

151 Nolan, *Cavalry: Its History and Tactics*, p. 164.

152 Anglesey, *History of the British Cavalry*, pp. 106–07.

153 Somerset John Gough Calthorpe, *Letters from Head-quarters, or, the Realities of the War in the Crimea*, vol. 1 (London, John Murray, 1856), pp. 23–4.

154 Ibid., pp. 37–8.

155 Thompson, 'The Turks in Kalafat', 449–61.

156 Ibid., pp. 291–308. Thompson recorded that the majority of the Bashi-Bazouks were mounted on little Anatolians.

157 John Thompson, 'Horse Dealing in Syria, 1854', *Blackwoods Edinburgh Magazine*, 75 (July–December 1859), pt. 1, 255–73.

158 Warwick Ball, *Syria: A Historical and Architectural Guide* (Essex, Scorpion Publishing and MCS, 1994), p. 52.

159 Thompson, 'Horse Dealing in Syria, 1854', 255–73.

160 Ibid., 273.

161 Ibid., 273.

162 Isa Khalil Sabbagh, *As the Arabs Say… Arabic Quotations Recalled and Interpreted* (Washington DC, Sabbagh Management Corporation, 1983), p. 35.

163 Thompson, 'Horse Dealing in Syria, 1854', p. 273.

164 Ibid., 255–73.

165 Ibid.

166 Ibid.

167 Ibid.

168 Ibid. Thompson wrote that their stay in the desert lasted from 22 May to 16 June 1854.

169 Sabbagh, *As the Arabs Say…*, p. 33.

170 Thompson, 'Horse Dealing in Syria, 1854', 419–34.

171 Ibid.

172 Anglesey, *History of the British Cavalry*, p. 106.

173 Thompson, 'Horse Dealing in Syria, 1854', 419–34.

174 Ibid.

175 Ibid.

176 Donald Thomas, *Charge! Hurrah! Hurrah! A Life of Cardigan of Balaclava* (London, Routledge & Kegan Paul, 1974), p. 193.

177 Frances Duberly, *Journal Kept during the Russian War: from the Departure of the Army from England in April, 1854, to the Fall of Sebastopol* (London, Longman, Brown, Green & Longmans, 1855), p. 47.

178 James Thomas Brudenell Cardigan, *Eight Months on Active Service* (London, Clowes and Sons, 1855), p. 54.

179 Royle, *The Great Crimean War*, p. 173.

180 William Russell, *The Great War with Russia* (London, Routledge & Sons, 1895), p. 115. As the war correspondent for *The Times*, Russell was eager to ingratiate himself with as many officers as possible and came to know Nolan quite well in Turkey and later in the Crimea.

Chapter 7: A Galloper for the QMG

181 TNA: WO6/74/1, Letter from the Duke of Newcastle to Lord Raglan, 10 April 1854.

182 Barker, *The Vainglorious War*, p. 41. The Russians had around 70,000 men in the Crimea at the time, including 3,500 cavalry and 2,500 artillerymen. The artillery had around 100 field artillery pieces, not to mention the guns defending Sevastopol itself or carried by the Black Sea fleet.

183 Moyse-Bartlett, *Nolan of Balaclava*, p. 175.

184 Hew Strachan, *The Reform of the British Army 1830-54* (Manchester, Manchester University Press, 1984), pp. 154–5.

185 Ibid., p. 148.

186 Moyse-Bartlett, *Nolan of Balaclava*, pp. 279–80.

187 Calthorpe, *Letters from Head-quarters*, p. 121. Calthorpe spoke of the Blue-Jackets (sailors) grabbing the legs of struggling horses, who were often sufficiently surprised at such confident treatment that they failed to react with the violence he expected.

188 NAM: 1989-06-41, Journal of Captain Louis Nolan, 15th Hussars. Note that Nolan's journal, presumably written in haste on many occasions, abounds with abbreviations. For example, Cavly – Cavalry, Dragn – Dragoon, etc.

189 Ibid.

190 Moyse-Bartlett, *Nolan of Balaclava*, p. 181.

191 Duberly, *Journal Kept during the Russian War*, pp. 79–80.

192 Calthorpe, *Letters from Head-quarters*, p. 88.

193 Moyse-Bartlett, *Nolan of Balaclava*, pp. 183–4.

194 NAM: 1989-06-41, Journal of Captain Louis Nolan, 15th Hussars.

195 Ibid.

196 Ibid.

197 Denis Judd, *The Crimean War* (London, Book Club Associates, 1976), p. 53.

198 Calthorpe, *Letters from Head-quarters*, pp. 168–9.

199 NAM: 1989-06-41, Journal of Captain Louis Nolan, 15th Hussars.

200 Kenneth Fenwick (ed.), *Voice from the Ranks* (London, Folio Society, 1954), p. 16.

201 Ibid., pp. 17–18.

202 Ibid., pp. 18–19. Gowing was promoted to sergeant following the battle, but his regiment had suffered terribly, the 7th Royal Fusiliers taking nearly

50 per cent losses during the battle. Considering that his part of the line was enfiladed by the guns of the Great Redoubt for much of the action, it is unsurprising. The 23rd Foot on their left also suffered similar losses.

203 Mabel Airlie (ed.), *With the Guards We Shall Go* (London, Hodder & Stoughton, 1933), p. 72. This was Captain Strange Jocelyn of the 2nd Battalion of the Royal Scots Fusiliers.

204 Calthorpe, *Letters from Head-quarters*, p. 173. Calthorpe later wrote: 'Nothing struck me more during the day than Lord Raglan's wonderful calmness and presence of mind during the whole battle. He rode everywhere, with round shot, shell and musket-balls flying about him, with an indifference that was really remarkable' (ibid., pp. 184–5).

205 Judd, *The Crimean War*, pp. 65–6.

206 Calthorpe, *Letters from Head-quarters*, pp. 182–3.

207 Barker, *The Vainglorious War*, pp. 113–14.

208 NAM: 1989-06-41, Journal of Captain Louis Nolan, 15th Hussars.

209 Calthorpe, *Letters from Head-quarters*, p. 184. Nolan recorded that this had been Captain Maude RHA, riding with the 11th Hussars, whose 'fiery zeal led him to pursue the enemy'. See NAM: 1989-06-41, Journal of Captain Louis Nolan, 15th Hussars.

210 Russell, *The Great War with Russia*, p. 116.

211 NAM: 1989-06-41: Journal of Captain Louis Nolan, 15th Hussars.

212 Peter Gibbs, *The Battle of the Alma* (London, Weidenfeld and Nicolson, 1963), pp. 173–5.

213 Russell, *The Great War with Russia*, p. 90.

214 NAM: 1989-06-41, Journal of Captain Louis Nolan, 15th Hussars.

215 Calthorpe, *Letters from Head-quarters*, pp. 217–18. Nolan recorded that they captured twenty-two baggage carts and horses, which included General Gorchakov's personal carriage and two of his thoroughbred horses.

216 Denison, *A History of Cavalry*, p. 428.

217 Kinglake, *Invasion of the Crimea*, p. 114.

Chapter 8: Balaklava

218 NAM: 1989-06-41, Journal of Captain Louis Nolan, 15th Hussars. It is possible that this soldier may have been involved in skirmishing elsewhere, but Nolan's account clearly suggests that he had been shot at during the assault on the Genoese fortress.

219 Kinglake, *Invasion of the Crimea*, vol. 3, p. 99. After his return from

captivity, Monto received considerable acclaim in Russia for this brief act of resistance.

220 Kinglake, *Invasion of the Crimea*, vol. 3, p. 104.

221 NAM: 1989-06-41, Journal of Captain Louis Nolan, 15th Hussars.

222 George Paget, *The Light Cavalry Brigade in the Crimea* (Wakefield, EP Publishing, 1975), p. 47. This patrol was carried out on 28 September.

223 Kinglake, *Invasion of the Crimea*, vol. 3, pp. 237–8.

224 NAM: 1989-06-41, Journal of Captain Louis Nolan, 15th Hussars.

225 Moyse-Bartlett, *Nolan of Balaclava*, p. 199.

226 Paget, *The Light Cavalry Brigade in the Crimea*, p. 61.

227 NAM: 1989-06-41, Journal of Captain Louis Nolan, 15th Hussars.

228 Ibid. According to Nolan's journal, this particular reconnaissance was made on 4 October.

229 Ibid. Most of the Turkish troops manning the redoubts were of Tunisian origin.

230 Outlying picquets were usually placed 4 to 5 miles in front of the lines and comprised one officer with thirty to forty men. In addition to watching for enemy movement, they were to raise the alarm if a threat was observed and delay the enemy advance if possible. Inlying picquets remained within the lines with their mounts saddled and prepared to support the outlying picquet at short notice. See Terry Brighton, *Hell Riders* (London, Penguin Books, 2005), p. 66.

231 Paget, *The Light Cavalry Brigade in the Crimea*, p. 67.

232 NAM: 1989-06-41, Journal of Captain Louis Nolan, 15th Hussars.

233 Ibid.

234 Brighton, *Hell Riders*, pp. 69–70. Historians are divided over whether Lucan's nickname originates from the action on the Bulganek or from this incident.

235 Paget, *The Light Cavalry Brigade in the Crimea*, pp. 56–7.

236 Duberly, *Journal Kept during the Russian War*, p. 105.

237 Kelly, Christine (ed.), *Mrs Duberly's War* (Oxford, Oxford University Press, 2007), p. 317.

238 Paget, *The Light Cavalry Brigade in the Crimea*, p. 65.

239 *The Times*, 22 November 1854, p. 7, quoting from a letter printed in the *Caledonian Mercury*.

240 Kinglake, *Invasion of the Crimea*, p. 313. Kinglake thought it possible that Morris's letter, taken from Nolan's body in the aftermath of the battle, was posted by mistake to his wife Amelia and the letter is still in the Morris

family papers: see M J Trow, *The Pocket Hercules* (Yorkshire, Pen & Sword, 2006), pp. 110–11.

241 Russell, *The Great War with Russia*, p. 127. By 'frock' Russell was referring to his 'frock coat'. He also recorded how several officers disapproved of Nolan's constant complaining (ibid., p. 128) but it was clear that he was not the only officer who had reservations about the way in which the campaign was being conducted. It was an army custom to auction off the unimportant personal effects of those killed, the proceeds being sent to their relatives.

242 Seaton, *The Crimean War*, p. 139. Although they had good cause to respect Turkish troops, the majority of those manning the Causeway redoubts were of Anatolian and Tunisian origin and as colonial troops the Russians judged them less likely to identify with the Turkish cause than Turkish nationals.

243 Kinglake, *Invasion of the Crimea*, vol. 4, p. 45.

244 Ibid., pp. 42–3.

245 Seaton, *The Crimean War*, p. 143. From the recollections of Uhlan officer Lieutenant K Kubitovich.

246 Calthorpe, *Letters from Head-quarters*, p. 300.

247 Seaton, *The Crimean War*, p. 143. This was recorded by Lieutenant Ushanov on Liprandi's Staff.

248 Kinglake, *Invasion of the Crimea*, p. 53.

249 Seaton, *The Crimean War*, pp. 143–4.

250 NAM: 1963-09-5 Recollections of Lieutenant Colonel (Major in 1854) William Forrest, 4th Dragoon Guards.

251 Calthorpe, *Letters from Head-quarters*, p. 304.

252 John Selby, *The Thin Red Line* (Newton Abbot, Hamish Hamilton, 1972), p. 121.

253 Seaton, *The Crimean War*, p. 145.

254 Nicolas Bentley (ed.), *Russell's Despatches from the Crimea* (London, Panther History, 1970), p. 122.

255 NAM: 1968-07-270, Lieutenant Colonel Anthony Sterling of the Highland Brigade.

256 Denison, *A History of Cavalry*, p. 429. It is also possible that the sudden appearance of the infantry as they crested the ridge came as quite a shock to the Russian cavalry and that they retired as soon as possible, not having expected to meet serious resistance this close to the causeway.

257 Kinglake, *Invasion of the Crimea*, p. 79.

258 Seaton, *The Crimean War*, p. 146. This comment made by Kubitovich referred of course to Marshal Joachim Murat, Napoleon's flamboyant cavalry commander, who was renowned for occasionally charging the enemy wielding nothing more lethal than a horsewhip. During the French invasion of Russia in 1812, the Cossacks developed a particular admiration for Murat's martial style and evident courage.

259 NAM: 1963-09-05, Lieutenant Colonel (Major in 1854) William Forrest, 4th Dragoon Guards. In addition, the heavy Russian greatcoats provided considerable protection against the swords of the Heavy Brigade.

260 Seaton, *The Crimean War*, p. 147. Lucan later estimated that the mêlée lasted around eight minutes and, considering how rapid cavalry clashes usually were, this was actually quite a long time.

261 Calthorpe, *Letters from Head-quarters*, p. 310. The Heavy Brigade eventually committed around 800 men to this action against at least 2,000 Russian cavalrymen. Some sources put the Russian figure as high as 3,000. Since most of the advances barely exceeded trotting speed, whether the action can truly be called a 'charge' is questionable.

262 Nolan, *Cavalry: Its History and Tactics*, p. 219.

263 Ibid., p. 219.

264 James Wightman, 'One of the "Six Hundred" on the Balaclava Charge', *The Nineteenth Century Magazine*, 31 (January–June 1892), pp. 850–63. In the absence of senior officers due to sickness, Captain Morris had been given temporary command of the 17th Lancers. In fact the whole brigade was greatly under strength at this time for similar reasons.

265 Nolan, *Cavalry: Its History and Tactics*, p. 63. In addition, Fortescue believed that Lucan should have ridden to the Light Brigade and ordered Cardigan to attack. He also criticized Ryzhov for advancing in such a large, unwieldy formation and suggested that a well-timed attack on its flank whilst engaged with the Heavy Brigade might have decimated the Russian squadrons. See Fortescue, *A History of the British Army*, p. 109.

266 Kinglake, *Invasion of the Crimea*, p. 208.

Chapter 9: The Fateful Message

267 *Morning Chronicle*, Tuesday, 14 November 1854, p. 4.

268 Kinglake, *Invasion of the Crimea*, vol. 4, p. 178.

269 Ibid., p. 179. Kinglake remarked that there was some doubt over whether the word 'to' was included in the original order as he was referring to a copy that Lucan later presented to Lord Raglan. Furthermore, advance

seemed to have been written with a capital A and there may have been a full stop after the word 'ordered'. Even so, the meaning of this instruction seems fairly plain.

270 Ibid., p. 192. John Blunt later made several copies of the orders at Lucan's behest but claimed that the exact wording of the Fourth Order was 'Lord Raglan wishes the Cavalry to advance rapidly to the front, follow the enemy and try to prevent the enemy carrying away the guns. Troop of Horse Artillery may accompany. French Cavalry is on your left'. See Douglas J Austin, 'Blunt Speaking', Special Publication 33, Crimean War Research Society, 2006, pp. 21–39. This version of the order is held by the National Army Museum.

271 Mark Adkin, *The Charge: The Real Reason Why the Light Brigade Was Lost* (London, Pimlico, 2000), p. 130.

272 Kinglake puts the number of guns at twelve (*Invasion of the Crimea*, vol. 4, p. 188) but Paget claimed as many as eighteen (Paget, *The Light Cavalry Brigade in the Crimea*, p. 182). More modern interpretations put the number at the usual eight field pieces. For example Mark Adkin believes that Obolensky's command consisted of around 200 men with four six pound guns and four nine pound howitzers. See Adkin, *The Charge*, p. 145.

273 Kinglake, *Invasion of the Crimea*, vol. 4, p. 189.

274 Wightman, 'One of the "Six Hundred" on the Balaclava Charge', pp. 850–63.

275 NAM: 07-288-2, Lord Cardigan's Memorandum on the Charge of the Light Brigade.

276 Moyse-Bartlett, *Nolan of Balaclava*, p. 219.

277 Hibbert, *The Destruction of Lord Raglan*, p. 144.

278 Paget, *The Light Cavalry Brigade in the Crimea*, p. 170. Paget was irritated at being asked to perform what he already considered his bound duty by his commander but perhaps this merely indicates Cardigan's nervousness over the awesome task before him. This instruction preyed on Paget's mind throughout the charge and its aftermath, although he did his utmost to carry out his task. Famously, he was also reluctant to sacrifice the cigar he was smoking at the time as they were so difficult to get hold of in the Crimea. With a cavalryman's panache, he rode all the way to the guns still smoking.

279 Wightman, 'One of the "Six Hundred" on the Balaclava Charge', pp. 850–63.

280 Kinglake, *Invasion of the Crimea*, vol. 4, p. 213.

281 Wightman, 'One of the "Six Hundred" on the Balaclava Charge', pp. 850–63. Though several accounts of the moment Nolan was killed exist, Wightman's is the best and, since he rode with the 17th, he was probably in a better position to see the incident than most. Several eyewitnesses relate how Nolan uttered an awful cry as he was struck; his wound was horrific, exposing his heart. Possibly the lungs were also penetrated, which may account for his eerie, high-pitched scream. Kinglake believed that this cry was probably an involuntary reaction of the body since Nolan was probably killed instantly. See Kinglake, *Invasion of the Crimea*, vol. 4, pp. 214–15.

282 Seaton, *The Crimean War*, p. 149.

283 George Loy Smith, *A Victorian RSM* (Tunbridge Wells, D J Costello, 1987), pp. 132–3.

284 Paget, *The Light Cavalry Brigade in the Crimea*, p. 179.

285 Albert Mitchell, *Recollections of one of the Light Brigade* (London, Hamilton, Adams & Co., 1885), p. 84.

286 Kinglake, *Invasion of the Crimea*, vol. 4, p. 282. It is unclear whether Lucan actually led the entire Heavy Brigade down the North Valley in support of Cardigan. Initially he stated that he led only two regiments forward, the Royals and the Scots Greys. However, he later changed his mind and in a speech to the House of Lords on 19 March 1855, claimed that all the heavy regiments took casualties in the incident. This implies that he led the entire brigade down the valley (see Hansard's Parliamentary Debates [series 3], vol. 137, p. 746).

287 Adkin, *The Charge*, pp. 142–3. Lucan later stated that this attack, which took place almost simultaneously with his own advance, undoubtedly spared the Heavy Brigade from further casualties as they retreated.

288 Woodham-Smith, *The Reason Why*, p. 248. Cardigan believed that he was only obliged to lead the brigade to its destination and that it was no part of a general's duty to engage in hand-to-hand combat. His decision to ride back and leave the rallying and recall of his brigade to subordinates later tarnished his reputation, ending in a court case for libel. After his heroic conduct in leading the Light Brigade into the battery, this was a pity.

289 Seaton, *The Crimean War*, p. 150. Kubitovich claimed that Ryzhov received severe criticism for counter-attacking with irregulars instead of using his hussars or lancers: 'the fault was indeed Ryzhov's for he should not have sent Cossacks ahead to meet the charge of line cavalry.' Ibid., p. 150. In his defence, he may have had little choice because of the disposition of his

troops and the fact that the action of the Light Brigade had been totally unexpected.

290 Paget, *The Light Cavalry Brigade in the Crime*a, pp. 186–7. This would conform with Nolan's belief that, even when greatly outnumbered, the advance of a determined and aggressive body of cavalry is likely to prevail if the enemy cannot match their resolve.

291 Loy Smith wrote that, despite having been on active service for four months, no gun spikes had been officially issued, at least to the Light Brigade. He and three other troop sergeant majors in the 11th Hussars had been given one each by an ADC at the Alma but these were the only ones he knew of in the brigade. See Loy Smith, *A Victorian RSM*, p. 131. Nevertheless, Kubitovich reported that some guns were actually spiked by the enemy (Seaton, *The Crimean War*, p. 150) and Edward Woodham, as Chairman of the Balaclava Committee, recalled in 1875 that 'each man had spikes in his pouch. All the cavalry regiments were supplied with gun-spikes whenever there was any likelihood of battle. We had no hammers, but drove the spikes in with the hilt of our swords or our hands – in any way we could.' See Supplement to the *Illustrated London News*, 30 October 1875, p. 438.

292 Michael Barthorp, *Heroes of the Crimea* (London, Blandford, 1991), p. 52.

293 Seaton, *The Crimean War*, p. 150.

294 Ibid., p. 151.

295 Ibid., p. 11. As uniform specialists will quickly point out, troopers of the Light Brigade did not wear redcoats. Presumably Kozukhov was either confusing them with troopers of the Heavy Brigade whom he may have seen earlier in the day or his memory was playing him false here.

296 Wightman, 'One of the "Six Hundred" on the Balaclava Charge', pp. 850–63.

297 NAM: 8602-75 Letter of Private Edward Firkins, 13th Light Dragoons. Dated Camp before Sebastopol 27 December 1854. It is unclear whether Firkins meant that these were regular lancers or Cossacks. At this point in the engagement they could have been either.

298 NAM: 8311-9, Captain Edward Seager, 8th King's Royal Irish Regiment of Light Dragoons.

299 Paget, *The Light Cavalry Brigade in the Crimea*, p. 188.

300 Ibid., p. 188.

301 Ibid., p. 192.

302 Loy Smith, *A Victorian RSM*, pp. 138–9.

303 Seaton, *The Crimean War*, p. 152.

304 Ibid., pp. 153–4.

305 Ibid.

306 Mitchell, *Recollections of one of the Light Brigade*, p. 87.

307 Moyse-Bartlett, *Nolan of Balaclava*, p. 227. Surgeon Mouat and Sergeant Wooden rescued the delirious Morris (who recovered) and assisted in carrying back Nolan's body. Their actions saw both of them awarded the newly commissioned Victoria Cross.

308 Anonymous, *Aldershottana: or Chinks in My Hut* (London, Ward & Lock, 1856), p. 120. It is likely that Dr Mouat is the anonymous officer referred to. There are very few pictures of Louis Nolan and most were not drawn from life. Whether he was 'ugly' or not is of course a matter of opinion, but the equestrian portrait of him in stable dress is generally felt to be one of the most accurate likenesses. It depicts him with black curly hair, a prominent nose and sharp features. Far more famous is the portrait that accompanied his obituary in the *Illustrated London News* in November 1854, which is said to be taken from an original then held in the Officers' Mess of the 15th King's Royal Hussars. This presents a more dashing aspect with Louis in full uniform but wearing a forage cap. Neat, moustachioed and gazing into the distance, this fits with the image that most people associate with Nolan. It also bears a similarity with the illustrations from 'The Training of Cavalry Remount Horses', which he may have modelled for.

309 Kinglake, *Invasion of the Crimea*, vol. 4, p. 321. Raglan later withdrew his remarks and absolved Cardigan of responsibility.

310 Ibid., p. 322.

311 Cyril Falls (ed.), *A Diary of the Crimea by George Palmer Evelyn* (London, Gerald Duckworth & Co., 1954), p. 97.

312 Fortescue, *A History of the British Army*, p. 106.

313 Wightman, 'One of the "Six Hundred" on the Balaclava Charge', pp. 850–63.

314 Seaton, *The Crimean War*, p. 154.

315 For many years the figure of 673 has been taken as the most reliable since it was the number recorded by Colonel Paget at roll-call that morning. However, many riders later joined the brigade or left it for one reason or another. In one of the most recent studies, Brighton judged that the figure could be no less than 666 but could have been more. See Brighton, *Hell Riders*, p. 292.

316 Seaton, *The Crimean War*, pp. 154–6.
317 NAM: 8311-9, Captain Edward Seager, 8th King's Royal Irish Regiment of Light Dragoons.
318 Duberly, *Journal Kept during the Russian War*, pp. 120–1.
319 TNA: WO 1/369 f.685, Casualty Returns for the period including the Battle of Balaklava (22–26 October 1854). All the Light Brigade casualty figures immediately previous to this were also taken from this source.
320 Robert G Richardson (ed.), *Nurse Sarah Anne – with Florence Nightingale at Scutari* (London, John Murray, 1977), p. 135.
321 Moyse-Bartlett, *Nolan of Balaclava*, p. 228. Tennyson's poem 'The Charge of the Light Brigade', which immortalized the charge, does include some lines describing the losses and tragedy of the incident. However, even today many readers are perhaps enamoured more by the romantic aspects of the poem without appreciating the human cost of the charge. Interestingly, his rough first draft of the poem referred to Nolan by name, though he later removed the ascription.

Chapter 10: Recriminations

322 Hibbert, *The Destruction of Lord Raglan*, p. 150.
323 Paget, *The Light Cavalry Brigade in the Crimea*, p. 73.
324 Hansard's Parliamentary Debates (series 3), vol. 137, p. 737. The Battle of Chillianwallah in 1849 witnessed an unfortunate incident during the Second Sikh War. A brigade of light cavalry (the 9th Lancers, 14th Light Dragoons and two native regiments) allegedly misheard the order of 'Threes right' as they were preparing to charge, thinking that the instruction was 'Threes about'. Wheeling about, they rode back through their own lines resulting in chaos in that sector of the field. Seeing the enemy supposedly in flight, the Sikhs counter-charged, inflicting some losses and capturing a number of guns. General Pope's reputation was irrevocably tarnished as a result of the incident. See Byron Farwell, *Queen Victoria's Little Wars* (Chatham, Wordsworth, 1999), pp. 56–7.
325 TNA: WO 1/369 ff.642-4, Raglan to Newcastle, 27 October 1854.
326 Bentley, *Russell's Despatches from the Crimea*, p. 125.
327 Ibid., p. 125. Russell was one of Raglan's most vocal critics and on occasion was denied access to some areas after the staff read some of his articles.
328 Woodham-Smith, *The Reason Why*, p. 264.
329 He wrote: 'the whole thing seems to have been misinterpreted by Captain Nolan to Lord Lucan, or at any rate misunderstood by him.' Calthorpe,

Letters from Head-quarters, p. 321.

330 TNA: WO 1/370 ff.483-6, Raglan to Newcastle, 16 December 1854.

331 Ibid.

332 Ibid. In a speech to the House of Lords, Lucan later claimed that the Light Brigade was so far forward as to be within long range fire of the Russians and he felt unwilling to send men out any further. (See Hansard's Parliamentary Debates [series 3], vol. 137, p. 744). However, the Russians would be unlikely to waste ammunition against small parties of men whose speed of movement would make them difficult targets. Furthermore, it would have been worth some degree of risk to gain a better vision of the enemy's positions, and reconnaissance was a central part of Lucan's task. Therefore this argument seems unconvincing.

333 Paget, *The Light Cavalry Brigade in the Crimea*, pp. 219–20. However, Paget was well aware of Nolan's disparaging remarks against Lucan amongst others.

334 Adkin, *The Charge*, p. 230.

335 NAM: 6309/5/1-2, Lieutenant Colonel (Major in 1854) William Forrest 4th Dragoon Guards, letters.

336 Adkin, *The Charge*, p. 240.

337 *The Times*, Friday, 2 March 1855, p. 7.

338 Blunt claimed that Lucan appeared 'to be surprised and irritated at the impetuous and disrespectful attitude and tone of Captain Nolan and looked at him sternly, but made no answer.' See Austin, 'Blunt Speaking', pp. 21–39. Since Blunt was a civilian, Lucan instructed him not to take part in the charge, although he was preparing to do so.

339 Hansard's Parliamentary Debates (series 3), vol. 136 (2 March–2 May 1855), p. 6. Under some circumstances a commander in chief might have to sacrifice some units for the safety of the entire army. This was one of Lucan's considerations upon reading the Fourth Order as he judged that Raglan may have needed to stop an attempt by the enemy of such importance that it justified heavy losses.

340 NAM: 1968-07-284 and 287, Lord Raglan's Papers.

341 Moyse-Bartlett, *Nolan of Balaclava*, pp. 237–8. Lucan wrote this in a letter to Lord Raglan on 7 December 1854 and brought up the matter again during his speeches in the House of Lords.

342 Moyse-Bartlett, *Nolan of Balaclava*, p. 240.

343 Hansard's Parliamentary Debates (series 3), vol. 136 (2 March–2 May 1855), p. 1118.

344 Ibid., p. 735. Taken from Lucan's speech on 19 March 1855.

345 Ibid., p. 750. However, several witnesses testify to the fact that the guns were being removed around this time.

346 Hansard's Parliamentary Debates, (series 3), vol. 136, p. 773. From the Duke of Newcastle's reply to Lucan's speech.

347 *The Times*, Monday, 20 November 1854, p. 7. The writer of the letter signed himself C.W., late 15th Hussars.

348 *Morning Chronicle*, Tuesday, 14 November 1854, p. 5. Note that the *Morning Chronicle* were at this stage unsure whether a written command had been issued.

349 *Daily News*, Tuesday, 14 November 1854, p. 5.

350 Ibid., Saturday, 18 November 1854, p. 5.

351 Royle, *The Great Crimean War*, pp. 503–04.

352 Kinglake, *Invasion of the Crimea*, vol. 4, p. 184. Kinglake also referred to his reputation for recklessness, remarking when Nolan carried a message to advance during the Alma: 'The order flew; for it was Nolan – the impetuous Nolan – who carried it to the 2d Division' (see Kinglake, *Invasion of the Crimea*, vol. 2, pp. 307–08).

353 Kinglake, *Invasion of the Crimea*, vol. 4, p. 185.

354 Ibid., p. 195.

355 NAM: 07-288-2, Lord Cardigan, Memorandum on the Charge of the Light Brigade.

356 Kinglake, *Invasion of the Crimea*, vol. 4, p. 362.

357 Ibid., p. 213.

358 Anonymous, *Aldershottana*, p. 119. This is an unusual and highly anecdotal book containing much humour but it appears to be an honest account and this passage certainly fits with the appearance of the battlefield today. The Sapouné Ridge dominates the plain but the Fedioukine Heights and the Causeway Heights in particular are not impressive features, blending very easily into the landscape with their shallow slopes. Indeed, the North and South Valleys are not really valleys at all but are classed as re-entrants in geographical terms. The fame of the charge leads many to expect a well-defined and striking location, but this is not in fact the case.

359 NAM: 8311-9, Captain Edward Seager, 8th King's Royal Irish Regiment of Light Dragoons.

Chapter 11: Nolan's Legacy

360 *Gentleman's Magazine*, January 1855, p. 88.

361 *Illustrated London News*, 25 November, 1854, p. 528.

362 *The Annual Register for 1854*, p. 332.

363 The idea that the Charge of the Light Brigade could be considered a partial success was supported by some of the survivors. Paget argued that they fulfilled the objective they had been given since they took the guns. The fact that they could not retain them as they were unsupported does not detract from this. See Paget, *The Light Cavalry Brigade in the Crimea*, p. 205. Loy Smith remarked that a great victory might have been achieved if a general attack had been made in their wake as they had nearly split the Russian army. See Loy Smith, *A Victorian RSM*, p. 148. In addition, Calthorpe believed that the serious effect on Russian morale and the bravery displayed meant that the charge could not be considered wholly futile. Brighton discusses this concept at some length, devoting a chapter to it in *Hell Riders*, pp. 295–302.

364 Moyse-Bartlett, *Nolan of Balaclava*, p. 130. Fortunately Moyse-Bartlett included a photograph of the marble scroll erected in Nolan's memory in his book as the monument has since been lost or stolen during renovation work on Holy Trinity Church.

365 Ibid., p. 250.

366 TNA: PROB 11/2208, the Last Will and Testament of Lewis Edward Nolan, 23 March 1855. This document is the official conformation of that written by Nolan the previous year. The original document was written on sheets of foolscap and Key was obliged to state that he recognized Louis's handwriting. Thompson also confirmed that the original documents were genuine.

367 Ibid.

368 Moyse-Bartlett, *Nolan of Balaclava*, pp. 251–2.

369 Supplement to the *Illustrated London News*, Saturday, 30 October 1875, pp. 439–42 (the quotation is separated by illustrations).

370 *Illustrated London News*, Saturday, 30 October 1875, p. 420.

371 Kinglake, *Invasion of the Crimea*, vol. 4, p. 198. The author has stood in the approximate position of the Light Brigade and the distance between No. 3 Redoubt and likely position of the Don Cossack battery is indeed slight. It is certainly possible that Nolan had pointed at the Causeway and Lucan had merely mistaken his gesture due to this perspective.

372 Loy Smith and Wightman refer to the conversation if not its contents, see Loy Smith, *A Victorian RSM*, p. 131 and Wightman, 'One of the "Six Hundred" on the Balaclava Charge', pp. 850–63. Numerous secondary

sources have alluded to this allegation but the author is yet to find a corroborating primary source. For secondary sources, see Thomas, *Charge! Hurrah! Hurrah!* p. 242. Also David, *The Homicidal Earl*, p. 398 and Robert B Edgerton, *Death or Glory* (Colorado, Westview, 1999), p. 97.

373 Adkin, *The Charge*, p. 242.

374 Paget, *The Light Cavalry Brigade in the Crimea*, p. 72. Paget's memoirs were published only in 1881 by his son after his death. Considering that Paget barely knew Nolan, his remarks could be perceived as a little harsh.

375 Paget, *The Light Cavalry Brigade in the Crimea*, p. 203.

376 Ibid., pp. 203–04. Since both Lords clearly disapproved of the order, it is likely that they would have discussed it further and possibly agreed to seek further confirmation had they been on friendlier terms.

377 Paget remarked that 'the nature of the ground must be considered; and I think I am right in saying that such an advance would have been attended with much difficulty, the ground being broke and uneven, and of such configuration that cavalry would have acted on it at a great disadvantage.' See Paget, *The Light Cavalry Brigade in the Crimea*, p. 205.

378 Henderson, *The Soldier of Three Queens*, pp. 193–5. Henderson arrived in the Crimea with the 10th Hussars well after the charge but did his best to find out about the circumstances surrounding Nolan's fate. Being well known in cavalry circles, he found it easy to talk with many of the survivors and the majority of them believed that Nolan had misinterpreted the order and, upon being challenged by Lucan, had replied, 'My Lord, there can be no mistake about it. There are the guns; and it is your duty to retake them.' They also commented that the conversation took less than two minutes. See Henderson, *The Soldier of Three Queens*, p. 309.

379 *The Times*, Saturday, 1 March 1856, p. 6.

380 Ibid., p. 6. The two aides along with Colonel Herbert in De Lacy Evans's command failed to find any trace of the Russian convoy.

381 George Higginson, *Seventy-One Years of a Guardsman's Life* (London, Smith, Elder & Co., 1916), pp. 185–6.

382 Calthorpe, *Letters from Head-quarters*, p. 316.

383 David Kelsey, 'Evidence and Belief: Captain Nolan's Final Moments', *Journal of the Society for Army Historical Research*, 81/325 (Spring 2003), p. 70. However, it should be borne in mind that many Victorians chose to remain anonymous under such circumstances and this does not necessarily imply dishonesty or unreliability. For example, Thompson did not put his name to his articles about the horse-buying mission to Syria and has only

been identified through army records. Many letters to the newspapers were submitted under pseudonyms. Editors would only accept this if they knew the true identity of the authors; presumably Kinglake knew the name of his source.

384 Colin Robins, 'Nolan Did Try to Redirect the Light Brigade – Who Says?', *War Correspondent*, 24/1 (April 2006), p. 7. Kinglake was a firm supporter of Raglan, believing that he performed well under the difficult circumstances that the campaign was fought in. He was also well acquainted with his family and went to great pains to defend Raglan's damaged reputation. Mark Adkin also raised his doubts over Kinglake's impartiality and thought that he was the first to argue that Nolan had tried to redirect the brigade. See Adkin, *The Charge*, p. 154.

385 Douglas J Austin, 'Nolan at Balaklava: A Reply', *War Correspondent*, 24/2 (July 2006), pp. 7–8. For Mitchell's account see Mitchell, *Recollections of one of the Light Brigade*, p. 83.

386 W Baring Pemberton, *Battles of the Crimean War* (London, Pan Books, 1972), p. 104.

387 Colin Robbins, 'Nolan and the Charge...', *War Correspondent*, 24/3 (October 2006), p. 19. See also John Harris, *The Gallant Six Hundred* (London, Hutchinson & Co., 1973), pp. 215–17.

388 Douglas J Austin, 'Nolan at Balaklava: Part IV – Soame Jenyns et al, a Hypothesis', *War Correspondent*, 24/4 (January 2007), pp. 15–21. Captain Jenyns commanded B Troop positioned slightly to the right of the centre in the first line of the charge.

389 Brighton, *Hell Riders*, p. 251. Nunnerley wrote these lines in 1884, see Nunnerley, James Ikin, *Short Sketch of the 17th Lancers and Life of Sergeant Major J.I. Nunnerley* (Liverpool, privately printed, 1884). Morley's recollections supported this view – see Thomas Morley, *The Cause of the Charge of Balaclava* (Nottingham, privately printed, 1899) pp. 8-9.

390 Adkin, *The Charge*, p. 155.

391 Ibid., pp. 156–7.

Bibliography

Archives consulted

Austrian State Archives (Österreichisches Staatsarchiv – Kriegsarchiv)
British Library
The National Army Museum (NAM)
The National Newspaper Archive (Colindale)
Public Record Office – The National Archives (TNA)
The University of Leicester

Archival sources
National Army Museum

NAM: 07-288-2, Lord Cardigan, Memorandum on the Charge of the Light Brigade.

NAM: 8602-75, Private Edward Firkins, 13th Light Dragoons, a letter to a close friend dated 27 December 1854.

NAM: 1963-09-05, Lieutenant Colonel (Major in 1854) William Forrest, 4th Dragoon Guards, letters to his family.

NAM: 1989-06-41, Journal of Captain Louis Nolan, 15th Hussars.

NAM: 1968-07-284 and 287, Lord Raglan's Papers.

NAM: 8311-9, Captain Edward Seager, 8th King's Royal Irish Regiment of Light Dragoons, 2 bound volumes of letters from 5 June 1854 to 15 August 1855.

NAM: 1968-07-270, Lieutenant Colonel Anthony Sterling of the Highland Brigade.

The National Archives

TNA: WO1/369 f.685, Casualty Returns for the period including the Battle of Balaklava (22–26 October 1854).

TNA: WO6/74/1, Duke of Newcastle to Lord Raglan, 10 April 1854.

TNA: FO 65/424/13, Sir George Hamilton Seymour to Lord John Russell.

TNA: WO 1/369 ff.642-4, Raglan to Newcastle, 27 October 1854.

TNA: WO 1/370 ff.483-6 Raglan to Newcastle, 16 December 1854.

TNA: PROB 11/2208, the Last Will and Testament of Lewis Edward Nolan, 23 March 1855.

Kriegsarchiv

KT 593, Conduitteliste for Unterlietenant Ludwig Nollan 1835–8.

KT 4345, Grundbuch – Ludwig Eduard von Nolan (Register for Lieutenant Nolan) 1832–9.

KT5406, two letters:

1st Letter – KT 5406 Letter to Geheime Haus, Hof unde Staatskanzlei 1840 (administration body to the Austrian Monarchy).

2nd Letter - KT 5406 Oberst Ezvik to General Command of Hungary 1840.

Published primary sources

Airlie, Mabel, Countess of (ed.), *With The Guards We Shall Go – A Guardsman's Letters in the Crimea 1854-1855*, London, Hodder & Stoughton Limited, 1933.

Anonymous, *Aldershottana: or Chinks in My Hut – Touch-and-Go Sketches from Court to Camp*, London, Ward and Lock, 1856.

Bapst, Germain, *Le Marechal Canrobert: Souvenirs d'un Siècle*, vol. 2, Paris, Librairie Plon, 1902 (I am grateful to Dr Douglas Austin for providing me with this source).

Bentley, Nicolas (ed.), *Russell's Despatches from the Crimea*, London, Panther History, 1970.

Boyd, Mark, *Reminiscences of Fifty Years*, London, Longmans, Green & Co., 1871.

Calthorpe, Somerset John Gough, *Letters from Head-quarters, or, the Realities of the War in the Crimea by an Officer of the Staff*, 2 vols, London, John Murray, 1856.

Cardigan, James Thomas Brudenell, *Eight Months on Active Service: Or, A Diary of a General Officer of Cavalry in 1854*, London, Clowes & Sons, 1855.

Duberly, Frances, *Journal Kept during the Russian War: from the Departure of the Army from England in April, 1854, to the Fall of Sebastopol*, London, Longman, Brown, Green & Longmans, 1855.

Falls, Cyril (ed.), *A Diary of the Crimea by George Palmer Evelyn*, London, Gerald Duckworth & Co., 1954.

Fenwick, Kenneth (ed.), *Voice from the Ranks: A Personal Narrative of the Crimean Campaign by a Sergeant of the Royal Fusiliers*, London, Folio Society, 1954.

Henderson, Robert, *The Soldier of Three Queens*, 2 vols, London, Saunders, Otley & Co., 1866.

Higginson, General Sir George, *Seventy-One Years of a Guardsman's Life*,

London, Smith, Elder & Co., 1916.

Kinglake, A W, *The Invasion of the Crimea: Its Origin, and an Account of its Progress Down to the Death of Lord Raglan*, 8 vols, Edinburgh and London, William Blackwood & Sons, 1863–1887.

Loy Smith, George, *A Victorian RSM: From India to the Crimea*, Tunbridge Wells, D J Costello, 1987.

Mitchell, Albert, *Recollections of one of the Light Brigade*, London, Hamilton, Adams & Co., 1885.

Nolan, L E, Captain, *Cavalry: Its History and Tactics*, London, Thomas Bosworth, 1853.

——, *Cavalry: Its History and Tactics*, Pennsylvania, Westholme Publishing, 2007.

——, *The Training of Cavalry Remount Horses: A New System*, London, Parker, Furnival & Parker, 1852.

Paget, General Lord George, *The Light Cavalry Brigade in the Crimea*, Wakefield, EP Publishing, 1975 (1st publ. John Murray, 1881).

Pool, Bernard (ed.), *The Croker Papers*, London, B T Batsford, 1967.

Richardson, Robert G. (ed.), *Nurse Sarah Anne: with Florence Nightingale at Scutari*, London, John Murray, 1977.

Rogers, Duncan (ed.), *Reminiscences of an English Cadet in the Austrian Service 1848-c1854*, Solihull, Helion & Company, 2006.

Russell, William, *The Great War with Russia*, London, Routledge & Sons, 1895.

The Queens Regulations and Orders for the Army, 1844, London, 1855.

Journals

Thompson, Captain John Wycliffe, 'The Turks in Kalafat', *Blackwoods Edinburgh Magazine*, 75 (January–June 1859), pt. 1, pp. 291–308, pt. 2, pp. 449–61

——, 'Horse Dealing in Syria, 1854', *Blackwoods Edinburgh Magazine*, 75 (July–December 1859), pt. 1, pp. 255–73, pt. 2, pp. 419–34

Vindex, 'The British Cavalry', *United Service Journal and Naval and Military Magazine*, pt. 3 (1831), pp. 473–6

Wightman, James, 'One of the "Six Hundred" on the Balaclava Charge', *Nineteenth Century Magazine*, 31 (January–June 1892), pp. 850–63

Newspapers and periodicals

Annual Register
Daily News

Gentleman's Magazine
Hansard's Parliamentary Debates
Illustrated London News
Morning Chronicle
The Times

Published secondary sources

Adkin, Mark, *The Charge: The Real Reason Why the Light Brigade Was Lost*, London, Pimlico, 2000.

Allen, Charles, *Plain Tales from the Raj*, London, Abacus, 2000.

Anglesey, Marquess of, *A History of the British Cavalry 1816 to 1919*, 8 vols, London, Leo Cooper, 1973–97.

Ball, Warwick, *Syria: A Historical and Architectural Guide*, Essex, Scorpion & MCS, 1994.

Barker, A J, *The Vainglorious War 1854-56*, London, Weidenfeld & Nicolson, 1970.

Barthorp, Michael, *Heroes of the Crimea: The Battles of Balaclava and Inkerman*, London, Blandford, 1991.

Bérenger, Jean, *A History of the Habsburg Empire 1700-1918*, London, Longman, 1997.

Brighton, Terry, *Hell Riders*, London, Penguin Books, 2005.

Compton, Piers, *Cardigan of Balaclava*, London, Robert Hale & Co., 1972.

David, Saul, *The Homicidal Earl: The Life of Lord Cardigan*, London, Abacus, 1999.

Denison, George T, *A History of Cavalry – from the Earliest Times with Lessons for the Future*, London, Macmillan, 1877.

Douet, James, *British Barracks 1600-1914*, London, HMSO, 1998.

Edgerton, Robert B, *Death or Glory*, Colorado, Westview Press, 1999.

Farwell, Byron, *Queen Victoria's Little Wars*, Chatham, Wordsworth Editions, 1999 (1st publ. 1973).

Fletcher, Ian, *Galloping at Everything: The British Cavalry in the Peninsular War and at Waterloo 1808-15*, Kent, Spellmount, 1999.

Fortescue, J W, *A History of the British Army*, 13 vols, London, Macmillan, 1899–1930.

Franks, Henry, *Leaves from a Soldier's Notebook*, Thirst 1904.

French, E G, *Good-Bye to Boot and Saddle – or The Tragic Passing of British Cavalry*, London, Hutchinson & Co., 1951.

Gibbs, Peter, *The Battle of the Alma*, London, Weidenfeld & Nicolson, 1963.

Grunwald, de Constantin, *Metternich*, London, Falcon Press, 1953.

Guedalla, Philip, *The Duke*, London, Hodder & Stoughton, 1933.

——, *Palmerston*, London, G P Putnam's Sons, 1927.

Hamley, General Sir Edward, *The War in the Crimea*, London, Seeley and Co., 1891.

Harries-Jenkins, Gwyn, *The Army in Victorian Society*, London, Routledge & Kegan Paul, 1977.

Haythornthwaite, Philip J, *The Napoleonic Source Book*, London, Guild Publishing, 1990.

Hibbert, Christopher, *The Destruction of Lord Raglan: A Tragedy of the Crimean War 1854–55*, Chatham, Wordsworth Editions, 1999 (1st publ. 1961).

Isa Khalil Sabbagh, *As the Arabs Say . . . Arabic Quotations Recalled and Interpreted*, Washington DC, Sabbagh Management Corporation, 1983.

Judd, Denis, *The Crimean War*, London, Book Club Associates, 1976.

Kelly, Christine (ed.), *Mrs Duberly's War: Journal and Letters from the Crimea, 1854-56*, Oxford, Oxford University Press, 2007.

Lee, Sidney, *Queen Victoria*, London, Smith, Elder & Co., 1904.

Longford, Elizabeth, *Queen Victoria*, Bath, Sutton Publishing, 1999.

Lunt, James, *Charge to Glory! A Garland of Cavalry Exploits*, London, William Heinemann, 1961.

Massie, Alastair, *The National Army Museum Book of the Crimean War: The Untold Stories*, London, Pan Books, 2005.

Mollo, John and Mollo Boris, *Into the Valley of Death: The British Cavalry Division at Balaclava 1854*, London, Windrow & Greene, 1996.

Moyse-Bartlett, Hubert, *Nolan of Balaclava*, London, Leo Cooper, 1975.

Newark, Peter, *Sabre & Lance*, Dorset, Blandford Press, 1987.

Okey, Robin, *The Habsburg Monarchy c. 1765-1918*, London, Macmillan, 2001.

Pavlovic, Darko, *The Austrian Army 1836-66*, vol. 1: *Infantry*; vol. 2: *Cavalry*, Oxford, Osprey, 1999.

Pemberton, W Baring, *Battles of the Crimean War*, London, Pan Books, 1972 (1st publ.1962).

Petre, Loraine, F, *Napoleon and the Archduke Charles*, London, Greenhill Books, 1991.

Rich, Norman, *Why the Crimean War? A Cautionary Tale*, Hanover, University Press of New England, 1985.

Royle, Trevor, *Crimea: The Great Crimean War 1854-1856*, London, Abacus, 2003.

Russell, J M, *The History of Maidstone*, London, Simpkin, Marshall & Co., 1881.

Seaton, Albert, *The Crimean War: A Russian Chronicle*, London, B T Batsford, 1977.

Selby, John, *The Thin Red Line*, Newton Abbot, Hamish Hamilton, 1972.

Simmons, Sue (ed.), *The Military Horse: The Equestrian Warrior through the Ages*, London, Marshall Cavendish, 1976.

Sked, Alan, *The Survival of the Habsburg Empire: Radetzky, the Imperial Army and the Class War*, 1848, London, Longman, 1979.

Strachen, Hew, *The Reform of the British Army 1830-1854*, Manchester, Manchester University Press, 1984.

Taylor, A J P, *Europe: Grandeur and Decline*, London, Penguin Books, 1967.

Thomas, Donald, *Charge! Hurrah! Hurrah! A Life of Cardigan of Balaclava*, London, Routledge & Kegan Paul, 1974.

Thomas, Robert H G and Scollins, Richard, *The Russian Army of the Crimean War 1854-56*, Oxford, Osprey, 1991.

Trow, M J, *The Pocket Hercules: Captain Morris & The Charge of the Light Brigade*, Barnsley, Pen & Sword, 2006.

Turnball, Peter Evan, *Austria*, 2 vols, London, 1840.

Warner, Philip *The Crimean War: A Reappraisal*, Chatham, Wordsworth, 2001 (1st publ. 1972).

Westwood, J N, *Endurance and Endeavour: Russian History 1812-1992*, Oxford, Oxford University Press, 1993.

Woodham-Smith, Cecil, *Queen Victoria: Her Life and Times*, 2 vols, London, Hamish Hamilton, 1972.

——, *The Reason Why*, London, Penguin Books, 1958.

Journals and magazines

Austin, Douglas J, 'Blunt Speaking', Special Publication 33, Crimean War Research Society, 2006, 21–39.

——, 'Nolan at Balaklava: Part IV – Soame Jenyns et. al., a hypothesis', *War Correspondent*, 24/4 (January 2007), pp. 15–21.

——, 'Nolan at Balaklava: a reply', *War Correspondent*, 24/2 (July 2006), pp. 7–8.

Buttery, David, 'Hunting as Training for War', *Soldiers of the Queen*, Journal for the Victorian Military Society, 115 (December 2003), pp. 3–10.

Gilchrist, M M, 'Louis Edward Nolan', *Dispatch*, Journal of the Scottish Military Historical Society (Spring 1998), pp. 12–15.

Kelsey, David, 'Evidence and Belief: Captain Nolan's Final Moments', *Journal of the Society for Army Historical Research*, 81/325 (Spring 2003), p. 70.

Noble, Duncan, 'Lance versus Sabre', *Military Illustrated*, 136 (September 1999), pp. 8–43.

Robins, Colin, 'Nolan and the Charge . . .', *War Correspondent*, 24/3 (October 2006), p. 19.

——, 'Nolan Did Try to Redirect the Light Brigade – Who Says?', *War Correspondent*, 24/1 (April 2006), p. 7.

Rothenberg, Gunther E, 'The Austrian Army in the Age of Metternich', *Journal of Modern History*, 40/2 (June 1968), pp. 155–65.

Secondary sources: electronic

Ackerl, Isabella, 'Austria's Military Academy Founded by Maria Theresa', Virtual Vienna Net, **http://www.virtualvienna.net/community**, 1–4.

http://www.silverwhistle.co.uk (this site contains an area dedicated to the Crimean War and includes biographical data on both Louis Nolan and Frances Duberley).

Index